T0259755

Scratch by Example

Programming for All Ages

Eduardo A. Vlieg

Apress®

Scratch by Example: Programming for All Ages

Eduardo A. Vlieg
Curacao, Curaçao

ISBN-13 (pbk): 978-1-4842-1945-4   ISBN-13 (electronic): 978-1-4842-1946-1
DOI 10.1007/978-1-4842-1946-1

Library of Congress Control Number: 2016953162

Managing Director: Welmoed Spahr
Lead Editor: Jonathan Gennick
Development Editor: Linda Laflamme
Technical Reviewer: Massimo Nardone
Editorial Board: Steve Anglin, Pramila Balan, Laura Berendson, Aaron Black, Louise Corrigan,
    Jonathan Gennick, Robert Hutchinson, Celestin Suresh John, Nikhil Karkal, James Markham,
    Susan McDermott, Matthew Moodie, Natalie Pao, Gwenan Spearing
Coordinating Editor: Jill Balzano
Copy Editor: Kim Burton-Weisman
Compositor: SPi Global
Indexer: SPi Global
Artist: SPi Global

Distributed to the book trade worldwide by Springer Science+Business Media New York,
233 Spring Street, 6th Floor, New York, NY 10013. Phone 1-800-SPRINGER, fax (201) 348-4505, e-mail orders-ny@springer-sbm.com, or visit www.springer.com. Apress Media, LLC is a California LLC and the sole member (owner) is Springer Science + Business Media Finance Inc (SSBM Finance Inc). SSBM Finance Inc is a **Delaware** corporation.

For information on translations, please e-mail rights@apress.com, or visit www.apress.com.

Apress and friends of ED books may be purchased in bulk for academic, corporate, or promotional use. eBook versions and licenses are also available for most titles. For more information, reference our Special Bulk Sales–eBook Licensing web page at www.apress.com/bulk-sales.

Any source code or other supplementary materials referenced by the author in this text are available to readers at www.apress.com. For detailed information about how to locate your book's source code, go to www.apress.com/source-code/. Readers can also access source code at SpringerLink in the Supplementary Material section for each chapter.

Printed on acid-free paper

Contents at a Glance

Contents

About the Author

Eduardo A. Vlieg was born and raised on the island of Curaçao, Dutch Antilles. In 1993, he received his Bachelor of Science degree in aircraft engineering technology from Embry-Riddle Aeronautical University in Daytona Beach, FL. In 2001, he received an MBA from the University of the Netherland Antilles. He has been working in the IT field since 1996 and has obtained various certifications since then. His background includes 20 years in the information security, auditing, financial, engineering, consulting, risk, and compliance industries.

If you have any questions, feedback, or remarks, the author would like to hear from you. You can contact him at vliege@hotmail.com.

About the Technical Reviewer

Massimo Nardone has more than 22 years of experience in security, web/mobile development, cloud, and IT architecture. His true IT passions are security and Android. He has been programming and teaching how to program with Android, Perl, PHP, Java, VB, Python, C/C++, and MySQL for more than 20 years. He holds a Master of Science degree in computing science from the University of Salerno, Italy, and has worked as a project manager, software engineer, research engineer, chief security architect, information security manager, PCI/SCADA auditor, and senior lead IT security/cloud/SCADA architect. He currently works as chief information security officer (CISO) for Cargotec Oy.

Massimo has reviewed more than 40 IT books for various publishing companies and is the coauthor of *Pro Android Games* (Apress, 2015).

Acknowledgments

I would like to thank the reviewers, Linda Laflamme and Massimo Nardone. This book wouldn't be what it is without you. I also would like to thank Jonathan Gennick for discovering me and giving me the chance to write this book. It's just the first of many more to come. Thank you, Jill Balzano, for managing this project and keeping me on track. Last, but not least, I would like to thank my lucky stars for having been born in and living on the island of Curaçao.

Live a life of "Oh wells," and not "What ifs…."

Introduction

One of the biggest obstacles in learning a programming language is learning the syntax of the language. Like the grammar of a language, the syntax is the set of rules that defines the combinations of symbols that are considered a correctly structured document or a fragment in that language.

Scratch removes this obstacle by using graphical blocks of code to represent programming commands. Instead of typing commands (or mistyping them and creating syntax errors), with Scratch you drag, drop, and snap graphical blocks of code. To create a program, or *project* as Scratch calls it, you simply snap those blocks of code together into stacks, much like Lego bricks. As with Lego bricks, connectors on the blocks suggest how they should be put together. With Scratch and its code blocks, you can control and mix graphics, animations, music, and sound to create interactive stories, games, simulations, art, and animations. You can even share your creations with others in the online community (more on this in a moment).

Block programming with Scratch is relatively easy, even for young children, and it's a good way to enter the world of programming. You can start by simply tinkering with the bricks, snapping them together in different sequences and combinations to see what happens. Along the way, you are also learning important computational concepts such as repeat loops, conditional statements, variables, lists, data types, events, and processes. In fact, Scratch has been used to introduce these concepts to students of many different ages, from elementary schools through universities. Creating with Scratch also encourages students to learn to think creatively, work collaboratively, and reason systematically. After learning Scratch, you can more easily transition to traditional text-based languages.

Why Was Scratch Created?

Developed by the MIT Media Lab's Lifelong Kindergarten Group, Scratch was conceived as an educational language that would make programming fun and accessible to a new generation. The researchers at the Lifelong Kindergarten Group noticed that children learn specific tasks and skills at school, but rarely get the opportunity to design things or learn about the process of designing things. Although many children know how to browse, chat, and play games on their electronic devices, far fewer understand how to create new devices, games, or applications. The Lifelong Kindergarten Group wanted to change this. They believed that it was very important for all children, from all backgrounds, to grow up knowing how to design, create, and express themselves. Inspired by how kindergarteners learn through a process of experimenting, creating, designing, and exploring, the Lifelong Kindergarten Group extended this style of learning to programming in general and Scratch in particular.

The Lifelong Kindergarten Group wanted to develop an approach to programming that would appeal to people who had never imagined themselves as programmers. They wanted to make it easy for everyone, of all ages, backgrounds, and interests, to program their own interactive stories, games, animations, and simulations, and share their creations with one another. The primary goal of the Scratch initiative was not to prepare people for careers as professional programmers but to nurture a new generation of creative, systematic thinkers comfortable using programming to express their ideas. Programming supports *computational thinking*, which helps you learn important problem-solving skills and design strategies that are applicable to several aspects of life and work. When you learn to code in Scratch, you learn important strategies for solving problems, designing projects, and communicating ideas.

Three core design principles were established for Scratch:

- **More tinkerable.** In Scratch, you can experiment and create by snapping blocks together, mixing graphics, animations, photos, music, and sound.

- **More meaningful.** In Scratch, you can create different types of projects. You can create stories, games, animations, and simulations, so people with widely varying interests are all able to work on projects they care about. Scratch also makes it easy for people to personalize their Scratch projects by importing photos and music clips, recording voices, and creating graphics.

- **More social than other programming environments.** Released in May 2013, Scratch 2.0 enables you to create projects online at the Scratch website (scratch.mit.edu). The Scratch website lets you share your projects, get feedback, look at other projects, modify them, and save them as your own. Online project sharing has been an important part of the Scratch philosophy since 2007, and the MIT Scratch Team works hard to foster a sense of community on the website, as you'll learn in the next section.

The Scratch Website

More than just a place to find Scratch guides and tutorials, the Scratch website (scratch.mit.edu) is an online community, where you can create Scratch projects, share, discuss, learn, get and give feedback, and modify and save one another's projects. The core audience on the site is between the ages of 8 and 16, although many adults participate as well. Everyone can use Scratch and learn from it, as well as learn from each other in the online community. As "Scratchers" program and share interactive projects, they learn important mathematical and computational concepts, as well as how to think creatively, reason systematically, and work collaboratively. The ultimate goal is to develop a shared community and culture around Scratch. Available in more than 40 languages, Scratch is now used in more than 150 countries, so you're likely to encounter a diverse set of fellow Scratchers online.

How to Use Scratch

You can use Scratch either online at the Scratch website or you can download the language and create projects offline on your own computer. You don't have to create an account to use Scratch online, but if you want to save and share your projects online, you will need one. Using Scratch online has the advantage that you can save and share your Scratch projects more easily. If you create Scratch projects on your computer, you then have to take the extra step of uploading them from your computer to the Scratch site to be able to share them online.

This book assumes that you will be using Scratch online. To go to the Scratch website, type **scratch.mit.edu** in your browser. The home page (see Figure I-1) displays several projects created by other Scratch users from all around the world. You can click, open, and run them.

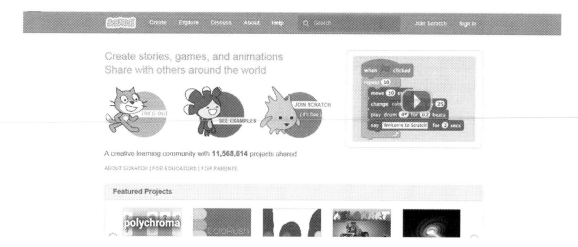

Figure I-1. *The Scratch website home page*

You can start creating Scratch projects by clicking **Create** at the top of the screen. (If you haven't yet created an account and signed in, you'll not be able to save your project, though.) Clicking **Explore** opens a page with more projects that you can explore. Clicking **Help** opens a page with lots of helpful resources for Scratch, including step-by-step guides, Scratch cards with quick tips on common tasks, and video tutorials.

In order to save and share your Scratch projects online, you need to create an account and sign in. To create an account, click **Join Scratch** at the top right of the Scratch site. In the window that opens, choose a username and password, type them the appropriate fields, and then click **Next** (see Figure I-2).

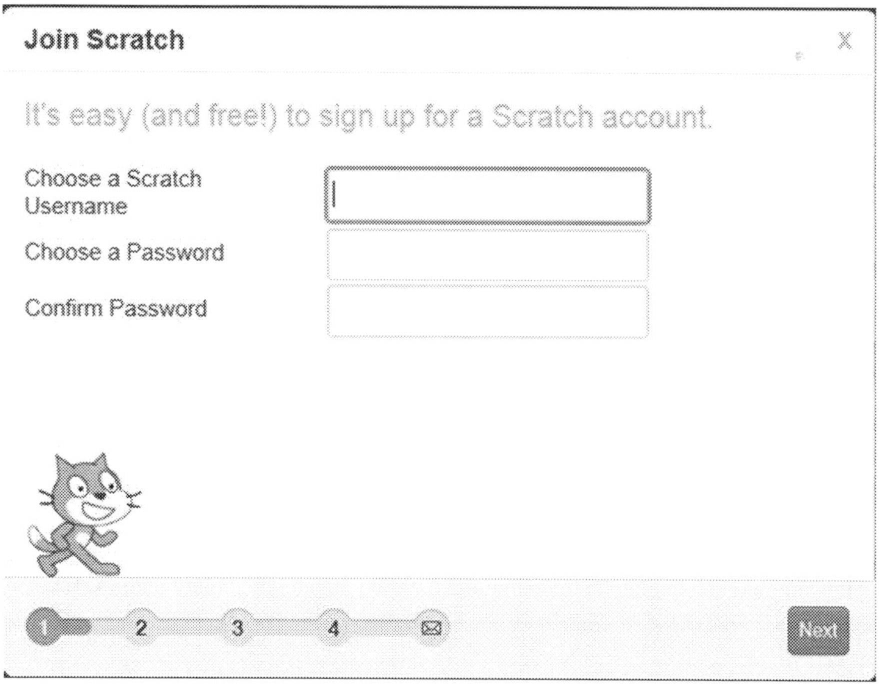

Figure I-2. *Create a Scratch username and password*

Tell the Scratch team a bit about yourself next. Select your birth month and year, gender, and country. Click **Next** (see Figure I-3).

Figure I-3. *Provide some details about yourself*

The next step is to provide your contact information. Type your email address in both fields, and then click **Next** (see Figure I-4).

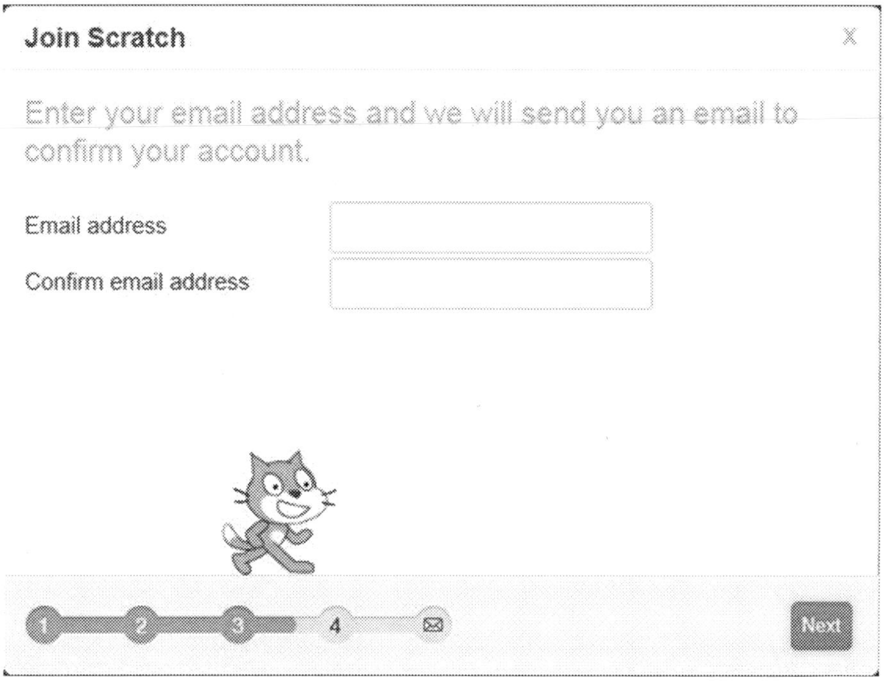

Figure I-4. Enter your email address

That's all there is to it. Your account has been created and you're automatically logged in. Click **OK Lets Go!** to start working with Scratch for the first time (see Figure I-5).

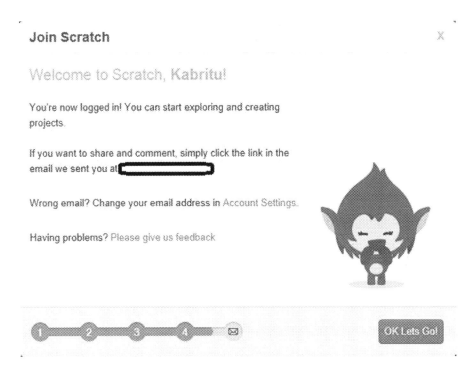

Figure I-5. *Click OK Lets Go! to start creating with Scratch*

About This Book

Following the Scratch philosophy of learning through experimentation, *Scratch by Example* introduces Scratch and programing through fun and simple example scripts that you can build, adapt, and reuse. From movement to sound to advanced interaction with users, web cams, and other scripts, each chapter focuses on a core concept. After a short discussion of the blocks you'll be using, you'll dive into creating example scripts. These start short and simple, but before long, you'll be building complete stories and even games.

Although *Scratch by Example* is intended for complete beginners to the world of programming and Scratch, by the time you complete this book, you will...

- Have a thorough understanding of the Scratch interface.

- Be able to create a variety of Scratch projects.

- Have a solid foundation upon which you can build further and create advanced Scratch projects in the future.

- Understand universal programming concepts that will help you learn complex languages more easily.

Are you ready to get started? Okay, let's go!

PART I

Learning the Basics

CHAPTER 1

Getting to Know the Scratch Interface

Scratch is a programming language based on graphical code blocks. Each block represents a different programming command, and you snap together the blocks to create a program, which Scratch calls *projects*. A lot like snapping together Legos, it's an easy and fun way to get introduced to the world of computer programming.

In this chapter, you will learn about the Scratch interface, which is where you create and run Scratch projects. Before you start creating programs, you need to learn your way around the various sections of the Scratch interface.

Getting Started

To access the interface and start creating Scratch projects, you can simply go to scratch.mit.edu and click **Create** at the Scratch site main menu bar at the top of the website (see Figure 1-1). If you want to save and share your projects, though, you first need to log in with your username and password. (For instructions on registering at the Scratch site and creating an account, see the Introduction.) After logging in, click **Create**. You will be redirected to the Scratch interface, where you can start creating Scratch projects.

Figure 1-1. Scratch site main menu bar

The Scratch interface (see Figure 1-2) consists of the following areas:

> **Stage**: This is where your project gets displayed when it's active.

> **Sprites pane**: This is where you add *sprites*, the objects that perform actions in your script, and display their properties.

> **Backdrops pane**: This is where you add a *backdrop*, which is similar to a background and is displayed in the stage area.

© Eduardo A. Vlieg 2016
E. A. Vlieg, *Scratch by Example*, DOI 10.1007/978-1-4842-1946-1_1

Tabs area: Here, you find three tabs: Scripts, Costumes, and Sounds. The **Scripts** tab contains the **block palette**, which is where you'll find the various categories of blocks of code and the code blocks themselves. The **Costumes** tab displays the *costumes*, or alternate appearances, of the selected sprite. A sprite can have one or multiple costumes. The **Sounds** tab displays the sounds you can apply to your Scratch project.

Scripts area: This is the area that you drag the blocks of code to and snap them together to create scripts—and eventually your project.

Backpack: This is a section where you save objects that you can use later in other projects. The objects can be costumes, sprites, backdrops, sounds, blocks of code, and scripts. You can drag and drop these objects into the backpack and later drag and drop them from the backpack to reuse in other Scratch projects.

Menu bar: This is where important overall controls, like Save, Revert, and New, are located.

Tool bar: Here you'll find five icons that represent important functions that you can use in Scratch.

Now let's take a closer look at each area.

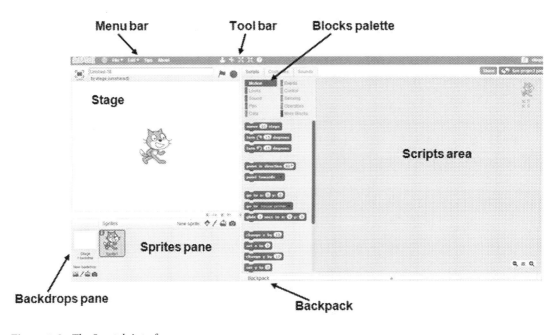

Figure 1-2. *The Scratch interface*

Stage

Just like a theater's stage, the stage (see Figure 1-3) in the Scratch interface is where you see all of a program's action happen. Programs are called *projects* in Scratch. A project (program) consists of one or multiple *scripts*, which you create by combining code blocks. When you run a project or activate a script, the result is displayed in the stage. The dimensions of the stage are 480 pixels wide in the horizontal direction, or X axis, and 360 pixels high in the vertical direction, or Y axis. When you want to indicate an exact position on the stage, you use a pair of X and Y values, or coordinates, similar to how you'd plot a point on a graph. (For a more detailed explanation of Scratch's coordinate system, see Chapter 3.)

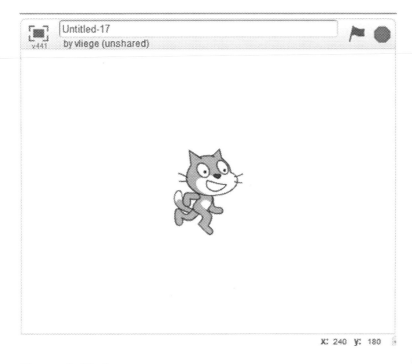

Figure 1-3. The Stage

The top of the stage provides some useful controls and information about the Scratch project. For example, the text area at the top of the stage area is where the name of the project is displayed. By default, Scratch names each new project *Untitled-* followed by a number. You can click in the text field to change the default name to something more memorable. Underneath the name of the project, the username of the person that is logged in is displayed, as well as a reminder of whether the project is shared or not. Clicking the green flag in the upper-right corner of the stage area can activate (trigger) a script that includes a corresponding green flag code block. Clicking the red octagon in the upper-right corner of the stage area will stop all the scripts in a project from running. You can also view the stage area in full-screen mode by clicking the blue square in the upper-left corner of the stage.

Sprites Pane

The Sprites pane (see Figure 1-4) is where Scratch displays thumbnails of the sprites that are being used in the current project. Sprites are objects that perform actions in a project. These actions are determined by the scripts that you create. The scripts tell the sprites what to do and what actions to perform. (More information about sprites can be found in Chapter 2.) The cat sprite called *Sprite1* always appears by default when you create a new project.

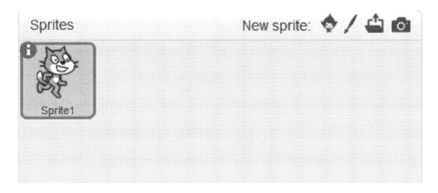

Figure 1-4. *The Sprites pane*

To add a new sprite to a Scratch project, you use the icons in the top-right corner of the pane. Click the leftmost icon (the one that looks like a character ◆) to choose a sprite from the library. To draw a new sprite, click the paintbrush icon. The file folder icon enables you to import a sprite from a file, while the camera icon enables you to import an image from a webcam as a sprite.

Backdrops Pane

The Backdrops pane (see Figure 1-5) is where Scratch displays a thumbnail of the current backdrop that is being used in your project. A backdrop is the background that appears behind your sprite in the stage, and every project has at least one. You can keep track of the backdrops used in a project with the Backdrops pane, which is to the left of the Sprites pane. Backdrops are explained more extensively in the next chapter of this book.

Figure 1-5. *The Backdrops pane*

The white backdrop always appears by default when you create a new project. If you click the white thumbnail in the Backdrops pane (see Figure 1-5), the **Costumes** tab changes to the **Backdrops** tab. This tab shows all the backdrops that are being used in the project. The difference between the Backdrops pane and Backdrops tab is that the Backdrops pane shows the thumbnail of the current backdrop displayed in the stage and the Backdrops tab shows all the backdrops that are used in a Scratch project. At the bottom of the Backdrops pane, there are four icons for adding a new backdrop. Click the landscape scene icon to choose a backdrop from the library, the paintbrush icon to draw a backdrop, the file folder to import one from a file, or the camera icon to import one from a webcam.

Block Palette

The block palette (see Figure 1-6) is where you find the different categories of code blocks. You drag and drop these code blocks to the scripts area and snap them together to create scripts.

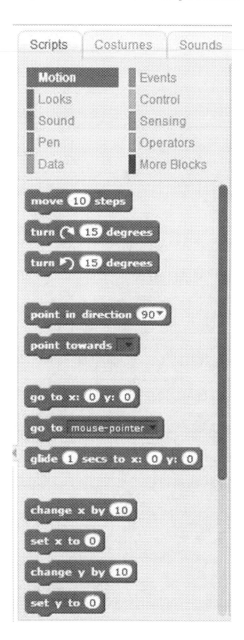

Figure 1-6. *The block palette*

The block palette contains ten categories of code blocks. Each category has its own color, so whenever you see blue blocks, for instance, you know they deal with motion. These are the categories:

Motion blocks: These blocks control the movement of the sprite. You'll learn how to use motion blocks in Chapter 3.

Looks blocks: This category includes several blocks of code that can be used to modify the appearance of a sprite. With these blocks, you can apply graphic effects to the sprite, change the color of the sprite, or change the size of the sprite. More about this category can be found in Chapter 5.

Sound blocks: These blocks add and control sound in your Scratch project. More about this category can be found in Chapter 6.

Pen blocks: These blocks control the pen, which you can use to draw on the stage. You'll learn more about this category in Chapter 4.

Data blocks: These blocks can hold values, either a number or a name, and be used to create variables to temporarily hold information needed in your project. Some data blocks enable you to create lists; these blocks contain more than one value. You'll learn more about this category in Chapters 8 and 9.

Event blocks: These blocks control when and how the scripts are activated. With these, you can control whether a script starts running when the user clicks the green flag or a sprite. You'll learn more about these blocks in Chapter 11.

Control blocks: These blocks control how the scripts run. For example, you can pause the script for a specified amount of time or you can repeat a sequence of blocks a specified number of times. More about this category can be found in Chapter 7.

Sensing blocks: These blocks are used if you need to detect things in your scripts. Some of these blocks also allow interaction with a webcam or interaction with the user. You'll learn more about these blocks in Chapters 7 and 10.

Operators blocks: These blocks perform math functions, such as adding, subtracting, and dividing numbers. You can also perform operations on strings of characters, such as comparing them and adding multiple sentences or words to create a new sentence. More about these blocks can be found in Chapter 7.

More blocks: In this section of the block palette, you can create your own code blocks or add extensions so that Scratch can interact with the PicoBoard or Lego WeDo. PicoBoard is a piece of hardware with sensors that enable Scratch projects to interact with the outside world. For example, the sound sensor on the PicoBoard can activate a script when it senses a certain level of noise. Lego WeDo is a Lego system consisting of sensors and motors. Using Scratch, you can use the Lego WeDo sensors to activate the Lego WeDo motors. You'll learn more about these blocks in Chapter 12.

Scripts Area

The scripts area (see Figure 1-7) is where you snap together the various blocks of code to create the scripts for your project. You can have just one script in the scripts area, but you can also create multiple scripts in this area at once.

Figure 1-7. *The scripts area*

The upper-right corner of the scripts area displays the selected sprite with the X and Y coordinates of the sprite's current location on the stage. In the scripts area's bottom-right corner are three icons. You can click the plus icon to increase the size of the displayed script or block of code. You click the minus icon to decrease it. Clicking the equals sign resets the script or block of code to its original location and size.

Backpack

You can find the backpack (see Figure 1-8) beneath the scripts area and block palette. Just like a real backpack, it's handy for storing things. Specifically, you can use it to save scripts, sprites, and other items that you want to reuse later in other projects.

Figure 1-8. *Collapsed backpack*

The backpack is collapsible. If you click the triangle icon (see Figure 1-8), the backpack will open and show what's saved in it. Or you can save items by dragging and dropping them into the backpack (see Figure 1-9). So if you are not using the backpack, you can collapse it. Collapsing the backpack closes it so that it will not take up too much space.

Figure 1-9. *The backpack with contents*

Menu Bar

As in any program or website, the menu bar (see Figure 1-10) offers easy access to basic but important controls. For instance, from the File menu, you can create a new project (**New**), save a project (**Save now**), revert to the last saved version of an open project (**Revert**), upload a project to the Scratch website, and download a project from the Scratch website to your computer. If your changes to a script don't go as planned, **Revert** enables you to undo all the changes that you've made since opening the project. When you upload a project using the File menu, it will be saved in the **My Stuff** section. Downloaded files end with the **.sb2** file extension.

Figure 1-10. *The menu bar*

The **Edit** menu offers the choices **Undelete** and **Small stage layout**. If you just deleted a block of code by mistake, choose **Edit ➤ Undelete** to get it back. Choose **Edit ➤ Small stage layout** to make the stage smaller and the scripts area larger.

From the menu bar, you can also find help on using Scratch and more information about Scratch. Click **Tips** to open a new window (to the right of the scripts area) that contains several how-to guides and Scratch tutorials. Click **About** to learn more about Scratch, such as the support and funding for Scratch, who uses Scratch, Scratch in schools, and research on how people use Scratch.

Tool Bar

The five icons in the tool bar (see Figure 1-11) offer one-click access to some useful functions.

Figure 1-11. *The tool bar*

On the far left of the tool bar, the **Duplicate** icon ![icon] looks like a stamp and lets you make an exact copy of a sprite, costume, backdrop, block of code, or complete script. Click the icon to change the cursor into a stamp icon, and then click the object that you want to duplicate (the sprite or block of code) to make the duplicate.

Next is the **Delete** icon ![icon]. Click it to change the cursor to a pair of scissors, and then click the object that you want to delete.

The next two icons, **Grow** ![icon] and **Shrink** ![icon], increase or decrease, respectively, the size of the object. Again, click the appropriate icon, and then click the object that you need to be larger or smaller.

The question mark at the far right is the **Block help** icon ![icon]. If you want to know more about a certain code block or any section of the Scratch interface, click the **Block help** icon, and then the block that you want to know more about. A window will open to the right of the scripts area with more information about the object that you selected.

Other Important Sections

Finally, the top-right corner of the Scratch interface contains a few more useful buttons and icons. In the top-right corner above the scripts area (see Figure 1-12), for example, the **Share** button ![Share] lets you share your project with the Scratch community, so other members of the community can see your projects, modify them, and leave comments. The **S** on the folder to the left of your username is an icon ![icon] for the **My Stuff** area. If you click it, it will take you to the link where all of your projects are saved.

Figure 1-12. *Scratch interface top-right corner*

In the top-left corner above the stage (see Figure 1-13), clicking the word Scratch will take you back to the Scratch home page (scratch.mit.edu), while clicking the globe icon will enable you to change the language of the Scratch interface (see Figure 1-14).

Figure 1-13. *Scratch interface top-left corner*

Figure 1-14. *Language selector*

Summary

The features and concepts explained in this chapter will become clearer in the next chapters, when you start working with Scratch to create scripts and projects. What you have learned in this chapter is very important, because you will use it every time that you create a script or project. This chapter taught you about the different sections of the Scratch interface. You learned about the following:

- Stage
- Sprites pane
- Backdrops pane
- Tabs area: Scripts tab (block palette), Costumes/Backdrops tab, Sounds tab
- Scripts area
- Backpack
- Menu bar
- Tool bar

The next chapter will teach you about two important topics: sprites and backdrops. After that, you will have gathered all the required basic Scratch knowledge, so that you can start creating some projects.

CHAPTER 2

Meet the Cat

After Chapter 1, you should feel comfortable navigating the Scratch interface. In this chapter, you'll use that interface to look more closely at sprites and backdrops. Sprites and backdrops are two important types of objects that can perform actions in a project. They follow the instructions that you provide when you snap together the code blocks into a script. Backdrops also function as the background of the stage area. In the sections that follow, you will learn how to add a sprite and a backdrop from the Scratch library. You will also learn how to create your own sprite and backdrop.

Sprites

Sprites are objects that perform actions in a project. An action can be, for example, making the sprite move or making a sound. Just like a movie script tells an actor what to say and where to move, the scripts you create tell the sprites what to do and what actions to perform. When you create a project, one of your first steps will be to choose your sprite from the Sprites pane. With the help of the Costumes tab and the Sprites info pane, you can easily change your sprite's appearance and keep track of its movements and more as you work on your project. This section not only introduces these key controls, but also provides some basic example scripts to get you started.

Sprites Pane

Located below the stage area, the Sprites pane is where you select, paint, import, and manipulate sprites (see Figure 2-1). The Sprites pane also provides a thumbnail view of all the sprites that are being used in the project.

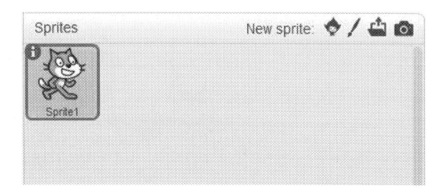

Figure 2-1. *The Sprites pane*

© Eduardo A. Vlieg 2016
E. A. Vlieg, *Scratch by Example*, DOI 10.1007/978-1-4842-1946-1_2

The default sprite that appears every time that you create a new project is the cat sprite named Sprite1. As shown in Figure 2-2, you can add a new sprite by...

- Choosing a new sprite from the library

- Painting a new sprite

- Uploading a sprite from a file

- Taking a picture with your webcam and using that picture as a sprite

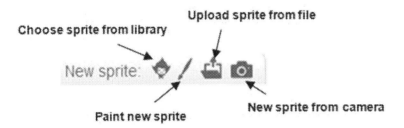

Figure 2-2. *New sprite*

Costumes

In Scratch, you can change the look of a sprite by using costumes. A costume is an alternate appearance of a sprite. Using multiple costumes or alternate appearances of a sprite gives the sprite the illusion of movement.

To see how you can change the look of a sprite by using costumes, let's create a new project. First, go to the Scratch website (scratch.mit.edu) and click **Sign in** at the top right of the screen. Enter your username and password, and then click the **Sign in** button to log in to the website. Click **Create** at the top left of the screen to start a new project. The project is immediately saved in the **My Stuff** section. If you'd like to change the title of your project to something other than the default (**Untitled-** followed by a number), click in the title field, type a new name, and press the Enter key.

By default, the project uses the Sprite1 cat in the Sprites pane. Let's try to change the way that the cat looks. To do so, you'll use the Costumes tab. First, select the thumbnail view of the sprite in the Sprites pane, and then click the **Costumes** tab (see Figure 2-3). The tab displays the cat's two costume choices: **costume1** and **costume2**. Click **costume2**. Notice that the thumbnail view and the stage now show the costume2 version of the cat.

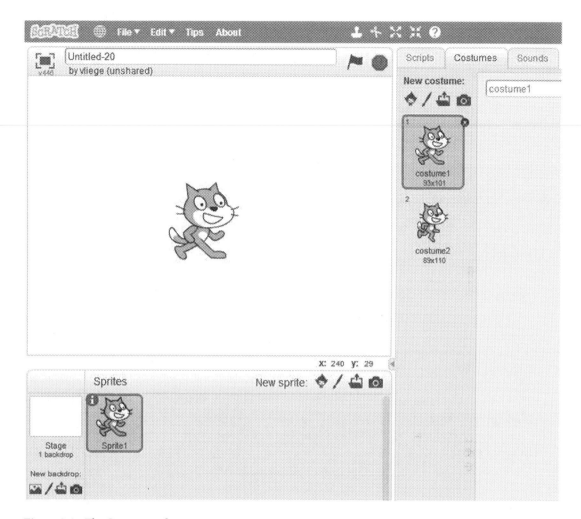

Figure 2-3. *The Costumes tab*

Not all, but many sprites consist of more than one costume. You can always check how many costumes a sprite has, see what they look like, and change a sprite's costume by going to the Costumes tab. When you select a costume in the Costumes tab, the thumbnail view in the Sprites pane changes to that costume.

Sprites Info Pane

To learn more information about a sprite in the Sprites pane, click the white letter **i** in the blue circle on the sprite's thumbnail (see Figure 2-4). The Sprites info pane will open to display some properties of the selected sprite (see Figure 2-5). For example, the Sprites info pane shows you the name of the selected sprite. Click in the name field to type a new name for your sprite, if you like. The pane also shows you the current position of the sprite in terms of its X and Y coordinates and the direction that the sprite is pointing in terms of degrees. In Figure 2-5, the cat sprite's direction is 90 degrees, which means the sprite is pointing to the right. To change a sprite's direction, click the blue line in the circle and drag it around the circle. Give it a try. Watch the direction of the sprite change in the stage area. You'll learn more about the **rotation style** in upcoming chapters, but basically, it controls which directions the sprite can face; selecting the two-sided arrow, for example, means that the sprite can only face left or right. When **show** is selected, the sprite is shown in the stage area. If you deselect **show**, the sprite will disappear from the stage area. Try it.

Figure 2-4. *The Sprites info pane*

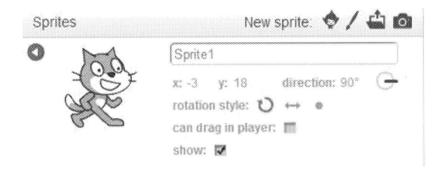

Figure 2-5. *The Sprites info pane properties*

Example 2-1: Playing with the Tool Bar Icons

In Chapter 1, you learned about the four tool bar icons above the stage: Duplicate, Delete, Grow, and Shrink.

In this example, you will try them. First, click the **Duplicate** icon (the one that looks like a stamp), and notice how your cursor changes to the Duplicate icon image (see Figure 2-6). Click the cat sprite to create an exact copy of that sprite.

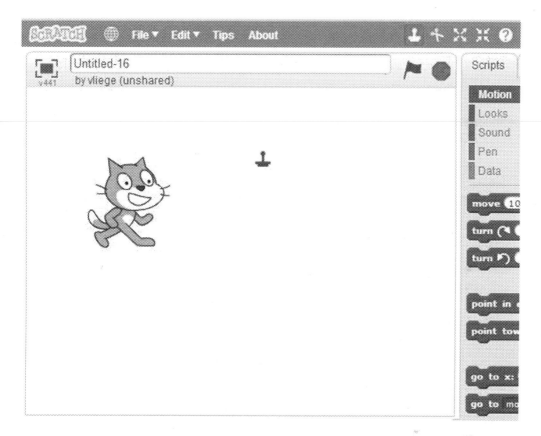

Figure 2-6. *Duplicate sprites with the Duplicate icon*

Next, delete the copy of the sprite that was created. Drag the copy that you just created so that the original sprite and its copy are side by side. Click the **Delete** icon ![scissors icon] (it looks like a pair of scissors), and notice that your cursor changes to a pair of scissors (see Figure 2-7). Click one of the sprites to delete it.

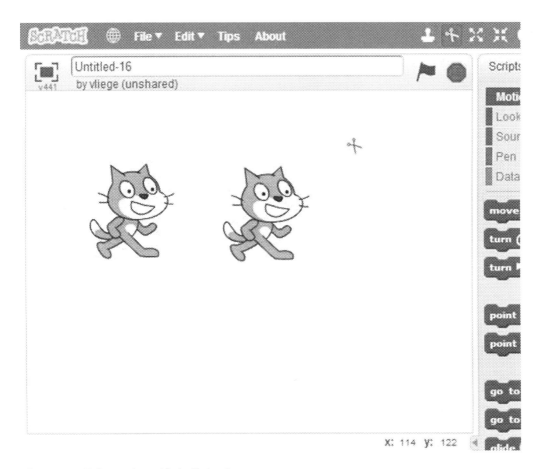

Figure 2-7. *Delete sprites with the Delete icon*

To change the size of your sprite, use the **Grow** and **Shrink** icons in the tool bar. Click either the Grow icon ![Grow icon] or the Shrink icon ![Shrink icon]. Then, after the cursor changes to match the icon that you chose, click the sprite that you want to be larger or smaller. To see how much Grow increases or Shrink decreases a sprite's size, you can check the ![size block] code block in the **Looks** block category. Go to the Scripts tab, click the **Looks** category in the block palette, and then select the ![size block] block. A size-reporting window opens on the stage and displays the sprite's current size (see Figure 2-8) as a percentage of its original size. The default size is 100, which is 100%. I clicked the Grow icon for the example cat, and it is now at 105% its default size.

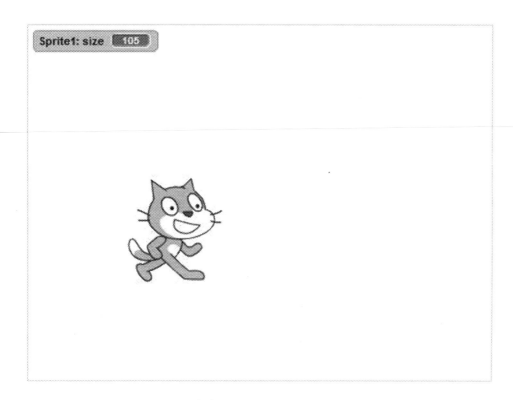

Figure 2-8. *Increase sprite size with the Grow icon*

Use the **Grow** or **Shrink** icons to increase or decrease the size of the sprite again, and notice how the number changes in the size-reporting window.

Example 2-2: Adding a New Sprite

In this example, you will add a new sprite from the library. Click the ◆ icon to open the **Sprite Library** window (see Figure 2-9). Make sure that underneath **Category** and **Type**, you have **All** selected. Click once on the sprite called **Adrian**. Notice that when you select a sprite, underneath that sprite's name, Scratch displays the number of costumes the sprite has. For example, Adrian has three costumes (see Figure 2-10).

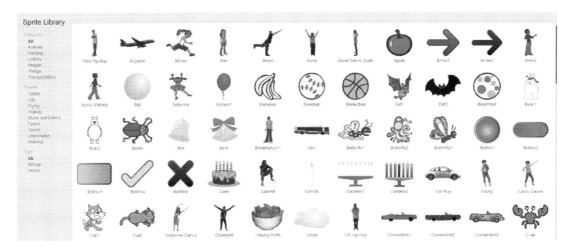

Figure 2-9. *The Sprite Library*

Figure 2-10. *Adrian sprite*

Click the **OK** button at the bottom-right corner of the **Sprite Library** to add the sprite named **Adrian** to your project. If you have other sprites in your project, please delete them by using the **Delete** icon in the tool bar so that your stage has only the Adrian sprite in it. Click the **Costumes** tab to see the three costumes that belong to the Adrian sprite (see Figure 2-11). Select any one of the costumes; not only does the appearance of the sprite change on the stage, the thumbnail view of the sprite in the Sprites pane changes to the current costume as well.

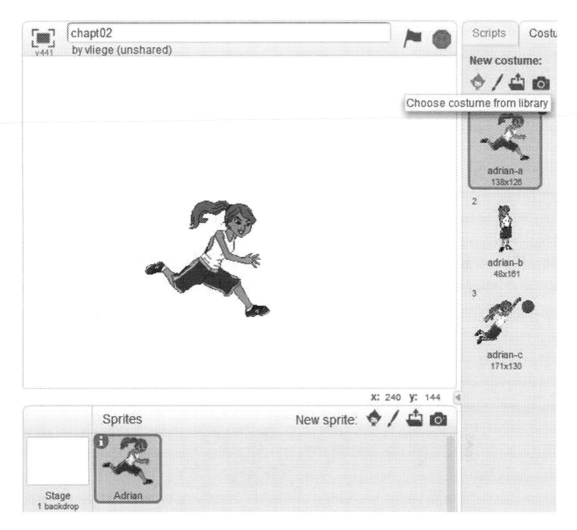

Figure 2-11. *Adrian's costumes*

Using the Costumes tab is only one way to change a sprite's costume. You can also use a single block of code, as you'll see in the next example.

Example 2-3: Changing Costumes

In this example, you will learn how to make the sprite change costumes. Select the thumbnail view of the sprite in the Sprites pane. Click the **Scripts** tab, select the **Looks** category, drag the `next costume` block, and drop it into the scripts area. Click the block in the scripts area. See how the costume changes in the stage and the thumbnail views? The faster you click the block of code, the faster the costume changes. This gives the illusion of movement to the sprite. Select the `costume #` block in the **Looks** category. Don't drag and drop it, just select it. This block reports the sprite's current costume number. A reporting window appears on the stage, showing the current costume number (see Figure 2-12) of the sprite. Notice how it changes every time you click the **next costume** block.

Figure 2-12. *The costume # reporting window*

Another block of code changes the sprite's costumes. The **switch costume to adrian-c ▼** block has a pull-down menu from which you can choose a specific costume name. Give it a try. Click the pull-down menu to the right of the block and select the costume that you want to change to. Click the block of code to activate it—and watch the costume change.

Example 4: Make the Sprite Dance

In this example, you will learn how to change the costumes of a sprite so that the sprite looks as if it's dancing. Let's start with a blank stage. Deselect the **costume #** block of code to remove it. Use the **Delete** tool bar icon to delete the sprite that you have on the stage. Now, click the icon to add a new sprite from the library. Choose the sprite named **1080 Hip-Hop** (see Figure 2-13) and click **OK** to add it to the stage. This sprite has 13 costumes.

Figure 2-13. *1080 Hip-Hop sprite*

Click as fast as you can on the `next costume` block in the **Looks** category. You don't need to drag and drop the block to the scripts area. Watch how the sprite dances hip-hop on the stage. In the next chapters, you will learn other ways to make the sprite dance or change costume without having to click the `next costume` block every time.

Example 2-4: Hide and Show

You can make sprites appear and disappear on the stage using code blocks in the **Looks** blocks category, as well as tool bar icons. Try it out. Make sure that the thumbnail view of the sprite is selected, and then click the `hide` block to remove the sprite from the stage. To make it come back, click the `show` block. The sprite reappears again on the stage.

Example 2-5: Painting a New Sprite

You can design your own sprite as well. This example will teach you how to create your own sprite. To do this, from the **File** menu, choose **New** to start with a clean stage and a new project. Delete the default cat sprite. In the Sprites pane, click the ✎ icon to paint a new sprite.

Notice the new paint area that opens to the right of the block palette. Also notice the new costume and new sprite thumbnail (see Figure 2-14).

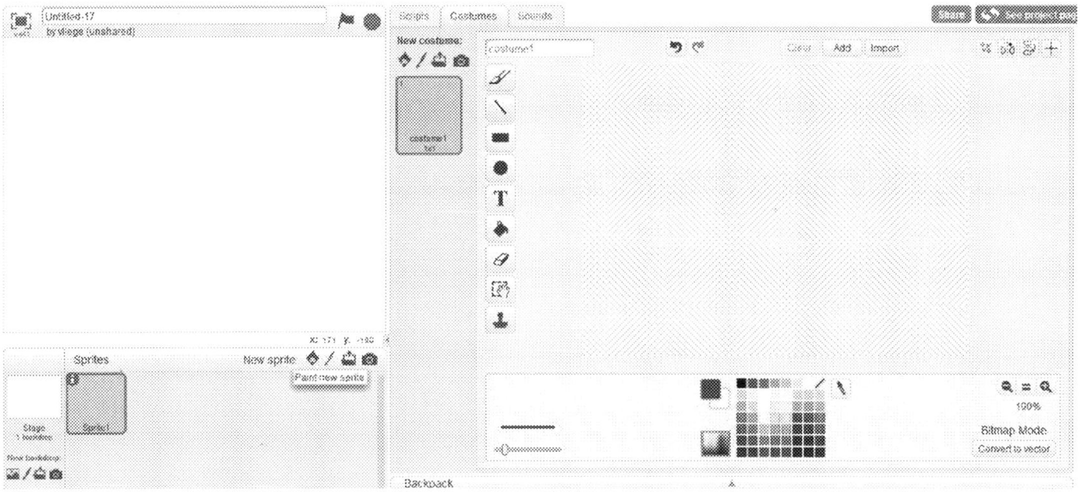

Figure 2-14. *The paint editor*

For this example, just try a simple shape. Later, you can draw whatever character or object that you want. Select the ellipse icon 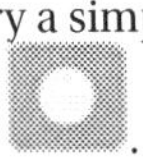. At the bottom of the paint area, make sure that you have the outline ellipse selected, not the solid ellipse (see Figure 2-15). Choose the black color from the color palette (see Figure 2-16). The outline of the circle we're going to draw will be black. Move your cursor to the right, and then draw the black outline of a circle in the paint area by holding your left mouse button and dragging the cursor (see Figure 2-17). If you make a mistake, you can always undo by clicking the undo icon 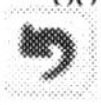 at the top of the paint area.

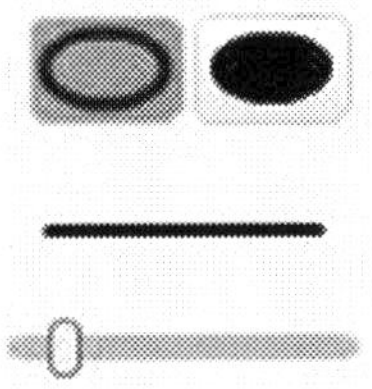

Figure 2-15. *Ellipse*

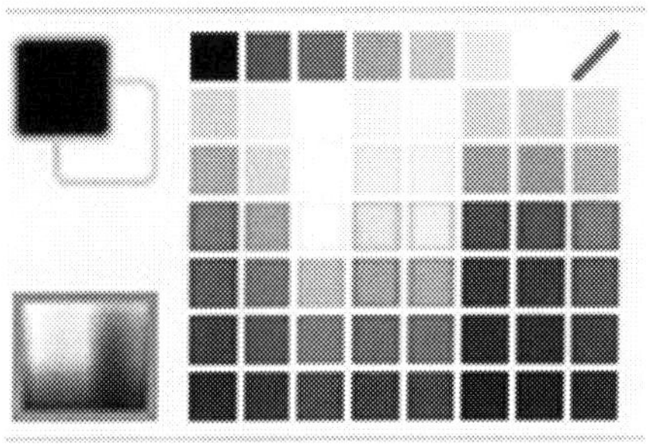

Figure 2-16. *The color palette*

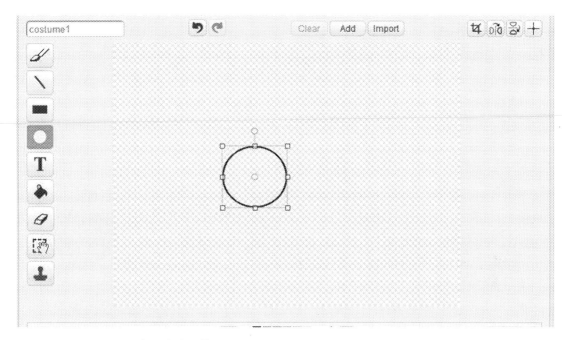

Figure 2-17. *Draw a circle with the Ellipse icon*

To center the circle, click the ✛ icon in the top-right corner of the paint area. A vertical and a horizontal line appear in the paint area (see Figure 2-18). Drag these lines to the center of the circle and let go. The circle will be positioned in the middle of the paint area.

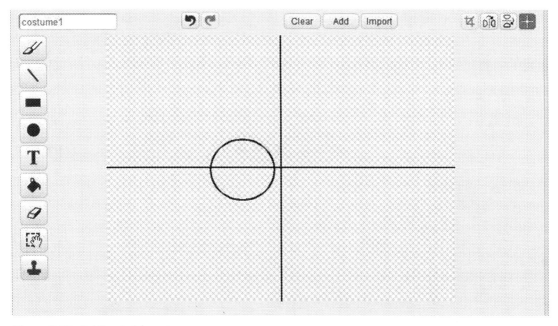

Figure 2-18. *Set the circle's center*

Next, fill the circle with the color yellow. Select yellow from the color palette and click the **fill with color** icon . At the bottom of the paint area, select the solid color icon (see Figure 2-19). Click in the center of the circle to fill the circle with the yellow color (see Figure 2-20).

Figure 2-19. *Select color*

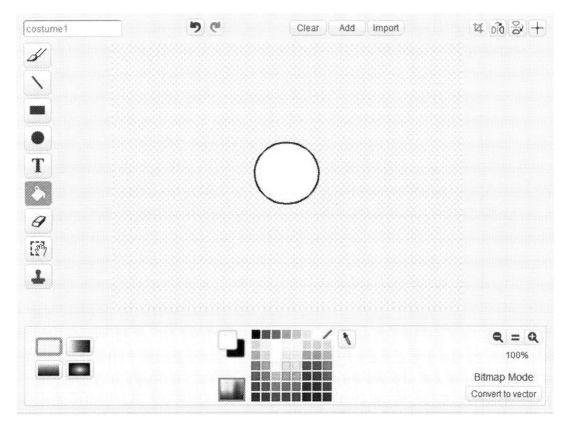

Figure 2-20. *Fill with color*

Let's give our circle a face using the **Line** icon ＼ . Select the black color before painting. Click the **Line** icon and click in the circle. Next, hold down your left mouse button and drag to draw the line. Add a few more lines to make your sprite look like what's shown in Figure 2-21.

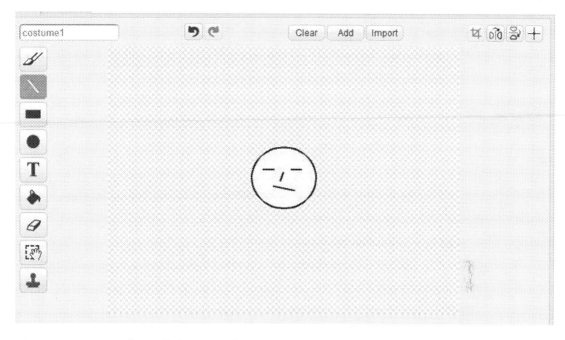

Figure 2-21. *Create a face with the Line tool*

After you create the sprite, it is saved automatically in the specific project that it was created in. Its costume is also saved. If you want to use the sprite in other projects, you need to drag it to the backpack and save it there.

Backdrops

A backdrop is the background of the stage area. By default, the background of the stage area is a white background, but this can be changed. Scripts can also instruct backdrops to perform actions like clearing the stage area or changing to another backdrop, but only the sprites can move.

Backdrops Pane

A backdrop is the background that appears behind your sprite on the stage, and every project has at least one. You can keep track of the backdrops used in a project with the Backdrops pane, which is to the left of the Sprites pane. As you can see in Figure 2-22, the Backdrops pane displays a thumbnail view of the current backdrop (in this case, the default backdrop is all white) with the name (**Stage** in this example) underneath it. Below this, the pane also states the number of backdrops that are used in your project.

Figure 2-22. *The Backdrops pane*

The same way that you can add new sprites to a project, you can add new backdrops. Simply click one of the icons in the **New backdrop** section of the Backdrops pane. Starting from the left, the icons enable you to do the following:

- Choose a new backdrop from the library

- Paint a new backdrop

- Upload a backdrop from a file

- Take a picture with your webcam and use that picture as a backdrop

If you want to see thumbnails of all the backdrops used in a project, click the thumbnail view of the current backdrop in the Backdrops pane. Scratch will replace the **Costumes** tab with the **Backdrops** tab, which displays thumbnails of all the backdrops that are in your project.

With the thumbnail view of the current backdrop selected, now click the **Scripts** tab. Notice that the available blocks of code change. The blocks of code that are available for use are dependent on which thumbnail view is selected: either a sprite or a backdrop thumbnail. For example, if you click the **Motion** category with a backdrop selected, no blocks of code will be available, because backdrops don't move. To get an idea of what you can do with backdrops, try the following examples.

Example 2-5: Adding a New Backdrop

Sometimes you want more than a plain white background for your sprite, so let's practice choosing and adding a backdrop. First, from the **File** menu, choose **New** to start a new project with a clean stage.

Adding a new backdrop is basically the same as adding a new sprite. In the Backdrops pane, click the ▓ icon to choose a backdrop from the library. When the **Backdrop Library** (see Figure 2-23) opens, select the **beach malibu** backdrop and click **OK**. Now the background of your stage area changes to the **beach malibu** backdrop, and the thumbnail view in the Backdrops pane changes to reflect this. Notice that Scratch replaces the Costumes tab with the Backdrops tab, which you see now lists two backdrops: the default white backdrop and the new that one you just added (see Figure 2-24).

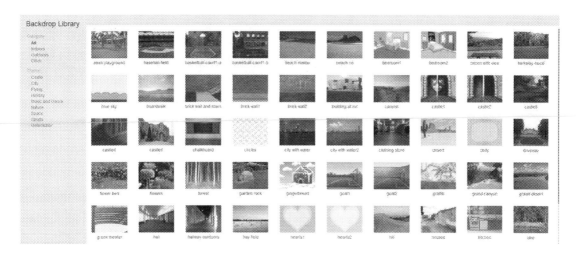

Figure 2-23. *The Backdrop Library*

Figure 2-24. *The beach malibu backdrop*

Example 2-6: Changing Backdrops

You can also use code blocks to change backdrops and learn more about the current backdrop. Select the thumbnail view in the Backdrops pane. Click the **Scripts** tab and within it click the **Looks** category to see the code blocks that apply to backdrops. Notice that you have a lot fewer blocks of code compared with when you had the sprite thumbnail view selected. Click the **next backdrop** block. Continuing to click the block will step through all the backdrops in your Backdrops pane. After the last backdrop, the first backdrop is displayed again. Notice how the backdrop changes on the stage and that the thumbnail view in the Backdrops pane changes to the current backdrop. As for the sprites, you can also change directly to a specific backdrop by name with the **switch backdrop to beach malibu** block. Use the block's pull-down menu to select the backdrop that you want on the stage, and then click the block to change the backdrop.

As you can see in Figure 2-24, each backdrop listed in the Backdrops pane also has a number assigned to it. To help you keep track of which one is the current backdrop, you can set a reporter block to appear on the stage and show the current backdrop number. In the Looks category, select the **☑ backdrop #** block. As you can see in Figure 2-25, a window appears on the stage, displaying the current backdrop's number. Click the **next backdrop** block to see the number change.

backdrop #   1

Figure 2-25. *Backdrop # reporter*

You can use another reporter block to display the current backdrop's name. In the **Looks** category, select the **☑ backdrop name** block to add a second reporter window to the stage, as shown in Figure 2-26.

30

Figure 2-26. Backdrop name reporter

Example 2-7: Painting a New Backdrop

You can also paint a new backdrop, just as you can draw your own sprites. In the Backdrops pane, click the

paintbrush icon ✎ to open the paint editor area for the backdrop (see Figure 2-27).

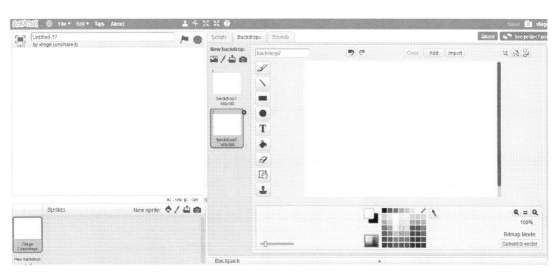

Figure 2-27. The backdrop paint editor

Let's paint a house. Choose black from the color palette and then click the **Rectangle** icon 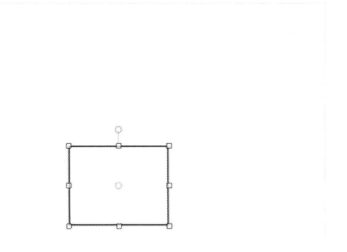 . In the paint area, hold the left mouse button as you drag to paint a square (see Figure 2-28).

Figure 2-28. *Square*

Next, click the **Line** icon . Starting at an upper corner of your rectangle, click and drag to draw the roof of the house (see Figure 2-29).

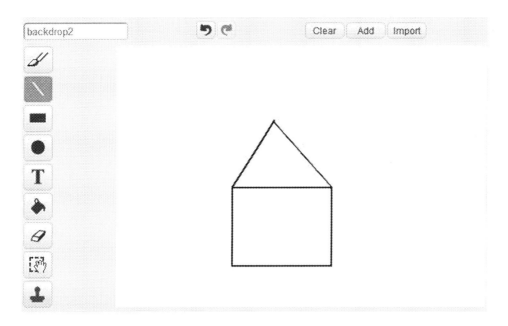

Figure 2-29. *Add a roof with the Line tool*

Next, use the **Rectangle** icon to add a door and windows to the house, as shown in Figure 2-30.

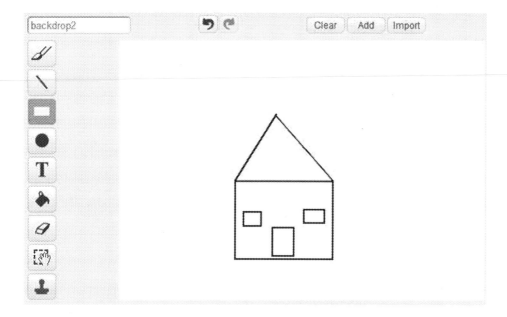

Figure 2-30. House

Now add some color to the house. Choose a color from the palette, click the **Fill with color** icon ![icon] , and then click in the roof to color it (see Figure 2-31). Use the same method to color the house (see Figure 2-32) and then the windows (see Figure 2-33).

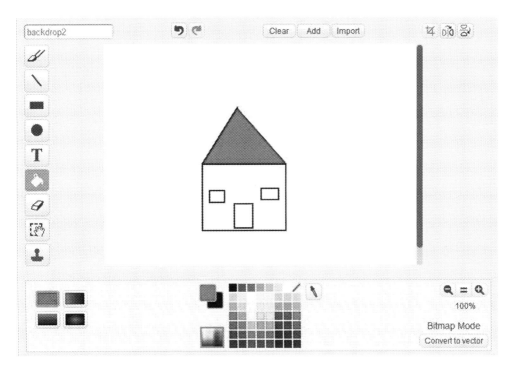

Figure 2-31. *Color the roof*

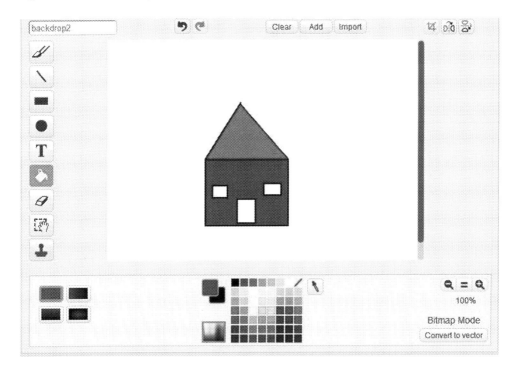

Figure 2-32. *Color the house*

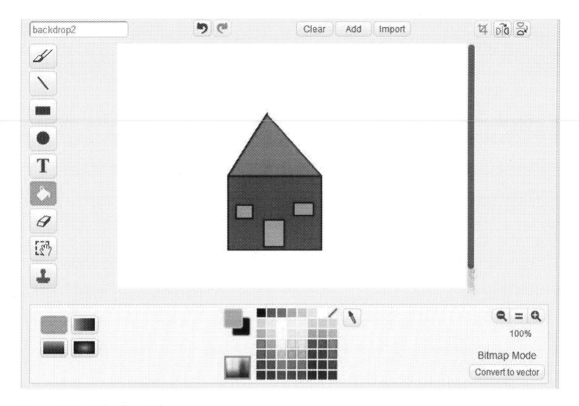

Figure 2-33. *Color the windows*

The house is now completed, and more importantly, you have painted a new backdrop. It shows up in the Backdrops tab and as the thumbnail view of the current backdrop in the Backdrops pane (see Figure 2-34). This new backdrop is also saved automatically in this project.

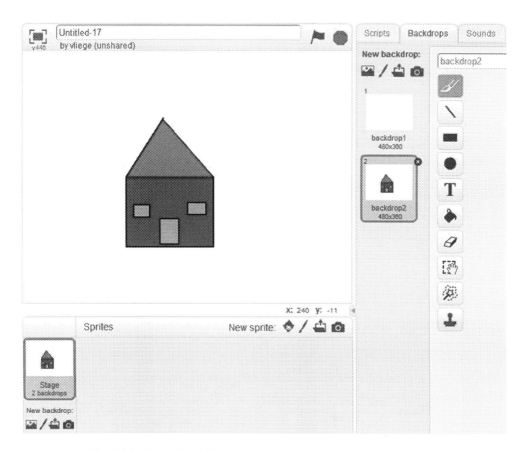

Figure 2-34. *The finished house backdrop*

Summary

In this chapter, you learned about two very important objects in Scratch: sprites and backdrops. From the scripts you create, sprites receive instructions telling them what to do. The backdrop, which is the background that is displayed on the stage, can also receive instructions from scripts, but only sprites can move.

There are many ways to add a sprite to a project. You can select a sprite from the Scratch library, for example, or you can create one yourself by painting it. A sprite consists of one or multiple costumes, which are alternate appearances of the sprite. Sequentially displaying these alternate appearances can give a sprite the illusion of movement.

Just as you can with sprites, you can add a backdrop to the stage in several ways, including selecting one from the Scratch library or painting one yourself. After learning about the interface, sprites, and backdrops, you now have the basic knowledge you need to start creating Scratch scripts, which is exactly what you'll do in the next chapter!

Exercises

1. Add a new sprite called **Avery Walking** from the library. Delete any other sprite on the stage. Only the new sprite should show on the stage.

2. Add a new backdrop called **bedroom1** from the library.

The answers to the exercises are available in Chapter 13.

CHAPTER 3

■ ■ ■

Make the Cat Move

This is the chapter that you've been waiting for. After reading the previous chapters, you now have all the background required to start programming in Scratch. In this chapter, you will learn about the blocks of code and how to use them to create scripts. You will also learn where to create scripts and where to run them. The focus of this chapter is specifically on the **Motion** category of code blocks. The blocks in this category instruct the sprite to move in various ways, and you'll learn how these blocks operate and how you can use them. Get ready, because you will start creating scripts in the second half of the chapter.

The Stage

You can think of the code blocks that you combine into a script as a series of instructions that tell your sprite what to do, as well as when and where to do it. To help you identify the point on the stage that your sprite currently occupies and specify exactly where to move it, Scratch uses a two-dimensional coordinate plane. To understand what that means, imagine the stage like a piece of graph paper with an *X axis* (a horizontal line) and a *Y axis* (a vertical line) crossing in the middle (see Figure 3-1). You can specify a location on the stage just like you'd plot a point on a graph, because every location on the stage is defined by a pair of X and Y positions, or *coordinates*. The X and Y axis cross, or intersect, in the middle of the stage, so the center of the stage is the point (0, 0).

© Eduardo A. Vlieg 2016
E. A. Vlieg, *Scratch by Example*, DOI 10.1007/978-1-4842-1946-1_3

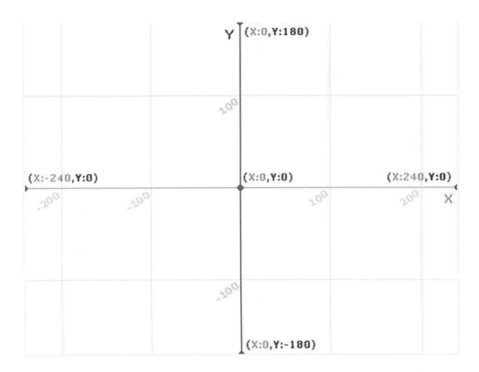

Figure 3-1. *Two-dimensional coordinate plane*

The stage is 480 pixels wide and 360 pixels high, so from the center of the stage (0, 0), the sprite can move 240 pixels to the right or 240 pixels to the left before hitting the edge. Likewise, a sprite can move only 180 pixels up or down from the center before hitting the edge of the stage. To specify the position of a sprite, use the X and Y coordinates that correspond to the position of the center of your sprite compared to the X axis and Y axis. For example, in Figure 3-2, the center of the cat is at (100, 100). You can check the position of your sprite by looking at the top-right corner of the scripts area. There you'll find the X, Y coordinates of the sprite beneath the small image of it (see Figure 3-3).

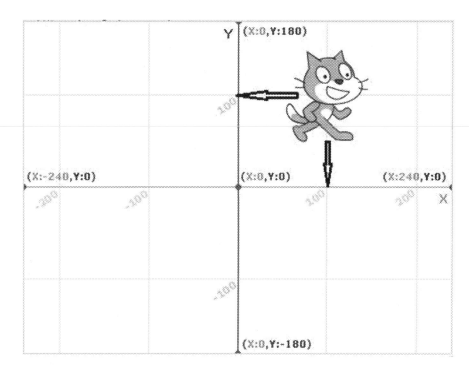

Figure 3-2. *The center of the sprite is at the position (100, 100)*

Figure 3-3. *The X, Y coordinates of the sprite*

While the X, Y coordinates tell you where the sprite is located, a measurement of degrees specifies in which direction the sprite is facing. Sprites can rotate 360 degrees on the stage. Facing to the right is 90 degrees. Facing toward the left is –90 degrees. Facing upward is 0 degrees and downward is 180 degrees. So, in Figure 3-2, the cat is at position (100, 100) and facing 90 degrees.

Scripts

In Scratch, scripts are the instructions that determine what happens on the stage. A script can have just one instruction (one block of code) or many. To create a script, you simply drag blocks of code from the block palette and snap them together in the scripts area. To snap one block to another, make sure that the notch of one block is aligned with the bump of the other one. When the blocks are close enough and ready to connect to each other, a white line (kind of like a glow) appears between them (see Figure 3-4). When you see it, let go of the block that you are dragging and it will snap automatically to the nearby block (see Figure 3-5).

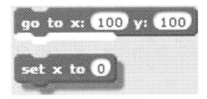

Figure 3-4. Before snapping together

Figure 3-5. After snapping together

There are six different block shapes that you can combine to create scripts. The shape of a block gives you a clue as to what the block does. The following describes the six shapes:

> **Hat blocks**: Sometimes called *triggers*, these blocks activate the script and start it running. Hat blocks are rounded at the top and sit on top of everything, like a real hat. You can snap other blocks can below them, but never above them. Most are found in the **Events** block category in the block palette. For example, the hat block in Figure 3-6 instructs the script to start when the green flag above the stage is clicked.

Figure 3-6. Example hat block

> **Stack blocks**: These blocks are the main instructions in a script. They have a notch at the top and a bump at the bottom, like a jigsaw puzzle piece, so you can snap other blocks below and above them (see Figure 3-7).

Figure 3-7. Example stack block

- **Boolean blocks**: Found in several categories in the block palette, these blocks contain conditions that are evaluated and then reported as either true or false. For example, the block in Figure 3-8 compares two items then reports *true* if the first is less than the second, and *false* if it isn't. In programming, conditions are used when a decision needs to be made; the result of the condition, whether true or false, determines the action to be taken. This may sound complicated, but you use the same Boolean logic in your daily life. For example, when you leave your office, whether you go left to the bus stop or right to walk home, depends on a condition: the weather. If it's raining, you dash to the left; if it's not, you go right and stroll home. You can embed Boolean blocks inside other blocks. You will find more about Boolean blocks in Chapter 7.

Figure 3-8. *Example Boolean block*

- **Reporter blocks**: These blocks hold values. The value can be either a number or a string of characters. Like the Boolean blocks, these blocks can only be embedded inside other blocks. No blocks can be snapped below or above them. The **direction** block (see Figure 3-9), found in the **Motion** blocks category, is an example of a reporter block. This block holds the current direction of the sprite. For example, if you want to know the current direction of the sprite, you can use this block in your script to display the direction on the stage. You will find more about reporter blocks, including how to use them, in Chapter 7.

Figure 3-9. *Example reporter block*

- **C blocks**: These blocks are found in the **Control** blocks category. Other blocks can be snapped inside them. For example, Figure 3-10 shows a C block that will repeat the sequence of the actions or blocks within it four times. You will use C blocks throughout this book, but Chapter 7 focuses on the Control blocks category.

Figure 3-10. *Example C block*

- **Cap blocks**: These blocks are snapped at the end of a script. Like a cap on the end of a pipe, cap blocks stop the flow of instructions (see Figure 3-11). There are only two cap blocks, both of which are found in the **Control** blocks category.

Figure 3-11. *Example cap block*

To start a script to run, just click it. A yellow glow appears around the script to indicate that it is activated and running (see Figure 3-12).

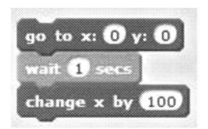

Figure 3-12. *Activated script*

Motion Blocks

Okay, so now that you have an understanding of the different block shapes and how to create scripts, let's take a closer look at the various **Motion** blocks, and then we'll start creating scripts. The Motion blocks category consists mostly of stack blocks. There are also some reporter blocks. With the blocks in the **Motion** category, you can make the sprite move in several ways. You can try out the following blocks by clicking to activate.

The ⟨move 10 steps⟩ block moves the sprite the number of steps you specify. Each step is equal to the length of a pixel. If the number is positive, the sprite moves in the direction that it is pointing toward. If the number is negative, the sprite moves in the opposite direction from which it's pointing. For instance, the example block moves the sprite 10 steps (10 pixels) in the direction that it's pointing.

Several blocks change the orientation of the sprite. The ⟨turn ↻ 15 degrees⟩ block turns the sprite clockwise according to the specified number of degrees. The ⟨turn ↺ 15 degrees⟩ block works the same way, but turns the sprite counterclockwise by the specified number of degrees. The examples here turn the sprite 15 degrees, but you can change the number in the blocks. Click each block to activate it and then watch the sprite turn in each direction. The ⟨point in direction 90▼⟩ block makes the sprite face toward a certain direction that you specify using the block's pull-down menu. Choose 90 to face the sprite to the right, –90 to face the sprite to the left, 0 to face it up, and 180 to face it down. The ⟨point towards ▼⟩ block points the sprite toward the mouse-pointer or another sprite in the project. Use the block's pull-down menu to display your options and choose what to point to. You can select the mouse-pointer or another sprite.

Sprites can move several ways. One way is by gliding, which gives the illusion of the sprite floating or gliding to a position. The ⟨glide 1 secs to x: -7 y: -283⟩ block makes the sprites glide for a specified number of seconds to a specified location. For instance, this block instructs the sprite to take 1 second to glide to the coordinates (–7, –283). Depending on the number of seconds, the sprite can move slower or faster. The **go to** blocks make the sprite move faster from one position to another. The ⟨go to x: -7 y: -283⟩ block moves the sprite to the specified location on the stage. Here the example block moves the sprite to the point (–7, –283). The ⟨go to mouse-pointer ▼⟩ block moves the sprite toward the mouse-pointer or another sprite in the project. You can use the pull-down menu to select another sprite or a random position for the sprite to go to.

The **change x by 10** block changes the current X coordinate by the specified number. For example, the block shown here adds 10 to the current X coordinate and moves the sprite to that X coordinate. If you use a negative number, the block will subtract that number from the current X coordinate. Similarly, the **change y by 10** block changes the current Y coordinate by the specified number.

The **set x to 0** block enables you to set only the X coordinate of the sprite to a specified value and move the sprite to that X coordinate. Likewise, the **set y to 0** block enables you to set only a Y coordinate and move the sprite to it.

If the sprite reaches the edge of the stage, the **if on edge, bounce** block makes the sprite bounce back in the opposite direction from where it was traveling. In other words, when the sprite reaches an edge of the stage, it will change orientation and travel back in the opposite direction from which it was traveling before hitting the edge.

The **set rotation style left-right** block sets the rotation style of the sprite. Using the pull-down menu in the block, you can choose one of three rotation styles: **left-right** means that the sprite can face only left or right; **all around** means that the sprite can face in any direction; and **do not rotate** means that the sprite always faces to the right (90 degrees) and cannot rotate.

Three blocks open monitor windows on the stage to report information about your sprite. The **x position** block holds the value of the current X coordinate of the sprite. If you select the box in front of it, a window opens on the stage and displays the current X coordinate of the sprite. The **y position** block works the same way for the Y coordinate of the sprite. Similarly, the **direction** block holds the value of the current direction of the sprite. Select the box in front of it to display the current direction of the sprite in a window on the stage.

Examples

It's time to start snapping some blocks together to create scripts that get your cat sprite moving. If you accidentally drag the wrong code block from the block palette to the scripts area, you can always unsnap the blocks from each other by clicking them and dragging them apart. To clean up the scripts area, you can also drag a block of code or a complete script back to the block palette. This is one way to erase a block of code or a complete script from the scripts area. If you want to start a new project for each script, you can always choose **File ➤ New** from the menu bar to create a new project with a clean scripts area.

Example 3-1: Move Forward

In this first example, let's take the cat on a forward walk. There are many ways to make the sprite move, and Script 3-1 demonstrates one of the simpler ways to do that.

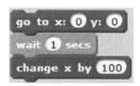

Script 3-1. *Move forward*

In the Sprites pane, select the thumbnail of Sprite1 (the cat) to tell Scratch to send instructions from the script that you're about to create to this sprite. In the block palette, click the **Motion** category to display its contents, and then drag the `go to x: 0 y: 0` block to the scripts area. If the block is not set to the coordinates (0, 0), please set the X value to 0 and the Y value to 0. Next, click the **Control** category in the block palette and drag the `wait 1 secs` to the scripts area and snap it to the previous block. If the block is not set to 1 second, please click in the number field to change it to 1 second. Finally, return to the **Motion** category, and drag and snap the `change x by 100` block to the script. If it's not set to 100, please change it so. To activate and run the script, click it in the scripts area.

The top block moves the sprite to the center of the stage. The next block, `wait 1 secs`, pauses the script for 1 second. The last code block adds 100 to the X coordinate of the sprite and moves the sprite to this new position. Because the sprite's X coordinate starts at 0, adding 100 changes it to 100. The Y coordinate stays the same, so the sprite moves to coordinates (100, 0).

Table 3-1 lists the blocks and describes the actions used in this example.

Table 3-1. *Code Blocks in Move Forward*

Blocks	Actions
`go to x: 0 y: 0`	Move the sprite to coordinates (X = 0, Y = 0), which is the middle of the stage.
`wait 1 secs`	The script waits 1 second. No actions are performed for 1 second.
`change x by 100`	Add 100 to the current value of the X coordinate and move the sprite to this new X coordinate.

Example 3-2: Move Backward

This example shows you how to create a script to make the sprite move backward. You can create Script 3-2 next to the previous one in the scripts area, or you can create it in a clean scripts area all by itself. Remember to select the thumbnail of the cat sprite first, and then drag the three blocks shown from the **Motion** and **Control** categories to snap them together in the scripts area. Be sure to set the values shown for each, as well.

Script 3-2. *Move backward*

Again, the top block of code will move the sprite to the center of the stage and the next pauses the script for 1 second. The last block of code moves the sprite 100 pixels in the opposite direction from which the sprite is facing, because the value specified is –100. Run the script, and then try changing the value for the final block to 100. Click to run the script again. This time, because the value is positive, the sprite moves in the same direction that it is facing.

Table 3-2 lists the blocks and describes the actions used in this example.

Table 3-2. *Code Blocks in Move Backward*

Blocks	Actions
go to x: 0 y: 0	Move the sprite to coordinates (X = 0, Y = 0), which is the middle of the stage.
wait 1 secs	The script waits 1 second. No actions are performed for 1 second.
move -100 steps	Move the sprite 100 pixels to the opposite direction from which it's facing.

Example 3-3: Move Up

Script 3-3 shows yet another way of moving the sprite. Because this script is the same as the previous ones, except for the last block of code, you can just remove the last block from Script 3-3, replace it with the

 block from the **Motion** category in the block palette, and set its value to 100.

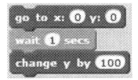

Script 3-3. *Move up*

Click the script to run it. This time, the cat moves up from the center of the stage to the coordinates (0, 100) because the final block adds 100 to the original Y coordinate value of 0.

Remember, you can always change the values in the code blocks' fields. Experiment with a new start

position by changing the values in the go to x: 0 y: 0 block. Pause the script for a longer length of time by increasing the second block's value or by moving the cat down by using a negative value in the final block. Run the script with your new values and watch how the sprite reacts.

Table 3-3 lists the blocks and describes the actions used in this example.

Table 3-3. *Code Blocks in Move Up*

Blocks	Actions
go to x: 0 y: 0	Move the sprite to coordinates (X = 0, Y = 0), which is the middle of the stage.
wait 1 secs	The script waits 1 second. No actions are performed for 1 second.
change y by 100	Add 100 to the current value of the Y coordinate and move the sprite to this new Y coordinate.

Example 3-4: Triggered Motion

Script 3-4 introduces a hat block as a trigger to activate the script when the user performs a certain action. You can find the hat blocks in the **Events** category in the block palette.

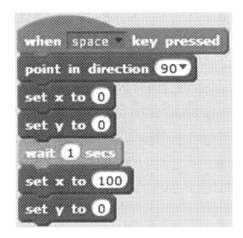

Script 3-4. *Triggered motion*

Drag the [when space key pressed] block from the **Events** category to the scripts area. Then choose **space** from the pull-down menu, if it's not already selected. Drag and snap together the remaining **Motion** and **Control** blocks needed to re-create Script 3-4, setting the parameters as shown.

The first block activates the script when the user presses the space bar (or you can choose a different key from the pull-down menu if you prefer). The next block makes the sprite face to the right (90 degrees). The third block of code sets the X coordinate to 0 and the next block sets the Y coordinate to 0. So the sprite begins by facing right and at the center of the stage. After a pause of 1 second, the last two blocks set the X and Y coordinates to 100 and 0, respectively, so that the sprite will move from the center to coordinates (100, 0).

Table 3-4 lists the blocks and describes the actions used in this example.

Table 3-4. *Code Blocks in Triggered Motion*

Blocks	Actions
when space ▾ key pressed	This block triggers the script. The script gets activated by pressing the space bar.
point in direction 90▾	Point the direction of the sprite to the right.
set x to 0	Set the value of the X coordinate to 0 and move the sprite to that location.
set y to 0	Set the value of the Y coordinate to 0 and move the sprite to that location.
wait 1 secs	The script waits 1 second. No actions are performed for 1 second.
set x to 100	Set the value of the X coordinate to 100 and move the sprite to that location.
set y to 0	Set the value of the Y coordinate to 0 and move the sprite to that location.

Example 3-5: Turn

Now try rotating your sprite. Drag the blocks from the **Events**, **Motion**, and **Control** categories of the block palette and snap together, as shown in Script 3-5. (Remember to select the thumbnail of the sprite in the sprites area first). This script uses the new hat block that activates the script when the user clicks the green flag above the stage. You still can activate the script by simply clicking it, though.

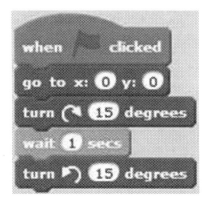

Script 3-5. *Turn*

After the user clicks the green flag, the next block moves the sprite to the center of the stage. The next block is new. It rotates the sprite 15 degrees clockwise from its current orientation. After a familiar 1 second pause, the last block rotates the sprite 15 degrees counterclockwise—back in its original orientation.

Remember that you can always change the values in the fields of the blocks to experiment and see how the sprite reacts.

Table 3-5 lists the blocks and describes the actions used in this example.

Table 3-5. *Code Blocks in Turn*

Blocks	Actions
when clicked	Clicking the green flag activates the script. The green flag is the trigger to start the script running.
go to x: 0 y: 0	Move the sprite to coordinates (X = 0, Y = 0), which is the middle of the stage.
turn ↻ 15 degrees	Turn the sprite clockwise 15 degrees.
wait 1 secs	The script waits 1 second. No actions are performed for 1 second.
turn ↺ 15 degrees	Turn the sprite counterclockwise 15 degrees.

Example 3-6: Backflip

This example rotates the sprite 360 degrees counterclockwise, creating the illusion of the sprite performing a backflip.

Take a look at Script 3-6. By now, you can probably tell what's going to happen. This time, the hat block activates the script when the user clicks the sprite on the stage. The next block makes the sprite face to the right. The third block moves the sprite to the center of the stage. Next is something new. It's a C block. Give it a try.

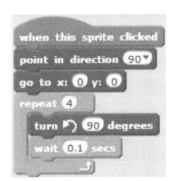

Script 3-6. *Backflip*

After dragging and snapping the first three blocks, go to the **Control** category and drag the

`repeat 4` block into place on the stage. Now snap the `turn ↺ 90 degrees` and

`wait 1 secs` blocks inside it. Make sure that each block's setting matches Script 3-6. After positioning the sprite at (0, 0), the script performs the first instruction inside the C block and turns the sprite counterclockwise 90 degrees from its current orientation. Next, the script pauses 0.1 second, and

then follows the arrow back to the top of the C block. Because it is set to 4, the `repeat 4` block repeats the sequence of instructions within it four times, flipping the cat 90 degrees from its current orientation each time. Run the script and watch it make the cat do a backflip.

You may think you're only snapping blocks together, but you're writing a real computer program. A Scratch script and a traditional computer program's lines of code are both lists of instructions telling the computer what to do. In this case, the blocks are telling the computer to move the sprite.

Table 3-6 lists the blocks and describes the actions used in this example.

Table 3-6. *Code Blocks in Backflip*

Blocks	Actions
when this sprite clicked	Clicking the sprite activates the script.
point in direction 90▼	Point the direction of the sprite to the right.
go to x: 0 y: 0	Move the sprite to coordinates (X = 0, Y = 0), which is the middle of the stage.
repeat 4	Repeat the actions represented by the blocks within this block four times.
turn ↺ 90 degrees	Turn the sprite counterclockwise 90 degrees.
wait 1 secs	The script waits 1 second. No actions are performed for 1 second.

Example 3-7: Square Pattern Motion

This time, you'll send the cat in a square pattern, from the center stage to coordinates (100, 0), (100, 100), and (0, 100), and then back to the center of the stage in its original position, facing to the right. Think about which blocks you might use to accomplish this, and then take a look at Script 3-7. Was your idea close? Drag and snap the blocks and adjust their settings to match the example script to try it.

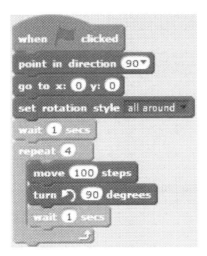

Script 3-7. *Square pattern motion*

According to the hat block, when the user clicks the green flag, the script starts. The next block makes the sprite face to the right. The third block moves the sprite to the center of the stage. The pull-down menu in the fourth block is set to give the sprite a rotation style of **all around**. This means that the sprite will be able to rotate all around (a 360-degree radius). The next block pauses the script for 1 second. The

block executes the blocks within it four times. The first block within it moves the sprite 100 pixels in the direction that it's facing. The next rotates the sprite 90 degrees counterclockwise, and the last block within the C block pauses the script for 1 second before repeating the three-block sequence.

Table 3-7 lists the blocks and describes the actions used in this example.

Table 3-7. *Code Blocks in Square Pattern Motion*

Blocks	Actions
when clicked	Clicking the green flag activates the script. The green flag is the trigger to start the script running.
point in direction 90	Point the direction of the sprite to the right.
go to x: 0 y: 0	Move the sprite to coordinates (X = 0, Y = 0), which is the middle of the stage.
set rotation style all around	Set the rotation style of the sprite so that it can rotate all around its axis.
wait 1 secs	The script waits 1 second. No actions are performed for 1 second.
repeat 4	Repeat the actions represented by the blocks within this block four times.
move 100 steps	Move 100 pixels.
turn ↺ 90 degrees	Turn the sprite counterclockwise 90 degrees.
wait 1 secs	The script waits 1 second. No actions are performed for 1 second.

Example 3-8: Glide and Bounce

The stage area has limits. If the sprite reaches any of the edges of the stage, it can get stuck. The
if on edge, bounce block prevents this, as you'll see in Script 3-8. Drag and snap the blocks together, and then watch what happens to the cat when it tries to glide past the edge of its world.

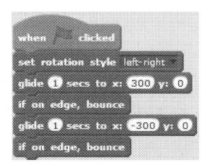

Script 3-8. *Glide and bounce*

The script starts running when the user clicks the green flag. The next block sets the rotation style of the sprite to **left-right**. This means that the sprite can only face left or right. The third block glides the block for 1 second to coordinates (300, 0). Remember that the limit of the X coordinate for the stage is 240, so the sprite will hit the edge (see Figure 3-13). The fourth block makes the sprite bounce when it hits the edge and travel in the opposite direction (see Figure 3-14). The next block will glide the sprite for 1 second to coordinates (–300, 0). Remember the limit of the X coordinate in that direction is –240. The last block will bounce the sprite when it hits the edge and make it travel in the opposite direction.

Figure 3-13. *Before reaching edge*

Figure 3-14. *After reaching the edge*

Table 3-8 lists the blocks and describes the actions used in this example.

Table 3-8. *Code Blocks in Glide and Bounce*

Blocks	Actions
when clicked	Clicking the green flag activates the script. The green flag is the trigger to start the script running.
set rotation style left-right	Set the rotation style of the sprite so that it can only turn left or right.
glide 1 secs to x: 300 y: 0	Glide the sprite for 1 second to coordinates, X = 300 and Y = 0.
if on edge, bounce	If the sprite reaches the edge of the stage, bounce in the opposite direction.
glide 1 secs to x: -300 y: 0	Glide the sprite for 1 second to coordinates, (X = –300, Y = 0).
if on edge, bounce	If the sprite reaches the edge of the stage, bounce in the opposite direction.

Example 3-9: Go to the Mouse-Pointer

It's time to let your cat have some fun with your mouse. Specifically, Script 3-9 demonstrates how to use your mouse-pointer to control the sprite. Drag and snap the necessary blocks together to try out this technique.

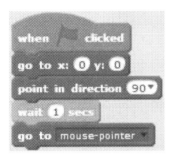

Script 3-9. *Go to the mouse-pointer*

The script starts when the user clicks the green flag. The next block moves the sprite to the center of the stage. The third block makes the sprite face to the right. The next block pauses the script for 1 second. The last block makes the sprite move toward the mouse-pointer.

Click the green flag, and then change the position of your mouse-pointer. Watch the sprite move toward it automatically.

Table 3-9 lists the blocks and describes the actions used in this example.

Table 3-9. *Code Blocks in Go to the Mouse-Pointer*

Blocks	Actions
when clicked	Clicking the green flag activates the script. The green flag is the trigger to start the script running.
go to x: 0 y: 0	Move the sprite to coordinates (X = 0, Y = 0), which is the middle of the stage.
point in direction 90	Point the direction of the sprite to the right.
wait 1 secs	The script waits 1 second. No actions are performed for 1 second.
go to mouse-pointer	Move the sprite toward the mouse-pointer.

Example 3-10: Move with the Mouse-Pointer

With the addition of a C block, you can keep your cat chasing your mouse forever—or at least until you click the stop button to stop the script.

As you snap together Script 3-10, you'll notice that it is identical to Script 3-9 until you reach the

block. Found in the **Control** category, this block will continue to execute the sequence of blocks within it until the script is stopped manually. In this case, there's only one block inside it: the

block. Click the green flag to run the script, and then move the mouse-pointer to watch how the sprite moves to it. To stop the script, click the red icon next to the green flag.

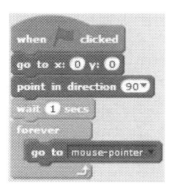

Script 3-10. *Move with the mouse-pointer*

Table 3-10 lists the blocks and describes the actions used in this example.

Table 3-10. *Code Blocks in Move with the Mouse-Pointer*

Blocks	Actions
when clicked	Clicking the green flag activates the script. The green flag is the trigger to start the script running.
go to x: 0 y: 0	Move the sprite to coordinates (X = 0, Y = 0), which is the middle of the stage.
point in direction 90	Point the direction of the sprite to the right.
wait 1 secs	The script waits 1 second. No actions are performed for 1 second.
forever	Repeat the actions represented by the blocks within this block forever—or until the script is stopped manually.
go to mouse-pointer	Move the sprite toward the mouse-pointer.

Example 3-11: Point Toward the Mouse-Pointer

What if you want your sprite to turn to face the mouse-pointer rather than move to its position? The answer is to use the 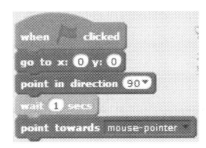 block, which makes the sprite face the direction of the mouse-pointer instead of moving toward it. Give Script 3-11 a try.

Script 3-11. *Point toward the mouse-pointer*

The actions of the first four blocks should be familiar. Clicking the green flag runs the script, the sprite moves to the center of the stage and faces to the right, and then the script pauses for 1 second. The last block of code faces the sprite toward the direction of the mouse-pointer. Activate the script and move the mouse-pointer to see how the sprite rotates to face its direction.

Table 3-11 lists the blocks and describes the actions used in this example.

Table 3-11. *Code Blocks in Point Toward the Mouse-Pointer*

Blocks	Actions
when ▢ clicked	Clicking the green flag activates the script. The green flag is the trigger to start the script running.
go to x: 0 y: 0	Move the sprite to coordinates (X = 0, Y = 0), which is the middle of the stage.
point in direction 90▾	Point the direction of the sprite to the right.
wait 1 secs	The script waits 1 second. No actions are performed for 1 second.
point towards mouse-pointer ▾	Point the direction of the sprite toward the mouse-pointer.

56

Example 3-12: Follow the Mouse-Pointer

Script 3-12 combines techniques from Scripts 3-10 and 3-11. Instead of making the sprite rotate to face the direction of the mouse-pointer once, it makes the sprite face the mouse-pointer continuously until the script is stopped.

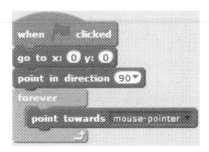

Script 3-12. *Follow the mouse-pointer*

The script starts running when the user clicks the green flag. The next two blocks of code will move the sprite to the center of the stage and make it face to the right. The next block, the C block, will execute the

block within it forever until the script is stopped manually. The block within the [forever] block will make the sprite face the direction of the mouse-pointer.

Create the script, activate it, and move the mouse-pointer around to watch how the sprite rotates.

Table 3-12 lists the blocks and describes the actions used in this example.

Table 3-12. *Code Blocks in Follow the Mouse-Pointer*

Blocks	Actions
when clicked	Clicking the green flag activates the script. The green flag is the trigger to start the script running.
go to x: 0 y: 0	Move the sprite to coordinates (X = 0, Y = 0), which is the middle of the stage.
point in direction 90▼	Point the direction of the sprite to the right.
forever	Repeat the actions represented by the blocks within this block forever—or until the script is stopped manually.
point towards mouse-pointer ▼	Point the direction of the sprite toward the mouse-pointer.

Summary

Congratulations, you now know how to build a basic script and move a sprite around the stage. You're a Scratch programmer! In this chapter, you learned how to create a script and how to activate it. You also learned about the various types of blocks of code and you specifically practiced using blocks in the **Motion** blocks category, among others.

In the next chapter, you continue using the knowledge that you gained here, but you focus on how to make the sprite draw on the stage.

Exercises

1.   Create a script to make the sprite **go to** positions (0, 0), (100, 100), and (–50, –100).

2.   Create a script that makes the sprite rotate 360 degrees on its axis. The user should activate the script by clicking the green flag.

The answers to the exercises are available in Chapter 13.

■ ■ ■

CHAPTER 4

Make the Cat Draw

With each chapter, you gain more knowledge about Scratch. You learn about more blocks of code and how to use them. This chapter focuses on the blocks in the **Pen** category. With these, you can write scripts that draw designs on the stage automatically. The blocks of code in this category are green and they perform different actions like drawing, changing the pen size and color, creating a copy of the sprite, and removing all marks previously created by the pen or stamp on the stage. After investigating how the various **Pen** blocks of code work, you'll practice using them in some examples scripts.

Pen Blocks

The blocks in the Pen category (see Figure 4-1) of the blocks palette enable you to draw on the stage and control the pen of the Scratch program. With these blocks, you can also set and change the color and width of the pen. Let's take a closer look at what each of the Pen category's blocks do before putting them to work in some example scripts.

© Eduardo A. Vlieg 2016
E. A. Vlieg, *Scratch by Example*, DOI 10.1007/978-1-4842-1946-1_4

Figure 4-1. Pen blocks

The  block removes all marks made previously by the pen or stamp on the stage. Think of it as your eraser, but a thorough one that erases all marks at once.

The stamp block creates a copy of the current sprite and stamps this image on the stage. In other words, it performs the same action as the tool bar's (**Duplicate**) icon.

When you draw with a real pen on a sheet of paper, you must perform three distinct actions: you first press the pen to the paper, you move it to create a mark, and then you lift the pen off the paper when you're finished. In Scratch, you use a combination of Pen and Motion blocks to accomplish the same three tasks. The **pen down** block performs the same action as pressing your pen to the paper; the pen is on the stage and ready to draw. The pen will draw a trail wherever the sprite goes on the stage. The pen follows the movements of the sprite. If the sprite moves in a square pattern and the **pen down** block is activated, for example, then pen will draw a square on the stage. When you're done drawing, you use the **pen up** block to lift the pen from the stage. Any motions performed after this block in a script will reposition the sprite, but will not draw a mark. When you're ready to draw again, simply snap on another **pen down** block.

Scratch offers several code blocks that enable you to customize the color that your pen draws with as well. For example, the **set pen color to** block sets the color of the pen. To set the color, click in the color box in the block. Your cursor will change into a pointing finger image, which you can use to then click and choose any color that's visible in the Scratch interface. Alternatively, you can set the pen color to a specific numeric value using the **set pen color to 0** block. Scratch offers 200 different colors, which are numbered from 0 (left end) to 199 (right end) along the color spectrum .

Using this same numbered spectrum, the **change pen color by 10** block changes the pen color by the specified increment compared to the current color. Positive numbers shift the color toward the right in the spectrum, while negative numbers shift the specified amount to the left.

You can also control the shade of each of Scratch's 200 colors. The **set pen shade to 50** block sets the shade of the pen color. A pen shade of 0 is completely black, a pen shade of 100 is completely white, and a pen shade of 50 is the pure color. Values between 0 and 50 mix the color with black. Values between 50 and 100 mix the color with white. If the value is greater than 100, it alternates every 100; so 100 to 200 goes white to black, and 200 to 300 goes black to white. Thus, changing the shade by 200 or any multiple of 200 will have no effect. For example, let's say that you are using the color green. Setting the shade to 50 is the pure color. If you want a lighter shade of green, you modify the number in the block to a value between 50 and 100, which mixes the pure color with white and creates a lighter shade. This **change pen shade by 10** block changes the shade of the pen color by the specified increment. So for example, if the pen color is green, you can change the value of this block and thereby change the shade of green.

Finally, you can easily change the width of the line that the pen draws with two additional blocks. The **set pen size to 1** block enables you to set the width of the line that the pen draws. The specified value is equal to the width of the line that the pen draws; for example, a value of 3 means that the width of the line that the pen draws is equal to three pixels. The value can range from 0 to 255.

The **change pen size by 1** block increases (positive values) or decreases (negative values) the width of the line that the pen draws by the specified number of pixels.

Examples

It's time to put the pen to the stage and start drawing. The following examples demonstrate how you can use the **Pen** blocks of code in scripts to draw several different shapes and apply various effects.

Example 4-1: How to Draw a Line

This example teaches you how to draw a line in Scratch. From the blocks palette, drag the blocks from the **Pen** and **Motion** categories to the scripts area and snap them together to create Script 4-1.

Script 4-1. *Draw a line*

The block clears the stage by removing all marks previously made by the pen or stamp. The next block sets the pen color and the third block sets the width of the line that the pen draws. As you remember from Chapter 3, the block set to 90 degrees makes the sprite face to the right and the block moves the sprite to the specified coordinates of (-100, 0). The block means that the sprite is ready to draw; wherever the sprite moves, the pen will draw a line. The next block makes the sprite glide for 1 second to coordinates (100, 0). The block essentially lifts the pen from the stage; so if the sprite moves, the pen will not draw.

To activate the script, just click it. Watch the sprite draw a horizontal line (see Figure 4-2) from (-100, 0) to (100, 0).

Figure 4-2. *Result of Script 4-1*

Table 4-1 lists the blocks and describes the actions used in this example.

Table 4-1. *Code Blocks in How to Draw a Line*

Blocks	Actions
clear	Remove all marks previously made by the pen or stamp.
set pen color to 10	Set the pen color to 10.
set pen size to 3	Set the pen size to 3.
point in direction 90▾	Make the sprite face to the right.
go to x: -100 y: 0	Move the sprite to coordinates (–100, 0).
pen down	The pen is on the stage and is ready to draw.
glide 1 secs to x: 100 y: 0	Make the sprite glide for 1 second to coordinates (100, 0). Because the **pen down** block was previously used, the pen will draw a trail wherever the sprite moves.
pen up	The pen is off the stage and cannot draw.

Example 4-2: How to Draw Lines

Take a look at Script 4-2. Based on what you learned in the last example, can you figure out what this one does without creating and running it?

Script 4-2. *Draw lines*

The first three blocks of code are the same as Script 4-1. They clear the stage, remove all previous marks, set the pen color, and set the pen size. This time, the forth block sets the rotation style of the sprite so that it can rotate in all directions, 360 degrees. The `point in direction 90` block then makes the sprite face to the right. The next block moves the sprite to coordinates, (–100, –100). The `pen down` block means that the sprite will draw wherever it moves until the scripts reaches the `pen up` block. The next block makes the sprite glide for 1 second to coordinates (100, –100), so the sprite draws a line from (–100, –100) to (100, –100). The next blocks make the sprite face upward, and then it glides for another 1 second to coordinates (100, 100) drawing a line as it moves (see Figure 4-3). The final block lifts the pen from the stage so that it will not draw anymore.

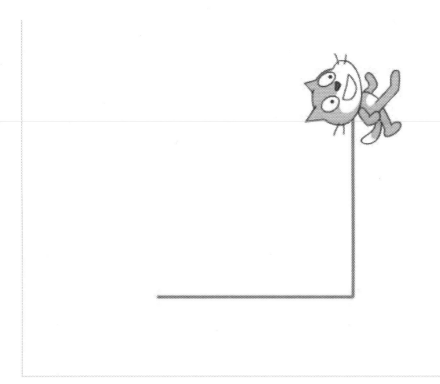

Figure 4-3. *Result of Script 4-2*

Table 4-2 lists the blocks and describes the actions used in this example.

Table 4-2. *Code Blocks in How to Draw Lines*

Blocks	Actions
clear	Remove all marks previously made by the pen or stamp.
set pen color to 10	Set the pen color to 10.
set pen size to 3	Set the pen size to 3.
set rotation style all around ▼	Set the rotation style of the sprite so that it can rotate all around its axis.
point in direction 90▼	Make the sprite face to the right.
go to x: -100 y: -100	Move the sprite to the position where X = –100 and Y = –100.
pen down	The pen is on the stage and is ready to draw.
glide 1 secs to x: 100 y: -100	Make the sprite glide for 1 second to coordinates (100, -100). Wherever the sprite moves, the pen will draw a trail.
point in direction 0▼	Make the sprite face up.
glide 1 secs to x: 100 y: 100	Make the sprite glide for 1 second to coordinates (100, 100). Wherever the sprite moves, the pen will draw a trail.
pen up	The pen is off the stage and cannot draw.

Example 4-3: How to Draw a Square

Remember a good way to learn any programming language, including Scratch, is to look at the script and try to figure out what it does. Many of the blocks in Script 4-3 will be familiar. Using the move 200 steps block enables you to move the pen a desired distance without needing to figure out the specific coordinates.

```
clear
set pen size to 3
set pen color to 20
point in direction 90▾
go to x: -100 y: -100
pen down
move 200 steps
wait 1 secs
point in direction 0▾
move 200 steps
wait 1 secs
point in direction -90▾
move 200 steps
wait 1 secs
point in direction 180▾
move 200 steps
point in direction 90▾
pen up
```

Script 4-3. *Draw a square*

The three first blocks of code of this script remove all previous marks from the stage and set the pen's size and color. The next two blocks face the sprite to the right and moves it to coordinates (–100, –100). The `pen down` block means that the pen is ready to draw. The `move 200 steps` block moves the sprite 200 pixels in the direction that it's facing. Because the pen is down, the pen will draw wherever the sprite moves. The next block pauses the script for 1 second. The `point in direction 0▾` block faces the sprite up and the next block moves it 200 pixels up. After another 1-second pause, the sprite's direction is set to –90 degrees to face the sprite to the left and the sprite moves 200 pixels to the left. After another 1-second wait and direction change, the sprite moves 200 pixels downward. The last `point in direction 90▾` block faces the sprite to the right again before the pen is lifted up, meaning that the sprite is done drawing.

Click the script to run it. In the previous chapter, Script 3-7 made the sprite move in a square pattern. This script uses a slightly different technique to make the sprite move in a square pattern, and because the `pen down` block is used, the pen will draw wherever the sprite moves. Because the sprite moves in a square pattern, the pen draws a square (see Figure 4-4).

Figure 4-4. *Result of Script 4-3*

Table 4-3 lists the blocks and describes the actions used in this example.

Table 4-3. *Code Blocks in How to Draw a Square*

Blocks	Actions
clear	Remove all marks previously made by the pen or stamp.
set pen size to 3	Set the pen size to 3.
set pen color to 20	Set the pen color to 20.
point in direction 90▼	Make the sprite face to the right.
go to x: -100 y: -100	Move the sprite to coordinates (–100, –100).
pen down	The pen is on the stage and is ready to draw.
move 200 steps	Move the sprite 200 pixels in the direction that it's facing. Wherever the sprite moves, the pen will draw a trail.

(continued)

Table 4-3. (*continued*)

Blocks	Actions
wait 1 secs	The script waits 1 second. No actions are performed for 1 second.
point in direction 0	Make the sprite face up.
move 200 steps	Move the sprite 200 pixels in the direction that it's facing. Wherever the sprite moves, the pen will draw a trail.
wait 1 secs	The script waits 1 second. No actions are performed for 1 second.
point in direction -90	Make the sprite face to the left.
move 200 steps	Move the sprite 200 pixels in the direction that it's facing. Wherever the sprite moves, the pen will draw a trail.
wait 1 secs	The script waits 1 second. No actions are performed for 1 second.
point in direction 180	Make the sprite face down.
move 200 steps	Move the sprite 200 pixels in the direction that it's facing. Wherever the sprite moves, the pen will draw a trail.
point in direction 90	Make the sprite face to the right.
pen up	The pen is off the stage and cannot draw.

Example 4-4: Same Square, Different Way

Remember that you can create multiple scripts in the same scripts area per project, but if you want to have one project for each script, you can go to the **File** menu and choose **New** to create a new project for your script. Script 4-4 produces the same result as Script 4-3, which is to draw a square, but it uses a

block like Script 3-7 did.

The actions that repeat in Script 4-3 are move the sprite, make the sprite face a certain direction, and wait 1 second. You'll snap the blocks for those three within the C block to repeat them, as shown in Script 4-4.

Script 4-4. *Same square, different way*

The three first blocks of code of this script remove all previous marks from the stage and set the pen's size and color. The next two block face the sprite to the right and move it to coordinates (–100, –100). The

block means that the pen is ready to draw. Next is the block that will repeat the blocks within it four times. The blocks within it move the sprite 200 pixels in the direction that it's facing, rotate the sprite 90 degrees counterclockwise, and pauses the script for 1 second. The last block stops the pen from drawing.

Notice how this script is shorter than Script 4-3, although they produce the same result, which is a square. Remember, if you have repeating actions in a script, try putting them in a repeat block to create a shorter and more efficient script.

Table 4-4 lists the blocks and describes the actions used in this example.

Table 4-4. *Code Blocks in Same Square, Different Way*

Blocks	Actions
clear	Remove all marks previously made by the pen or stamp.
set pen size to 3	Set the pen size to 3.
set pen color to 20	Set the pen color to 20.
point in direction 90▾	Make the sprite face to the right.
go to x: -100 y: -100	Move the sprite to coordinates (–100, –100).
pen down	The pen is on the stage and is ready to draw.
repeat 4	Repeat the actions represented by the blocks within this block four times.
move 200 steps	Move the sprite 200 pixels in the direction that it's facing. Wherever the sprite moves, the pen will draw a trail.
turn ↺ 90 degrees	Turn the sprite counterclockwise 90degrees.
wait 1 secs	The script waits 1 second. No actions are performed for 1 second.
pen up	The pen is off the stage and cannot draw.

Example 4-5: How to Draw a Triangle

Drawing a triangle uses the same concepts as drawing a square. The main differences are the number of steps and the angle of the direction change. Drag and snap together the blocks for Script 4-5 to see how it works.

Script 4-5. *Draw a triangle*

The three first blocks of code in this script remove all previous marks from the stage and set the pen's size and color. The next two blocks face the sprite to the right and move it to coordinates (–100, –100).

The ![pen down] block means that wherever the sprite moves next, the pen will draw a trail.

The ![repeat 3] block repeats the action within it three times. Those actions are to move the sprite 300 pixels in the direction that it's facing, turn the sprite 120 degrees counterclockwise, and pause the script for 1 second. The pen will draw three lines, each one in a different direction (as shown in Figure 4-5). The last block tells the sprite that it is done drawing.

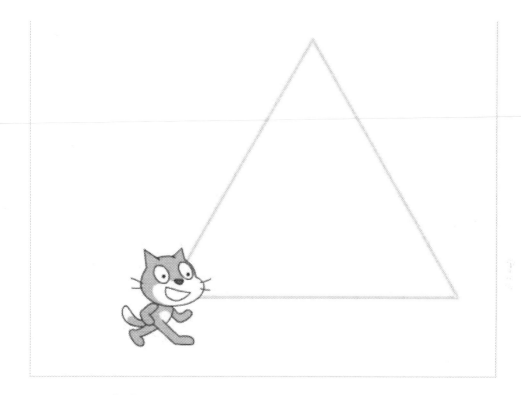

Figure 4-5. *Result of Script 4-4*

Remember, you can always change the size and color of the pen by simply changing the value in the blocks. Give it a try and see how the width and color of the lines change.

Table 4-5 lists the blocks and describes the actions used in this example.

Table 4-5. *Code Blocks in How to Draw a Triangle*

Blocks	Actions
clear	Remove all marks previously made by the pen or stamp.
set pen size to 3	Set the pen size to 3.
set pen color to 50	Set the pen color to 50.
point in direction 90▾	Make the sprite face to the right.
go to x: -100 y: -100	Move the sprite to coordinates (–100, –100).
pen down	The pen is on the stage and is ready to draw.
repeat 3	Repeat the actions represented by the blocks within this block three times.
move 300 steps	Move the sprite 300 pixels in the direction that it's facing. Wherever the sprite moves, the pen will draw a trail.
turn ↺ 120 degrees	Turn the sprite counterclockwise 120 degrees.
wait 1 secs	The script waits 1 second. No actions are performed for 1 second.
pen up	The pen is off the stage and cannot draw.

Example 4-6: How to Draw an Octagon

You have learned how to draw a line, a square, and triangle. By increasing the repeats to 8 and changing the turn angle to 45 degrees, you can draw an octagon by using the same technique.

In Script 4-6, the three first blocks of code again remove all previous marks from the stage and set the pen's size and color. The next two blocks face the sprite to the right and move it to coordinates (–50, –100).

The **pen down** block means that the pen is ready to start drawing. Within the C block, the sequence of actions repeats eight times: the sprite moves 100 pixels in the direction that it's facing, rotates 45 degrees counterclockwise, and pauses for 1 second. So the script draws a 100-pixel line eight times with each line at a 45-degree angle to the previous one. The last block of code stops the pen from drawing. Now, click the script to activate it and watch it draw an octagon (see Figure 4-6).

Script 4-6. *Draw an octagon*

Figure 4-6. *Result of Script 4-6*

If you change the number of steps that the sprite moves, you can make the octagon smaller or bigger. Remember, you can always change the pen size and color, as well.

Table 4-6 lists the blocks and describes the actions used in this example.

Table 4-6. *Code Blocks in How to Draw an Octagon*

Blocks	Actions
clear	Remove all marks previously made by the pen or stamp.
set pen size to 6	Set the pen size to 6.
set pen color to 30	Set the pen color to 30.
point in direction 90	Make the sprite face to the right.
go to x: -50 y: -100	Move the sprite to coordinates (–50, –100).
pen down	The pen is on the stage and is ready to draw.
repeat 8	Repeat the actions represented by the blocks within this block eight times.
move 100 steps	Move the sprite 100 pixels in the direction that it's facing. Wherever the sprite moves, the pen will draw a trail.
turn ↺ 45 degrees	Turn the sprite counterclockwise 45 degrees.
wait 1 secs	The script waits 1 second. No actions are performed for 1 second.
pen up	The pen is off the stage and cannot draw.

Example 4-7: How to Draw a Circle

Although it doesn't appear to have straight sides, you can draw a circle using the same technique as you did for a triangle, square, and octagon. Again, the key is in the number of repeats and the angle of the sprite's turn. A full circle is composed of 360 degrees. Therefore, if you change the pen's direction by 10 degrees 36 times, you'll draw a full circle ($36 \times 10 = 360$). Drag and snap the blocks for Script 4-7 to see how this works.

```
clear
set pen color to 10
set pen size to 3
go to x: 0 y: -100
point in direction 90▾
wait 1 secs
pen down
repeat 36
    move 20 steps
    turn ↻ 10 degrees
pen up
```

Script 4-7. *Draw a circle*

The first five blocks of code clear all previous marks from the stage, set the pen's color and size, move the sprite to its starting position of (0, –100), and make the sprite face to the right. The next block pauses the

whole script for 1 second, and then the pen is readied to draw. The ⬚ block will repeat the sequence of actions within it 36 times: move the sprite 20 pixels in the direction that it's facing, and then rotate the sprite 10 degrees counterclockwise. The last stops the pen from drawing anymore.

Click the script to activate it and watch Scratch draw a circle (see Figure 4-7).

Figure 4-7. *Result of Script 4-7*

Table 4-7 lists the blocks and describes the actions used in this example.

Table 4-7. *Code Blocks in How to Draw a Circle*

Blocks	Actions
clear	Remove all marks previously made by the pen or stamp.
set pen color to 10	Set the pen color to 10.
set pen size to 3	Set the pen size to 3.
go to x: 0 y: -100	Move the sprite to coordinates (0, –100).
point in direction 90	Make the sprite face to the right.
wait 1 secs	The script waits 1 second. No actions are performed for 1 second.

(continued)

Table 4-7. (*continued*)

Blocks	Actions
pen down	The pen is on the stage and is ready to draw.
repeat 36	Repeat the actions represented by the blocks within this block 36 times.
move 20 steps	Move the sprite 20 pixels in the direction that it's facing. Wherever the sprite moves, the pen will draw a trail.
turn ↺ 10 degrees	Turn the sprite counterclockwise 10 degrees.
pen up	The pen is off the stage and cannot draw.

Example 4-8: Circle Art

Now that you have learned how to draw some basic shapes, it's time to create some art. Script 4-8 draws 24 circles of different colors by putting one C block inside another.

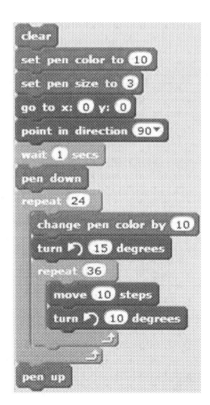

Script 4-8. *Circle art*

As you drag the blocks into place, you'll notice Script 4-8 starts with a familiar pattern. The first five blocks of code clear all previous marks from the stage, set the pen's color and size, move the sprite to its starting position of (0, 0), and make the sprite face to the right. The next block pauses the whole script for

1 second, and then the pen is readied to draw. The script then enters the first ⬚ block to perform its sequence of instructions. Inside, the first the action is to change the pen color's value by 10. The next block rotates the sprite 15 degrees counterclockwise. Then the script moves to the inner repeat

block, ⬚. This block performs the sequence of instructions inside it (move and draw 10 steps, then turn 10 degrees) 36 times before looping back to repeat the beginning of the sequence in the outer C block. So, each of the 24 times that it repeats the outer repeat block, Scratch changes the pen color, rotates the sprite, and then draws a circle using the inner repeat block's instructions. The last block, which is outside both repeating blocks, instructs the pen to stop drawing.

Click the script to see the beautiful art that it creates (see Figure 4-8). It will draw 24 circles, each with a different color and each starting at the same location (0, 0), but with the sprite facing a different direction because it rotates around its axis. If you don't see the sprite rotate on the stage, set its rotation style to **all around**.

Figure 4-8. Circle art

Table 4-8 lists the blocks and describes the actions used in this example.

Table 4-8. *Code Blocks in Circle Art*

Blocks	Actions
clear	Remove all marks previously made by the pen or stamp.
set pen color to 10	Set the pen color to 10.
set pen size to 3	Set the pen size to 3.
go to x: 0 y: 0	Move the sprite to the center of the stage.
point in direction 90▾	Make the sprite face to the right.
wait 1 secs	The script waits 1 second. No actions are performed for 1 second.
pen down	The pen is on the stage and is ready to draw.
repeat 24	Repeat the actions represented by the blocks within this block 24 times.
change pen color by 10	Change the pen color by 10.
turn ↻ 15 degrees	Turn the sprite counterclockwise 15 degrees.
repeat 36	Repeat the actions represented by the blocks within this block 36 times.
move 10 steps	Move the sprite 10 pixels in the direction that it's facing. Wherever the sprite moves the pen will draw a trail.
turn ↻ 10 degrees	Turn the sprite counterclockwise 10 degrees.
pen up	The pen is off the stage and cannot draw.

Example 4-9: Triangle Art

Using Script 4-8's same basic technique of a repeat block within a repeat block, you can create art with triangles. See if you can figure out what happens in Script 4-9 before creating and running it. Remember, the script sends instructions to the sprite, starting from the top to the bottom, and performs all the instructions and repeats of the inner repeat block before moving on to the next instruction in the outer repeat block.

Script 4-9. *Triangle art*

The first five blocks of code clear all previous marks from the stage, set the pen's size and color, make the sprite face to the right, and move the sprite to its starting position of (-100, -100). The next block readies the pen to draw. Next, the action moves into the outer repeat block. The first block inside is the start of the inner repeat block, so Scratch begins the instructions inside it and repeats them three times to draw the three sides of a triangle, pausing 0.2 seconds at the end of each sequence.

After completing the inner block, the script moves the sprite 100 pixels in the direction that it's facing, rotates the sprite 60 degrees counterclockwise, and changes the pen color. One repeat of the sequence of actions within the outer repeat block is then complete, so the script loops back to the start of the

block until all 30 repeats are complete. When they are, the block stops the pen from drawing.

So, this script draws a triangle 30 times, and each triangle will be in a different position and a different color. Why in a different position? Because at the end of each repeat, the script moves the sprite 100 pixels and rotates it 60 degrees counterclockwise before drawing a new triangle (see Figure 4-9).

Figure 4-9. *Result of Script 4-9*

Table 4-9 lists the blocks and describes the actions used in this example.

Table 4-9. *Code Blocks in Triangle Art*

Blocks	Actions
clear	Remove all marks previously made by the pen or stamp.
set pen color to 10	Set the pen color to 10.
set pen color to 50	Set the pen size to 50.
point in direction 90▾	Make the sprite face to the right.
go to x: -100 y: -100	Move the sprite to coordinates (–100, –100).
pen down	The pen is on the stage and is ready to draw.
repeat 30	Repeat the actions represented by the blocks within this block 30 times.
repeat 3	Repeat the actions represented by the blocks within this block three times.
move 200 steps	Move the sprite 200 pixels in the direction that it's facing. Wherever the sprite moves, the pen will draw a trail.

(*continued*)

Table 4-9. (*continued*)

Blocks	Actions
turn ↺ 120 degrees	Turn the sprite counterclockwise 120 degrees.
wait 0.2 secs	The script waits 0.2 seconds. No actions are performed for 0.2 seconds.
move 100 steps	Move the sprite 100 pixels in the direction that it's facing. Wherever the sprite moves, the pen will draw a trail.
turn ↺ 60 degrees	Turn the sprite counterclockwise 60 degrees.
change pen color by 20	Change the pen color by 20.
pen up	The pen is off the stage and cannot draw.

Example 4-10: Fill the Circle

Using a similar technique to Script 4-9, Script 4-10 draws a circle 23 times, but each time it changes the pen color and increases the pen size.

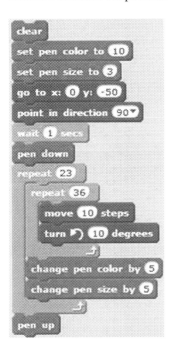

Script 4-10. *Fill the circle*

You should be very familiar with the first seven blocks of code from the previous scripts in this chapter. The first clears the stage by removing all marks made by the pen or stamp; the next two set the pen's color and size; the next pair move the sprite to (0, –50) and face it to the right; the script pauses; and then the pen is made ready to draw. Now wherever the sprite moves, the pen will draw a trail.

Next, the action enters the outer **repeat 23** block. The first instruction in its sequence is the inner **repeat 36** block, which draws a circle using 36 repeats of the **move 10 steps** and **turn 10 degrees** blocks. After the final repeat of the inner repeat block, the action exits to the last two blocks of the outer repeat block, which increment the pen's color by 10 and increase its size by 5. Next, the script loops back to the start of the outer repeat block to repeat the sequence. After 23 repeats of drawing a circle, and then changing the pen size and color, the script exits the outer repeat block (see Figure 4-10). The last block lifts the pen to signal that it is done drawing.

Figure 4-10. *Result of Script 4-10*

Table 4-10 lists the blocks and describes the actions used in this example.

Table 4-10. *Code Blocks in Fill the Circle*

Blocks	Actions
clear	Remove all marks previously made by the pen or stamp.
set pen color to (10)	Set the pen color to 10.
set pen size to (3)	Set the pen size to 3.
go to x: (0) y: (-50)	Move the sprite to coordinates (0, –50).
point in direction (90▾)	Make the sprite face to the right.
wait (1) secs	The script waits 1 second. No actions are performed for 1 second.
pen down	The pen is on the stage and is ready to draw.
repeat (23)	Repeat the actions represented by the blocks within this block 23 times.
repeat (36)	Repeat the actions represented by the blocks within this block 36 times.
move (10) steps	Move the sprite 10 pixels in the direction that it's facing. Wherever the sprite moves, the pen will draw a trail.
turn ↺ (10) degrees	Turn the sprite counterclockwise 10 degrees.
change pen color by (5)	Change the pen color by 5.
change pen size by (5)	Change the pen size by 5.
pen up	The pen is off the stage and cannot draw.

Example 4-11: Color the Stage

Script 4-11 makes the sprite draw a line while moving from left to right on the stage. When the sprite reaches the edge of the stage, it bounces in the opposite direction from which it was traveling, moves up 10 pixels, changes the line color, and then repeats the actions. The result is a stage covered in different colored lines from left to right. The blocks you use should all be familiar. Before you check the script or Table 4-11, which blocks would you use and how would you arrange them?

```
clear
set pen size to 20
set pen color to 50
point in direction 90▾
set rotation style left-right ▾
go to x: 0 y: -100
pen down
repeat 100
    move 300 steps
    if on edge, bounce
    change pen color by 10
    change y by 10
pen up
```

Script 4-11. *Color the stage*

Script 4-11 starts with four familiar blocks of code. The first clears the stage by removing all marks made by the pen or stamp, the next two set the pen's color and size and color, and the next faces the sprite to the right. When you snap in the `set rotation style left-right ▾` block, be sure to choose **left-right** from the pull-down menu to restrict the sprite to face only left or right. The next two blocks move the sprite to the location with coordinates (0, –100) and readies the pen to draw a trail wherever the sprite moves. The following repeat block repeats the sequence of instructions within it 100 times. The first action is to move the sprite 300 pixels in the direction that it's facing. The second block bounces the sprite back in the opposite direction from which it was traveling. The next block increases the pen's color number by 10. The last block in the **sequence** increases the Y coordinate by 10 pixels, and then the sequence loops back to the beginning of the repeat block and repeats. After 100 repeats, the action exits the repeat block and the last block of code at the bottom of the script disables the pen from drawing.

Click the script to activate it and watch the screen fill (see Figure 4-11).

Figure 4-11. *esult of Script 4-11*

Table 4-11 lists the blocks and describes the actions used in this example.

Table 4-11. *Code Blocks in Color the Stage*

Blocks	Actions
clear	Remove all marks previously made by the pen or stamp.
set pen size to 20	Set the pen size to 20.
set pen color to 50	Set the pen color to 50.
point in direction 90	Make the sprite face to the right.
set rotation style left-right	Set the rotation style of the sprite so that it can only turn left or right.
go to x: 0 y: -100	Move the sprite to coordinates (0, –100).
pen down	The pen is on the stage and is ready to draw.

(continued)

Table 4-11. (*continued*)

Blocks	Actions
repeat 100	Repeat the actions represented by the blocks within this block 100 times.
move 300 steps	Move the sprite 300 pixels in the direction that it's facing. Wherever the sprite moves, the pen will draw a trail.
if on edge, bounce	If the sprite reaches the edge of the stage, bounce in the opposite direction.
change pen color by 10	Change the pen color by 10.
change y by 10	Add 10 to the current value of the Y coordinate and move the sprite to that new Y coordinate.
pen up	The pen is off the stage and cannot draw.

Example 4-12: Clone the Cat

In this example, you'll send the cat stamping around the stage—literally. The Pen category's **stamp** block of code does the same as the ▣ (Duplicate) icon in the tool bar; it creates an exact copy of the sprite on the stage.

Drag and snap the indicated blocks to create Script 4-12. The first block clears the stage of all marks made by the pen or stamp. The next pair of blocks move the sprite to the location (-150, 0) and makes the sprite face to the right. The **stamp** block creates a copy of the sprite. The next block pauses the script for 1 second, and then the copy moves 100 pixels in the direction that it's facing. The next three blocks stamp a copy of the sprite on the stage, pause the script for 1 second, and move the copy another 100 pixels in the direction that it's facing. The next **stamp** block stamps another image of the sprite at that new location, the script pauses again for 1 second, and finally the last block moves the copy 100 pixels again in the direction that it's facing.

```
clear
go to x: -150 y: 0
point in direction 90▾
stamp
wait 1 secs
move 100 steps
stamp
wait 1 secs
move 100 steps
stamp
wait 1 secs
move 100 steps
```

Script 4-12. *Clone the cat*

Run the script. When it's done, you'll see four images of the sprite on the stage (see Figure 4-12).

Figure 4-12. *Result of Script 4-12*

You may also notice several sequences of repeated blocks in the script. How could you write this script more efficiently?

repeat 3

If you guessed using a [repeat 3] block to contain the stamp, wait, and then move the sequence of blocks, you were right! Remember, you can modify all the scripts shown in this book. Change the values in the blocks of code and modify them to your liking.

Table 4-12 lists the blocks and describes the actions used in this example.

Table 4-12. *Code Blocks in Clone the Cat*

Blocks	Actions
clear	Remove all marks previously made by the pen or stamp.
go to x: -150 y: 0	Move the sprite to coordinates (–150, 0).
point in direction 90▾	Make the sprite face to the right.
stamp	Create an image of the sprite and stamp this image on the stage.
wait 1 secs	The script waits 1 second. No actions are performed for 1 second.
move 100 steps	Move the sprite 100 pixels in the direction that it's facing. Wherever the sprite moves, the pen will draw a trail.
stamp	Create an image of the sprite and stamp this image on the stage.
wait 1 secs	The script waits 1 second. No actions are performed for 1 second.
move 100 steps	Move the sprite 100 pixels in the direction that it's facing. Wherever the sprite moves, the pen will draw a trail.
stamp	Create an image of the sprite and stamp this image on the stage.
wait 1 secs	The script waits 1 second. No actions are performed for 1 second.
move 100 steps	Move the sprite 100 pixels in the direction that it's facing. Wherever the sprite moves, the pen will draw a trail.

Summary

With each chapter, you learn more about Scratch. In this chapter, you learned about the **Pen** blocks of code and tried creating several example scripts that make use of Pen blocks. As well as reinforcing lessons from previous chapters, the scripts taught you several new techniques, like how to draw and change the pen size and color.

The next chapter focuses on the Looks blocks of code. These blocks change the appearance of the sprite, and you'll learn several different techniques.

Exercises

1. Create a script that draws a blue pentagon. (It will help to remember that a pentagon has five sides and its five angles add up to 360 degrees.)

    Pentagon:

2. Create a script that draws three squares of equal size, but each in a different color, side by side, on the stage.

    Three squares side by side:

The answers to the exercises are available in Chapter 13.

CHAPTER 5

The Playful Cat

By now, you and the cat sprite have been through a lot. You have learned how to move it in various ways and make it draw all kinds of shapes and patterns. In this chapter, you'll learn to give it a new look with costumes and effects, as well as a little personality with speech and thought bubbles. The blocks you need for this are in the **Looks** category. These purple blocks control the way the sprite looks. After investigating what each of the blocks in this category does, you can put them to work in several examples to better learn how to use them.

Looks Blocks

The blocks in the Looks category allow you to change the size of the sprite, apply graphic effects to the sprite, change the sprite's costume, and create speech and thought bubbles for the sprite. Like all the other blocks categories, the Looks category can be found in the block palette (see Figure 5-1).

© Eduardo A. Vlieg 2016
E.A. Vlieg, *Scratch by Example*, DOI 10.1007/978-1-4842-1946-1_5

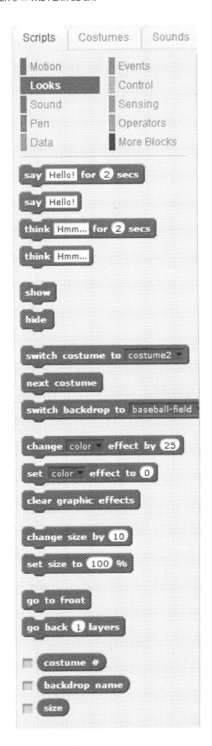

Figure 5-1. Looks blocks

Four blocks in the Looks category enable your sprites to speak and think—or at least add speech and thought bubbles for your sprite on the stage. The say Hello! for 2 secs block creates a speech bubble filled with the specified text that stays on the stage for a specified number of seconds. This

Hello!

example displays a bubble for two seconds. The say Hello! block also creates a speech bubble around the text that you supply, but its bubble remains on the stage until another speech or thought block is activated or until the script is manually stopped. If your sprite is more of a thinker than a talker, you can use the think Hmm... for 2 secs block to create a thought bubble filled with the specified text that stays on stage for the specified time. The think Hmm... block creates a similar thought

Hmm...

bubble with the specified text, . The bubble stays on the stage until another speech or thought block is activated or until the script is manually stopped.

This show and hide blocks make the sprite display on and disappear from the stage, respectively. If a sprite is already visible, then the show block has no effect. If a sprite is already hidden, hide has no effect. These two blocks perform the same actions as selecting and deselecting **show** in the Sprites info pane (see Figure 5-2).

Figure 5-2. *Sprites info pane*

The **switch costume to costume2** block changes the active sprite's costume to one you choose from the pull-down menu. You can see what your choices look like in the Costumes tab. In this example, the active sprite will change to its costume called **costume2**. The **next costume** block changes the active sprite to the next costume available for it in the Costumes tab. You can use this block to sequentially cycle through all the costumes available for a sprite. To help you keep track of which costume is visible, you can use the **costume #** block. When you select this reporter block by clicking in the box in front of it, a window opens on the stage to display the current costume number of the sprite. The **change color effect by 25** block applies the chosen graphical effect to the sprite by the specified amount. The graphic effects available in the pull-down menu are color, fisheye, whirl, pixelate, mosaic, brightness, and ghost. If you need to return the active sprite to its original state, use the **clear graphic effects** block to reset all the graphic effects on the sprite.

You can also adjust the size of your sprite from the Looks category. The **change size by 10** block changes the size of the sprite by the percentage that you specify. Setting the block to 0 does not change the size of the sprite. Setting it to an amount less than 0 shrinks the sprite, and an amount greater than 0 increases the size of the sprite. In the preceding example, the percentage is set to 10. This means that 10% will be added to the current size of the sprite; so if the current size of the sprite is 100%, adding 10% to it will result in a size of 110%. If the percentage was set to –50, this means that 50% would be subtracted from the current size of the sprite. If you prefer, you can resize your sprite using a specific percentage with the **set size to 100 %** block. The default size of the sprite is 100%. A setting of less than 100% shrinks the size of the sprite, whereas a setting greater than 100% increases the size of the sprite. To keep track of your active sprite's size, use the **size** reporter block. When you select this block, a window appears on the stage that shows the current size of the sprite.

Examples

Next, try the **Looks** blocks in action by creating some scripts. These scripts will help you practice creating speech bubbles, applying graphical effects to the sprite, and more. Remember that to create scripts, you need to drag the blocks from the block palette and drop them in the scripts area. You can always modify the scripts in the examples by changing the values in the blocks.

Example 5-1: Meet the Cat

Let's start with something easy and add some speech bubbles for the cat. You'll find the blocks that you need for Script 5-1 in the Control, Motion, and Looks categories.

Script 5-1. *Meet the cat*

The first block of code is a trigger; when a user clicks the green flag above the stage, the script activates. The next block moves the sprite to the middle of the stage. The third block creates a speech bubble for the sprite that lasts 2 seconds. The speech bubble displays the *Hello!* text. The last block of code creates a speech bubble that also lasts for 2 seconds and contains the text *My name is Cat the Sprite*.

After you have created this script, click the green flag to chat with the cat.

Table 5-1 lists the blocks and describes the actions used in this example.

Table 5-1. *Code Blocks in Meet the Cat*

Blocks	Actions
when ⚑ clicked	Clicking the green flag activates the script. The green flag is the trigger to start the script running.
go to x: 0 y: 0	Move the sprite to the position where X = 0 and Y = 0.
say Hello! for 2 secs	The sprite gets a speech bubble that displays *Hello!* for 2 seconds
say My name is Cat the Sprite for 2 secs	The sprite gets a speech bubble that displays *My name is Cat the Sprite* for 2 seconds.

Example 5-2: Think

Thought bubbles work just like speech bubbles, as you can see in Script 5-2.

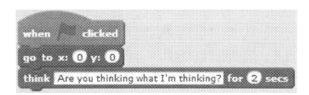

Script 5-2. *Think*

The first block of code starts the script running when the green flag is clicked. The second block of code moves the sprite to the center of the stage at coordinates (0, 0). The last block of code creates a thought bubble for the sprite that displays *Are you thinking what I'm thinking?* and lasts for 2 seconds.

Click the green flag to run the script and produce the thought bubble (see Figure 5-3).

Figure 5-3. *Result of Script 5-2*

Table 5-2 lists the blocks and describes the actions used in this example.

Table 5-2. *Code Blocks in Think*

Blocks	Actions
when [🏴] clicked	Clicking the green flag activates the script. The green flag is the trigger to start the script running.
go to x: ⓪ y: ⓪	Move the sprite to the position where X = 0 and Y = 0.
think [Are you thinking what I'm thinking?] for ② secs	The sprite gets a speech bubble that displays *Are you thinking what I'm thinking?* for 2 seconds.

Example 5-3: Color Change

This example introduces three new blocks: a trigger from the **Events** category and two effects-related blocks from the **Looks** category.

The trigger block in Script 5-3 requires the user to click the sprite to activate the script. The  block acts like an eraser for effects: it resets the sprite to its original state and removes any graphic effects that may have been applied to the sprite. If no graphic effects were applied, nothing happens. The last block of code changes the color of the sprite by the specified amount, in this case 25. So basically, what this script does is change the color of the sprite once (see Figure 5-4). If you'd like to try a different effect, you can choose it from the block's pull-down menu, or change the value to see a different color.

Script 5-3. *Color change*

Figure 5-4. *Result of Script 5-3*

Table 5-3 lists the blocks and describes the actions used in this example.

Table 5-3. *Code Blocks in Color Change*

Blocks	Actions
when this sprite clicked	The script starts running by clicking the sprite. Clicking the sprite is the trigger that activates the script.
clear graphic effects	Reset all graphic effects on the sprite. It will return the sprite to its original state (before any graphic effects were applied to it).
change color effect by 25	Change the color of the sprite by the amount of 25.

Example 5-4: Colorful Sprite

Have you already figured out what this Script 5-4 does? The addition of a **repeat** block enables the effect from Script 5-3 to repeat. In addition, this example demonstrates yet another way to start the script.

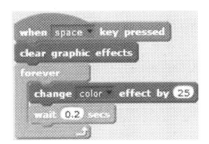

Script 5-4. *Colorful sprite*

The first block of code is a trigger block that starts the script running when the user presses the space

bar. The second block resets all graphic effects applied to the sprite. Next is the block, which is found in the **Control** blocks category. This **repeat** block repeats the sequence of actions within it forever; you must stop the script manually. The sequence of actions within the **repeat** block is as follows: change the color of the sprite by 25 and pause the script by 0.2 seconds. The script continues looping through these actions until the user clicks the red button icon (next to the green flag) above the stage.

Table 5-4 lists the blocks and describes the actions used in this example.

Table 5-4. *Code Blocks in Colorful Sprite*

Blocks	Actions
when space key pressed	The script starts running by clicking the space bar. Clicking the space bar is the trigger that activates the script.
clear graphic effects	Reset all graphic effects on the sprite. It will return the sprite to its original state (before any graphic effects were applied to it).
forever	The actions within the forever block will be repeated forever or until the script is stopped manually.
change color effect by 25	Change the color of the sprite by the amount of 25.
wait 0.2 secs	The script waits 0.2 seconds. No actions are performed for 0.2 seconds.

Example 5-5: Hide and Show

You can easily make your sprite appear on and disappear from the stage. All you need is a few familiar blocks and Script 5-5.

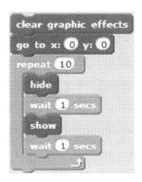

Script 5-5. *Hide and show*

The first block of code resets all graphic effects that were applied to the sprite previously. The next block of code will move the sprite to the center of the stage. The C block then repeats the sequence of actions within it 10 times. The first block within that sequence is the **hide** block, which makes the sprite disappear from the stage. The next block stops the script for 1 second. The **show** block then makes the sprite appear on the stage. The next block will make the script stop for 1 second, and then the sequence loops. So, Script 5-6 moves the sprite to the center of the stage and then makes the sprite disappear and reappear 10 times.

If you'd like to make your sprite disappear and then reappear in a new position, try adding a

 block or a block, and adjusting its settings before the

block in your repeat loop.

Table 5-5 lists the blocks and describes the actions used in this example.

Table 5-5. *Code Blocks in Hide and Show*

Blocks	Actions
clear graphic effects	Reset all graphic effects on the sprite. It will return the sprite to its original state before any graphic effects were applied to it.
go to x: 0 y: 0	Move the sprite to the position where X = 0 and Y = 0, which is the center of the stage.
repeat 10	Repeat the actions represented by the blocks within this block 10 times.
hide	Make the sprite disappear from the stage.
wait 1 secs	The script waits 1 second. No actions are performed for 1 second.
show	Make the sprite appear on the stage.
wait 1 secs	The script waits 1 second. No actions are performed for 1 second.

Example 5-6: Pixelate

Let's try a different effect and repeat it.

The first block of Script 5-7 makes the sprite appear on the stage if it was hidden. The next block resets all graphic effects that were applied to the sprite. If no graphic effects were applied to the sprite, nothing happens. The script then pauses for 1 second before entering the **repeat** block, which repeats the action within it five times. It contains a single block, which applies the **pixelate** graphic effect by the amount of 15. Remember, you can change this number and see how it affects the sprite.

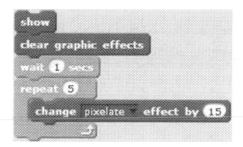

Script 5-6. *Pixelate*

Click the script to activate it and watch how it performs (see Figure 5-5).

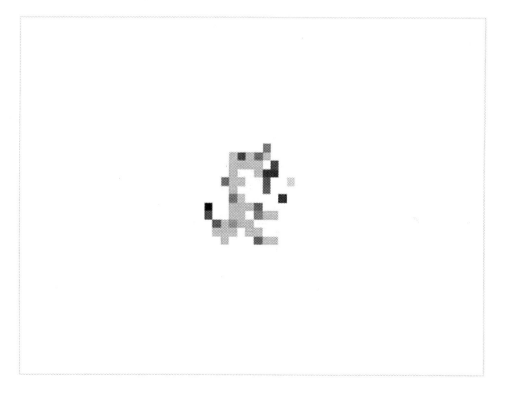

Figure 5-5. *Result of Script 5-6*

Table 5-6 lists the blocks and describes the actions used in this example.

Table 5-6. *Code Blocks in Pixelate*

Blocks	Actions
show	Make the sprite appear on the stage.
clear graphic effects	Reset all graphic effects on the sprite. It will return the sprite to its original state before any graphic effects were applied to it.
wait 1 secs	The script waits 1 second. No actions are performed for 1 second.
repeat 5	Repeat the actions represented by the blocks within this block five times.
change pixelate effect by 15	Apply the pixelate effect to the sprite by the amount of 15.

Example 5-7: Change Costume

In this example, the sprite will change its costume 10 times in a row. This will give the illusion of the cat moving its legs and walking in place. Give it a try.

Script 5-7 begins by resetting all graphic effects that were applied previously to the sprite, and then moves the sprite to the center of the stage (0, 0). Next, the `repeat 10` block repeats the sequence of actions within it 10 times. The first action of the sequence is to change the costume of the sprite to the sprite's next available costume in the **Costumes** tab. The script keeps cycling through all the costumes available. So if the last costume is used, it will go back to the first one and start all over again. The last block of code in the sequence stops the script for 1 second, and then the action loops back to the start of the sequence.

Script 5-7. *Change costume*

Table 5-7 lists the blocks and describes the actions used in this example.

Table 5-7. *Code Blocks in Change Costume*

Blocks	Actions
clear graphic effects	Reset all graphic effects on the sprite. It will return the sprite to its original state before any graphic effects were applied to it.
go to x: 0 y: 0	Move the sprite to the position where X = 0 and Y = 0, which is the center of the stage.
repeat 10	Repeat the actions represented by the blocks within this block 10 times.
next costume	Change the sprite to the next costume in the costumes tab.
wait 1 secs	The script waits 1 second. No actions are performed for 1 second.

Example 5-8: Grow and Shrink

This example doubles the size of the sprite and decreases the size back to the default size as it loops

through a ⎯⎯⎯⎯⎯ block.

Script 5-8 starts by moving the sprite to the center of the stage, if it's not there already. The next block of code sets the size of the sprite to 100%, which is the default size. The third block then resets all graphic effects that were applied to the sprite. The action then reaches the C block, which will repeat the sequence of actions within it 10 times. The first action in the sequence is to change the size of the sprite by 100. Because the size of the sprite was 100, adding another 100 to it doubles the sprite's size. The sequence pauses for 1 second, and then the next block changes the size of the sprite by –100. Because the size of the sprite was previously 200, subtracting 100 from it brings the size back to 100 (the default size). The last block in the sequence stops the script again for 1 second, after which the action loops back to the start of the sequence. The sprite grows and shrinks 10 times.

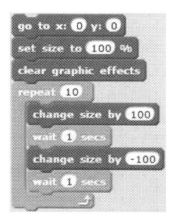

Script 5-8. *Grow and shrink*

Table 5-8 lists the blocks and describes the actions used in this example.

Table 5-8. *Code Blocks in Grow and Shrink*

Blocks	Actions
go to x: 0 y: 0	Move the sprite to the position where X = 0 and Y = 0, which is the center of the stage.
set size to 100 %	Set the sprite to its default size.
clear graphic effects	Reset all graphic effects on the sprite. It will return the sprite to its original state before any graphic effects were applied to it.
repeat 10	Repeat the actions represented by the blocks within this block 10 times.
change size by 100	Double the default size of the sprite.
wait 1 secs	The script waits 1 second. No actions are performed for 1 second.
change size by -100	Shrink the sprite to half its size.
wait 1 secs	The script waits 1 second. No actions are performed for 1 second.

Example 5-9: Shrink and Grow

Script 5-9 is almost the same as the previous example, except that it decreases the size of the sprite first and then increases it. This script also shows another way to change the size of the sprite. In programming, often there is more than one way to achieve the same result.

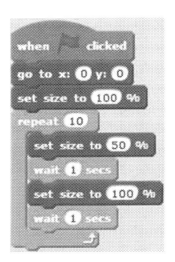

Script 5-9. *Shrink and grow*

The script activates when the user clicks the green flag and the sprite moves to the center of the stage. If the sprite is already at the center of the stage, nothing happens. The second block sets the size of the sprite to

100% (the default size). Next is a block that repeats the sequence of actions within it 10 times. The first block in the sequence sets the size of the sprite to 50%, which is half its default size. The sequence pauses for 1 second, and then the next block sets the size of the sprite back to its original size (100%). After another pause of 1 second, the sequence repeats.

When you run the script, the sprite shrinks to half its original size and then grows back to its original size 10 times before the script stops.

Table 5-9 lists the blocks and describes the actions used in this example.

Table 5-9. *Code Blocks in Shrink and Grow*

Blocks	Actions
when clicked	Clicking the green flag activates the script. The green flag is the trigger to start the script running.
go to x: 0 y: 0	Move the sprite to the position where X = 0 and Y = 0, which is the center of the stage.
set size to 100 %	Set the sprite to its default size.
repeat 10	Repeat the actions represented by the blocks within this block 10 times.
set size to 50 %	Shrink the sprite to half its size.
wait 1 secs	The script waits 1 second. No actions are performed for 1 second.
set size to 100 %	Reset the sprite to its default size.
wait 1 secs	The script waits 1 second. No actions are performed for 1 second.

Example 5-10: Move and Grow

Have you already figured out what Script 5-10 does? It builds on the concepts in Script 5-9, increasing the size of the sprite as it moves.

Script 5-10. *Move and grow*

The first block is the trigger that starts the script running when the user clicks the green flag. The next block moves the sprite to the coordinates (–220, 0), which is to the left on the stage area along the X axis. The next pair of code blocks makes the sprite face to the right and sets the size of the sprite to 100%. The

block repeats the sequence of actions within it 35 times. The first block in that sequence moves the sprite 10 pixels in the direction it's facing, which is to the right. The next block in the sequence increases the sprite's size by 5, and then the action loops back to the start of the sequence.

Script 5-10 increases the size of the sprite as it moves from left to the right across the stage, which gives the illusion of the sprite traveling from distance and coming nearer. This technique is handy if you want a 3D effect in your Scratch project.

Table 5-10 lists the blocks and describes the actions used in this example.

Table 5-10. *Code Blocks in Move and Grow*

Blocks	Actions
when [flag] clicked	Clicking the green flag activates the script. The green flag is the trigger to start the script running.
go to x: -220 y: 0	Move the sprite to the position where X = -220 and Y = 0, which is the center of the stage.
point in direction 90▾	Make the sprite face to the right.
set size to 100 %	Set the sprite to its default size.
repeat 35	Repeat the actions represented by the blocks within this block 35 times.
move 10 steps	Move the sprite 10 pixels in the direction it's facing.
change size by 5	Increase the sprite by 5%.

Example 5-11: A Short Story

Here's where you put together all that you've learned so far. Script 5-11 is one long script that tells a short story. The cat starts going for a walk, but then changes its mind and goes for a run. At the end, the sprite stops and says that it's tired. Don't let the length of this example intimidate you—give it a try!

```
when    clicked
go to x: 0 y: 0
point in direction 90 ▾
set rotation style left-right ▾
set size to 100 %
switch costume to costume1 ▾
say Let's go for a walk for 2 secs
repeat 100
    move 10 steps
    next costume
    wait 0.2 secs
    if on edge, bounce
think We better run! for 2 secs
repeat 200
    move 10 steps
    next costume
    wait 0.001 secs
    if on edge, bounce
say I'm tired! for 2 secs
```

Script 5-11. *A short story*

The first block activates the script when the user clicks the green flag. The next pair of blocks moves the sprite to the center of the stage and makes the sprite face to the right. The fourth block sets the rotation style of the sprite to **left-right**, meaning the sprite will be able to face left or right only. The next block sets the size of the sprite to 100%, which is its default size. The next block changes the sprite's costume to

costume1. The `say Let's go for a walk for 2 secs` block creates a speech bubble for the sprite that

displays *Let's go for a walk.* Next, the `repeat 100` block repeats the sequence of actions within it 100 times. The sequence of actions begins by moving the sprite 10 pixels in the direction that it's facing, changing the sprite to its next costume. The action pauses for 0.2 seconds. The last block within the sequence block makes the sprite bounce and travel in the opposite direction, if it reaches the edge of the stage. After 100 repeats of this sequence, the block creates a thought

bubble for the sprite that displays *We better run!* The next block, , repeats the sequence of actions within it 200 times. That sequence moves the sprite 10 pixels in the direction that it's facing, changes the sprite to its next costume, stops the script for 0.001 seconds, and finally instructs the sprite to bounce and travel in the opposite direction if it hits the edge of the stage, and then the sequence repeats. The last block in this script creates a speech bubble for the sprite that displays *I'm tired!*

This example shows how you can combine techniques from previous examples to tell a story. Experiment with this script, modify it to your liking, and create your own story.

Table 5-11 lists the blocks and describes the actions used in this example.

Table 5-11. *Code Blocks in a Short Story*

Blocks	Actions
	Clicking the green flag activates the script. The green flag is the trigger to start the script running.
	Move the sprite to the position where X = 0 and Y = 0, which is the center of the stage.
	Make the sprite face to the right.
	Set the rotation style of the sprite, so it can only turn left or right.
	Set the sprite to its default size.
	Switch the sprite to the costume called **costume1**.
	The sprite gets a speech bubble that displays *Let's go for a walk* for 2 seconds.
	Repeat the actions represented by the blocks within this block 100 times.
	Move the sprite 10 pixels in the direction that it's facing.
	Change the sprite to the next costume in the costumes tab.
	The script waits 0.2 seconds. No actions are performed for 0.2 seconds.

(continued)

Table 5-11. (*continued*)

Blocks	Actions
`if on edge, bounce`	If the sprite reaches the edge of the stage, bounce in the opposite direction.
`think We better run! for 2 secs`	The sprite gets a thought bubble that displays *We better run!* for 2 seconds.
`repeat 200`	Repeat the actions represented by the blocks within this block 200 times.
`move 10 steps`	Move the sprite 10 pixels in the direction that it's facing.
`next costume`	Change the sprite to the next costume in the Costumes tab.
`wait 0.001 secs`	The script waits 0.001 seconds. No actions are performed for 0.001 seconds.
`if on edge, bounce`	If the sprite reaches the edge of the stage, bounce in the opposite direction.
`say I'm tired! for 2 secs`	The sprite gets a speech bubble that displays *I'm tired!* for 2 seconds.

Summary

You've a come a long way, but there are still exciting things ahead. In this chapter, you learned how to change the look of the sprite and how to add graphic effects to it. You have also learned how to create speech and thought bubbles for the sprite and change its costume, resulting in the illusion that the sprite is moving.

The next chapter focuses on the **Sound** block category. These blocks add sound to your Scratch project. After that chapter, you start the second part of this book. The second part of this book puts together all the basic concepts that you have learned and creates more advanced and complex scripts.

Exercises

1. Select the **Avery Walking** sprite. Create a script that makes the sprite walk across the stage, back and forth. Change its costume while moving and activate the script when the space bar is pressed.

2. Select any sprite. Apply the **Brightness** effect. Apply the **Ghost** effect to make the sprite disappear. At the end, make the sprite show up again.

The answers to the exercises are available in Chapter 13.

CHAPTER 6

The Noisy Cat

In the last chapter, you learned how to add speech bubbles for your sprite, but the cat was still silent. That's about to change. In this chapter, you'll learn about the blocks in the **Sound** category, which enable you to add sound to your Scratch scripts. Combining the blocks in this category, you can add sound effects to your projects. You can create a song by playing different musical instruments and playing specific music notes. You can even record custom sounds to add dialog that helps tell a story in your Scratch project.

This chapter starts with an explanation of how to add sound to a Scratch project. You can upload a sound, add a sound from the Scratch library, or record a sound. Once sound is added to your project, you'll want to play it. For that, you need the **Sound** blocks. After a tour of the Sound category's blocks, we'll go through some script examples that show these Sound blocks in action.

Choosing and Recording Sounds

Scratch enables you to add sounds to your project in three ways. You can select a sound from the Scratch library, you can record your own sound, or you can upload a sound file. To do any of these, you first need to click the **Sounds** tab (see Figure 6-1). By default, the **meow** sound is selected from the library (see Figure 6-2). At the bottom of the sound thumbnail, you see how long the sound lasts. In the case of the **meow** sound file, it lasts 00:00:84 seconds.

© Eduardo A. Vlieg 2016
E. A. Vlieg, *Scratch by Example*, DOI 10.1007/978-1-4842-1946-1_6

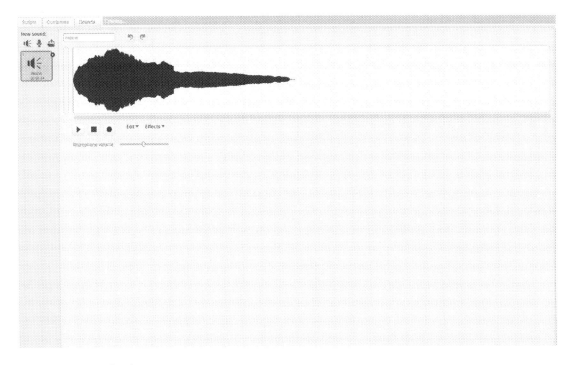

Figure 6-1. *Sounds tab*

Figure 6-2. *The meow sound is selected by default*

To hear it, or any sound file in the Sounds tab, select the sound file's thumbnail to display the sound's waveform on the right side of the Sounds tab. Below it, you will find Play, Stop, and Record icons (see Figure 6-3). Click Play to hear the sound. In this same area, you can change the name of the sound file by clicking in the text field at the top, as well as edit and apply effects to the sound with the pull-down menus.

Figure 6-3. *Sound controls and the selected sound's soundwave*

The icons below **New sound** enable you to add sound files in three ways (see Figure 6-4). To select a sound from the library, simply click the [icon] icon. To record a sound, click the [icon] icon. To upload a sound file, click the [icon] icon.

Figure 6-4. *New sound icons*

When you click the [icon] icon, the Sound Library (see Figure 6-5) opens, displaying all the sound files that you can choose. To add a sound file to your script, all you need to do is select the file and click **OK**. The sound file will appear in the **Sounds** tab. You can also preview each sound file before adding it to your project by clicking the [icon] icon belonging to the sound file in the Sound Library.

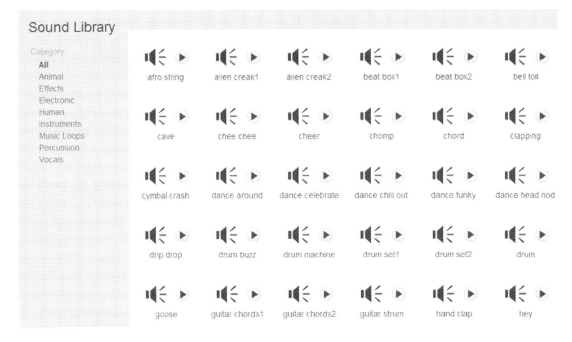

Figure 6-5. *Sound Library*

You can also create your own sound file by recording a sound. To do so, first click the 🎤 icon. When you do, Scratch adds a sound file called **recording1** to the **Sounds** tab (see Figure 6-6). The waveform window to the right is empty because the recording1 file doesn't yet contain any sound (see Figure 6-7). To add some, click the ⏺ icon and record your sound using your computer's microphone. You can always rename the file to something more descriptive using the text field on the top-right side. In Figure 6-8's example, I recorded a sound and renamed it to Boo.

Figure 6-6. *recording1*

Figure 6-7. *Empty sound file*

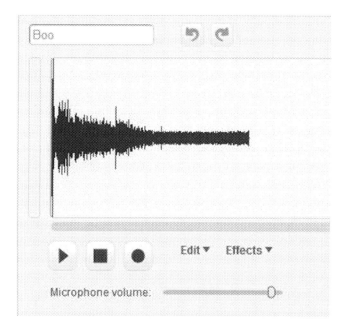

Figure 6-8. *Boo recorded sound*

To upload an existing sound file to your Scratch project, click the ⬆ icon. A window opens where you can select the sound file. Navigate to where you have the sound file saved and click **Open**. Keep in mind that Scratch can only read WAV and MP3 sound files.

Sound Blocks

The blocks in the **Sound** category control sounds in a Scratch project (see Figure 6-9). Not only can you control the sound files that were added to the project, but you can also play several different musical instruments and music notes. You can adjust the tempo and the sound volume, as well.

Figure 6-9. *Sound blocks*

Two blocks enable you to play the sounds loaded in your Sounds tab. The **play sound meow** block plays the sound that you select from the pull-down menu. In this example, it plays the meow sound. If you have multiple sounds added to your project that are displayed in the **Sounds** tab, you can use the pull-down menu in the block to select another sound. The **play sound meow until done** block also plays the sound file that you choose from the pull-down menu. Unlike with the previous block, with this one, Scratch will not execute the next block of code until it has finished playing the sound. For example, if you want a sprite representing a car to move while an engine noise plays, you might choose the **play sound** block, but you'd choose the **play sound until done** block if you don't want the car to move until the door slam noise completes. To silence all of your sounds, use the **stop all sounds** block, which instructs the script to stop playing all sounds.

Several of the code blocks work together to enable you to play music. All music is based on a tempo, so you need to set one for your Scratch music too. You use the `set tempo to 60 bpm` block to set the tempo, which is the number of beats per minute that can occur. In this example, there are 60 beats in a minute, so 1 beat is 1 second long. The more beats you have per minute, the shorter the beat. The fewer the beats per minute, the longer the beat lasts. You can later adjust the tempo to be faster or slower with the `change tempo by 20` block. Specifying a positive number speeds the tempo with more beats per minute (bpm), and a negative number slows the tempo with fewer beats. In the previous example, 20 beats will be added to the current value for the tempo or bpm. The `tempo` block holds the value of the tempo in case you lose track. Select the box in front of this block in the blocks palette to display the current tempo in a monitor window on the stage.

In addition to your tempo, you must also choose an instrument to play your music with the `set instrument to 1▾` block. There are 21 musical instruments that you can choose from. Each number corresponds to a musical instrument. Click the pull-down menu to display the list of musical instruments and see which number corresponds to which musical instrument. In the previous example, 1 corresponds to **piano**. To instruct the specified instrument to play a note, use the `play note 60▾ for 0.5 beats` block to specify a note and a number of beats for which to play it. Each number corresponds to a note. Clicking the pull-down menu displays a keyboard and the music note corresponding to a number. In this example, 60 corresponds to the **middle C** note. If you need drums, use the `play drum 1▾ for 0.25 beats` block for the drum number you chose from the pull-down menu and enter the specified number of beats. There are 18 types of percussion instruments that you can choose from. Clicking the pull-down menu displays the list and the instrument that belongs to the specific number. In this example, 1 belongs to **snare drum**.

Similar to the `wait 1 secs` block or a rest in a musical score, the `rest for 0.25 beats` block pauses the script and does not play any sound for the specified number of beats.

Finally, you can set and change the volume of your music and other sounds. The `set volume to 100 %` block sets the sound volume to a specific level, with 100% as the default. Using the `change volume by -10` block is like twisting your volume control dial. A negative number decreases the volume and a positive number increases it. A value of 0 does not change the volume. The `volume` block holds the value of the sound volume. Select the box in front of it in the blocks palette to display a monitor on the stage.

Examples

So far, you have learned the theory of how to add sound to a Scratch project. Now it's time to listen to what happens when you combine the blocks into scripts. The following examples will give you some practice with the sound blocks in action.

Example 6-1: Meow

Giving your sprite a voice is simple, as you can see in Script 6-1.

Script 6-1. *Meow*

Drag the  block from the from the **Events** category, and then drag the

block from the **Sound** category and snap them together. Finally, choose **meow** from the **play sound** block's drop-down menu. When the user clicks the green flag, the next block will play the specified meow sound.

Table 6-1 lists the blocks and describes the actions used in this example.

Table 6-1. *Code Blocks in Meow*

Blocks	Actions
	Clicking the green flag activates the script. The green flag is the trigger to start the script running.
	Play the **meow** sound.

Example 6-2: Say Meow

If you combine a speech bubble with a sound, everyone will know who is talking. You just need to add one extra block of code to Example 6-1's script.

Script 6-2. *Say Meow*

When the user clicks the green flag, the script activates. The next block plays the meow sound. The last block creates a speech bubble for the cat, which displays *Meow* for 2 seconds.

Table 6-2 lists the blocks and describes the actions used in this example.

Table 6-2. *Code Blocks in Say Meow*

Blocks	Actions
when clicked	Clicking the green flag activates the script. The green flag is the trigger to start the script running.
play sound meow ▾	Play the **meow** sound.
say Meow for 2 secs	The sprite gets a speech bubble that says *Meow* for 2 seconds.

Example 6-3: Play Sound Until Done

To better understand the difference between the  used in Example 6-2 and the play sound meow ▾ until done block used in this example, create Script 6-3 and observe what happens when you click the green flag to run it.

```
when clicked
play sound meow ▾ until done
say Meow for 2 secs
```

Script 6-3. *Play until done*

The play sound meow ▾ until done block plays the entire **meow** sound before executing any blocks after it. Create the script and click the green flag to run it.

Did you notice the difference between this script and the previous one? Script 6-2 starts playing the **meow** sound and displays the speech bubble immediately before the sound has finished playing. Script 6-3 plays the sound all the way to the end and then displays the speech bubble only after the sound has finished playing.

Table 6-3 lists the blocks and describes the actions used in this example.

Table 6-3. *Code Blocks in Play Sound until Done*

Blocks	Actions
when clicked	Clicking the green flag activates the script. The green flag is the trigger to start the script running.
play sound meow ▾ until done	Play the meow sound until done and then move to the next block.
say Meow for 2 secs	The sprite gets a speech bubble that says *Meow* for 2 seconds.

Example 6-4: Change Volume

By adding a block, you can extend a sound by repeating it. As you can see in Script 6-4, this script uses the pop sound. Before creating the script, remember to select the **pop** sound in the library and add it to the **Sounds** tab, so that it will be available from the block's pull-down menu. If you don't select a sound from the library first, it will not be available in the block's pull-down menu.

Script 6-4. *Change volume*

After the user clicks the green flag, the script starts in silence, because the block specifies 0% volume. The block is set to repeat the sequence of actions within it 20 times. The first action in the sequence increases the volume by the specified amount (5%). The next block plays the selected sound (**pop**), the script pauses for 1 second, and then the sequence of actions within the C block repeat. Because each time through the sequence the volume increases by 5%, 20 repeats increases the volume to 100% by the end of the script.

Table 6-4 lists the blocks and describes the actions used in this example.

Table 6-4. *Code Blocks in Change Volume*

Blocks	Actions
when clicked	Clicking the green flag activates the script. The green flag is the trigger to start the script running.
set volume to 0 %	Turn the volume all the way down.
repeat 20	Repeat the actions represented by the blocks within this block 20 times.
change volume by 5	Increase the volume by 5%.
play sound pop	Play the **pop** sound.
wait 1 secs	The script waits 1 second. No actions are performed for 1 second.

Example 6-5: Let's Waltz

This script plays the rhythm of a waltz. By experimenting with the different instruments, tempo, and beats, you can create your own rhythms and songs.

Script 6-5 starts running when the user clicks the green flag. The next block sets the tempo to 100 beats per minute. The next block will repeat the sequence of actions within it 10 times. The first action in the sequence plays the bass drum (drum number 2) for 0.25 beats. After a silent pause of 0.25 beats, the next two blocks in the sequence play the **open hi-hat** (drum number 5) for 0.5 beats each.

Script 6-5. *Waltz*

Run the script and listen. Sounds like a waltz rhythm, doesn't it?

Table 6-5 lists the blocks and describes the actions used in this example.

Table 6-5. *Code Blocks in Let's Waltz*

Blocks	Actions
when [flag] clicked	Clicking the green flag activates the script. The green flag is the trigger to start the script running.
set tempo to 100 bpm	Set the tempo to 100 beats per minute.
repeat 10	Repeat the actions represented by the blocks within this block 20 times.
play drum 2▾ for 0.25 beats	Play bass drum for 0.25 beats.
rest for 0.25 beats	Don't play anything for 0.25 beats.
play drum 5▾ for 0.5 beats	Play **open hi-hat** for 0.5 beats.
play drum 5▾ for 0.5 beats	Play open **hi-hat** for 0.5 beats.

Example 6-6: Change Tempo

Script 6-6 shows how changing the tempo while running a script affects the sound.

Script 6-6. *Change tempo*

Script 6-6 starts when the user clicks the green flag. The next block sets the tempo to 20 beats per minute. The

block then repeats the sequence of actions within it 50 times. The first block in the sequence plays the snare drum (drum number 1) for 0.25 beats, and then the bass drum (drum number 2) plays for 0.25 beats. The third block in the sequence makes the script stop playing any sound for 0.25 beats. The last block in the sequence increases the tempo by 10 beats per minute. So, each repeat through the loop increases the tempo.

Table 6-6 lists the blocks and describes the actions used in this example.

Table 6-6. *Code Blocks in Change Tempo*

Blocks	Actions
when clicked	Clicking the green flag activates the script. The green flag is the trigger to start the script running.
set tempo to 20 bpm	Set the tempo to 20 beats per minute.
repeat 50	Repeat the actions represented by the blocks within this block 50 times.
play drum 1 for 0.25 beats	Play snare drum for 0.25 beats.
play drum 2 for 0.25 beats	Play bass drum for 0.25 beats.
rest for 0.25 beats	Don't play anything for 0.25 beats.
change tempo by 10	Increase the tempo by 10 beats per minute.

Example 6-7: Nursery Rhyme

This example demonstrates how you can create songs with Sound blocks. In fact, it's a lot like playing a musical instrument. In Script 6-7, you'll play part of the "Frère Jacques" ("Brother John") nursery rhyme with Scratch's vibraphone.

Script 6-7. *Nursery rhyme*

The script begins when the user clicks the green flag. The next block sets the volume to 100%, which is all the way up. If it's too loud, you can lower the volume by setting a smaller number in the block. The next

block sets the musical instrument to the vibraphone (instrument number 14). The first block then repeats the sequence of actions within it twice. Specifically, each time through the loop, the notes C, D, E, and then C play for 0.5 beats each in sequence. The second **repeat** block then also repeats the sequence of actions that it contains twice, playing the notes E, F, and G for 0.5 beats each.

After you run the script, try changing the instrument to see how it affects the sound. Or, if you're musically inclined, try scripting a different tune. Maybe the cat would enjoy "Three Blind Mice".

Table 6-7 lists the blocks and describes the actions used in this example.

Table 6-7. *Code Blocks in Nursery Rhyme*

Blocks	Actions
	Clicking the green flag activates the script. The green flag is the trigger to start the script running.
	Turn the volume all the way up.
	Select vibraphone as the instrument.
	Repeat the actions represented by the blocks within this block 2 times.

(continued)

Table 6-7. (*continued*)

Blocks	Actions
play note 60▾ for 0.5 beats	Play the middle C note for 0.5 beats.
play note 62▾ for 0.5 beats	Play the D note for 0.5 beats.
play note 64▾ for 0.5 beats	Play the E note for 0.5 beats.
play note 60▾ for 0.5 beats	Play the middle C note for 0.5 beats.
repeat 2	Repeat the actions represented by the blocks within this block 2 times.
play note 64▾ for 0.5 beats	Play the E note for 0.5 beats.
play note 65▾ for 0.5 beats	Play the F note for 0.5 beats.
play note 67▾ for 0.5 beats	Play the G note for 0.5 beats.
rest for 0.5 beats	Don't play anything for 0.5 beats.

Example 6-8: The Marching Cat

It's time to combine several of the techniques you've learned—movement, costume changes, and sound into a more complete story. In this example, you'll make the cat march back and forth across the stage to the accompaniment of drums playing at varying volumes.

Script 6-8 activates when the user clicks the green flag. After a Sound block sets the volume to 100%, two **Motion** blocks make the sprite face to the right and set the rotation style so that the sprite can face left or

right. The two [repeat 100] blocks contain the core of the script's instructions. The first one repeats the sequence of actions within it 100 times. The first block within the sequence makes the sprite move 5 steps in the direction that it's facing. The sprite changes to its next costume, and then the snare drum (drum number 1) plays for 0.25 beats. The script pauses for 0.2 seconds, and then the volume decreases by 1%. The final block in the sequence checks if the sprite has reached the edge of the stage and bounces it back in the opposite direction, if necessary. The action then loops back to the first block in the sequence.

Script 6-8. *Marching cat*

After the final repeat of the first C block, the script moves to the second  block to repeat the sequence of actions within it 100 times. The first block in its sequence moves the sprite 5 steps in the direction that it's facing. The next block changes the sprite to its next costume. Next, the bass drum (drum number 2) plays for 0.25 beats, and then the script pauses for 0.2 seconds. The next block increases the volume by 1% and the last block in the loop makes sure that if the sprite reaches the edge of the stage, it bounces back in the opposite direction.

Table 6-8 lists the blocks and describes the actions used in this example.

Table 6-8. *Code Blocks in the Marching Cat*

Blocks	Actions
when [green flag] clicked	Clicking the green flag activates the script. The green flag is the trigger to start the script running.
set volume to 100 %	Turn the volume all the way up.
point in direction 90 ▾	Make the sprite face to the right.
set rotation style left-right ▾	Set the rotation style of the sprite so that it can only face left or right.
repeat 100	Repeat the actions represented by the blocks within this block 100 times.
move 5 steps	Move the sprite 5 pixels in the direction that it's facing.
next costume	Change the sprite to the next costume in the Costumes tab.
play drum 1 ▾ for 0.25 beats	Play snare drum for 0.25 beats.
wait 0.2 secs	The script waits 0.2 seconds. No actions are performed for 0.2 seconds.
change volume by -1	Decrease volume by 1%.
if on edge, bounce	If the sprite reaches the edge of the stage, bounce in the opposite direction.
repeat 100	Repeat the actions represented by the blocks within this block 100 times.
move 5 steps	Move the sprite 5 pixels in the direction that it's facing.
next costume	Change the sprite to the next costume in the Costumes tab.
play drum 2 ▾ for 0.25 beats	Play bass drum for 0.25 beats.
wait 0.2 secs	The script waits 0.2 seconds. No actions are performed for 0.2 seconds.
change volume by 1	Increase volume by 1%.
if on edge, bounce	If the sprite reaches the edge of the stage, bounce in the opposite direction.

Example 6-9: Playing Drums

Script 6-9 simulates playing drums. This script is almost the same as Scripts 6-5 and 6-6, but it shows another variation of a drum sequence. Remember that you can adjust it to your liking, so you play your own drum sequence.

Script 6-9. *Playing drums*

The script starts running when the user clicks the green flag. The first ⟨repeat 3⟩ block repeats the sequence of actions within it 3 times. The block in the sequence is to play the snare drum (drum number 1) for 1 beat. After a rest in which nothing plays for 0.25 beats, the third block in the sequence plays the snare drum again for 1 beat. After another silent rest for 0.25 beats, the bass drum (drum number 2) plays for 0.25 beats. The last block in the sequence pauses the script for 1 second.

When all three repeats are complete, the script moves to the second ⟨repeat 2⟩ block, which repeats the actions within it 2 times. The first block in the sequence plays the crash cymbal (drum number 4) for 1 beat. The next block pauses the script for 0.5 seconds. The last block in this repeating loop plays the crash cymbal again for 1 beat.

Go ahead. Create the script and run it.

Table 6-9 lists the blocks and describes the actions used in this example.

Table 6-9. *Code Blocks in Playing Drums*

Blocks	The bass drum
when [flag] clicked	Clicking the green flag activates the script. The green flag is the trigger to start the script running.
repeat 3	Repeat the actions represented by the blocks within this block 3 times.
play drum 1▾ for 1 beats	Play snare drum for 1 beat.
rest for 0.5 beats	Don't play anything for 0.5 beats.
play drum 1▾ for 1 beats	Play snare drum for 1 beat.
rest for 0.5 beats	Don't play anything for 0.5 beats.
play drum 2▾ for 0.25 beats	Play bass drum for 0.25 beats.
wait 1 secs	The script waits 1 second. No actions are performed for 1 second.
repeat 2	Repeat the actions represented by the blocks within this block 2 times.
play drum 4▾ for 1 beats	Play crash cymbal for 1 beat.
wait 0.5 secs	The script waits 0.5 seconds. No actions are performed for 0.5 seconds.
play drum 4▾ for 1 beats	Play crash cymbal for 1 beat.

Example 6-10: Galloping Horse

Are you ready to tell another story? In this example, you'll make a horse gallop across the stage to the sound of hoof beats, and then stop, rear, and neigh in the middle of the stage. It may sound complicated, but scripting these actions in Scratch is easier than instructing a real horse to do them.

Before creating Script 6-10, make sure that you have all the elements that you need. Add the **Horse1** sprite from the Sprite Library (see Figure 6-11). This sprite consists of two costumes, which will be displayed in the Costumes tab (see Figure 6-12). You can delete any other sprite from the stage. Also, add the **horse gallop** and **horse** sounds from the Sound Library to the Sounds tab.

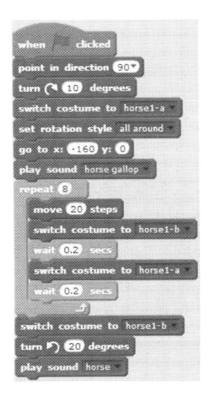

Script 6-10. *Galloping horse*

The script starts running when the user clicks the green flag. The next pair of blocks makes the horse face to the right, and then rotate 10 degrees clockwise. The fourth block switches the costume to **horse1-a**. The next block sets the rotation style to **all around**, so the horse is able to turn around its axis. The next block moves the horse to the position (–160, 0). The next block plays the sound **horse gallop**.

The ![repeat 8 block] block then repeats the sequence of actions within it 8 times. The sequence moves the horse 20 steps in the direction that it's facing, switches the sprite to the **horse1-b** costume, pauses the script for 0.2 seconds, switches the sprite to the **horse1-a** costume, and then pauses the script for 0.2 seconds again.

After the final loop through the ![repeat 8 block] block sequence, the next block switches the sprite to the **horse1-b** costume. The ![turn 20 degrees block] block then rotates the horse 20 degrees counterclockwise and the final block in the script plays the **horse** sound (see Figure 6-10).

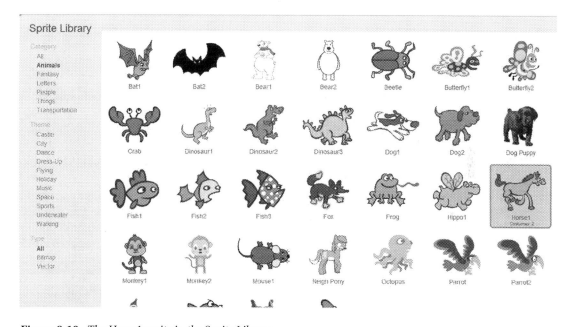

Figure 6-10. The Horse1 sprite in the Sprite Library

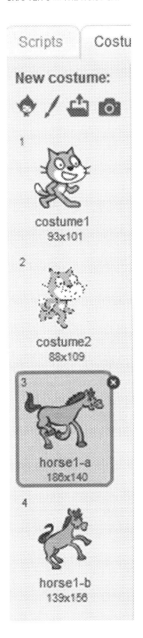

Figure 6-11. *The Costumes tab*

Figure 6-12. *Result of Script 6-10*

Table 6-10 lists the blocks and describes the actions used in this example.

Table 6-10. *Code Blocks in Galloping Horse*

Blocks	Actions
when ⚑ clicked	Clicking the green flag activates the script. The green flag is the trigger to start the script running.
point in direction 90▾	Make the sprite face to the right.
turn ↻ 10 degrees	Turn the sprite clockwise 10 degrees.
switch costume to horse1-a ▾	Switch the sprite to the **horse1-a** costume.
set rotation style all around ▾	Set the rotation style of the sprite so that it can rotate all around its axis.
go to x: -160 y: 0	Move the sprite to the position where X = –160 and Y = 0.

(*continued*)

Table 6-10. (*continued*)

Blocks	Actions
repeat 8	Repeat the actions represented by the blocks within this block 8 times.
move 20 steps	Move the sprite 20 pixels in the direction that it's facing.
switch costume to horse1-b	Switch the sprite to the **horse1-b** costume.
wait 0.2 secs	The script waits 0.2 seconds. No actions are performed for 0.2 seconds.
switch costume to horse1-a	Switch the sprite to the horse1-a costume.
wait 0.2 secs	The script waits 0.2 seconds. No actions are performed for 0.2 seconds.
switch costume to horse1-b	Switch the sprite to the horse1-b costume.
turn 20 degrees	Turn the sprite counterclockwise 20 degrees.
play sound horse	Play the **horse** sound.

Summary

In this chapter, you learned how to add sound to a Scratch project and to control sound in a Scratch project. You now have all the basic knowledge to create some cool projects in Scratch. You know how to add sprites and backdrops. You know how to move the sprite and change its appearance, create speech and thought bubbles, and add sound to a project. Before you move on, try creating some stories of your own using other sounds and sprites. Have some fun!

This chapter completes the first part of this book, which taught you basic Scratch knowledge. The next chapter starts the second part of the book, which covers advanced concepts that are also used in high-level computer programming languages.

Exercises

1. Create a script to play the sound called **bird**. Set the volume at 100% and each time you play the sound decrease the volume by 10% until the sound level is 0.

2. Create a script and set the instrument to **piano**. Play notes C, D, and E. Set the instrument to **cello** and play the notes E, D, and C.

The answers to the exercises are available in Chapter 13.

PART II

Becoming a Programmer

CHAPTER 7

Advanced Concepts

Now that you've mastered the basics of the Scratch programming language, you're ready to tackle some more advanced concepts. In this chapter, you will investigate how to work with user input, with control blocks that enable your project to take different actions depending on circumstances, with Boolean blocks that evaluate whether conditions are true or false, and with operator blocks that manipulate values. Along the way, you'll learn some important concepts that are common to all high-level programming languages, but are still as simple to use as dragging and snapping blocks in Scratch. Your first step is to take a closer look at the blocks in the **Control**, **Sensing**, and **Operators** categories in the block palette.

Control Blocks

Blocks in the **Control** category (see Figure 7-1) literally control the flow of the action within your scripts by looping repetitively through a sequence of instructions, or by evaluating and reacting to conditions, or by pausing or stopping the action entirely.

© Eduardo A. Vlieg 2016
E. A. Vlieg, *Scratch by Example*, DOI 10.1007/978-1-4842-1946-1_7

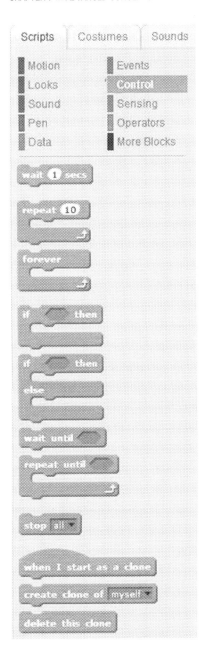

Figure 7-1. *Control blocks*

You're already very familiar with three blocks housed here: the `repeat 10` block, which repeats the sequence of actions within it a specified number of times to create what is called a *loop* in programming language; the `forever` block, which repeats (loops) the sequence of actions forever, or until the script is stopped manually; and the `wait 1 secs` block, which pauses the script for the specified time. Those blocks, however, are only the beginning of the programming power and flexibility that the Control category offers.

When combined with Boolean blocks, several more Control blocks add flexibility to your scripts, enabling you to issue instructions based on specific conditions. As you remember from Chapter 3, Boolean blocks evaluate conditions and then report them as either true or false. Because you can snap Boolean blocks inside Control blocks, you can then tell your script to take an action when a certain condition is met.

For example, the `wait until` block pauses the script until the Boolean block that you snap into it reports its condition as true. So, instead of waiting a specific number of seconds, you can use this block to wait until the mouse is clicked, a value is entered, or a timer reaches a certain value. Similarly, the

`repeat until` block continues repeating the sequence of actions within it until the Boolean block that you snap into it reports its condition as true. This type of loop is called a *while loop* in traditional programming language, because it repeats while a specific condition exists.

Sometimes you might want to perform a different action depending on the circumstances in your script. For instance, if a user answers "yes" to a question, then you would want to take a different action than if the answer is "no," or you might want the pen to draw only when the user holds down the mouse button. To react to circumstances this way, you need what is called a *conditional statement* or an *If/Then statement* in programming language and the `if then` block in Scratch. If the Boolean block that you snap into the `if then` block evaluates as true, then this C block executes the instructions (or sequence of instructions) within it. If the condition is false, the script skips to the block immediately after the C block and executes it. The `if then else` block works in a similar way. If the Boolean block that you snap into it reports its condition as true, then the sequence of instructions in the first part of the block execute. If the condition is false, the script ignores the first sequence of blocks and executes the second sequence of instructions within the block after the word *else*.

The last block in the Control category, the `stop all` block, stops scripts in a project from executing any instructions. You can use the pull down menu to select all scripts in a project (as in the example) or just one particular script.

Sensing Blocks

The **Sensing** category (see Figure 7-2) contains a combination of Boolean blocks and reporter blocks that help you sense and evaluate what the user of your script and your sprites are doing. Many of these blocks snap into, or *embed*, in the various **Control** or **Operators** blocks, enabling your script to take action depending on their value or condition.

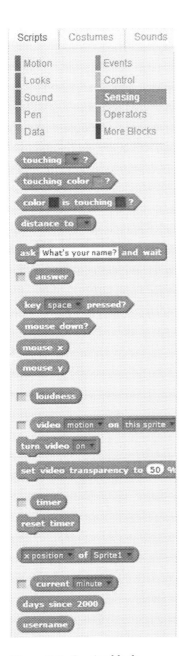

Figure 7-2. *Sensing blocks*

The four Boolean blocks all evaluate a condition that you specify, and then return a value of either true or false to the block they're embedded into. For example, the **touching ▼ ?** block evaluates whether the sprite touches the item that you choose from the pull-down menu: the mouse-pointer, the edge of the stage, or another sprite. The **touching color ? ** block returns a value of true if the sprite is touching the specified color. You select the color by clicking in the color box in the block and then clicking the desired color anywhere in the Scratch interface. The **key space ▼ pressed?** block checks if the specified key is pressed. You can select which key to test for, by using the pull down menu. The last Boolean block, **mouse down?**, checks if the primary mouse button is held down.

The Sensing category also contains six reporter blocks that store information about the mouse position, sprite position, user input, and more. You can then embed these blocks into to other blocks to pass on that information for evaluation and action. For instance, the **mouse x** and **mouse y** blocks, respectively, hold the mouse-pointer's current X and Y coordinates on the stage. Using its two pull-down menus, you can set the **x position ▼ of Sprite1 ▼** block to hold the value of a specified sprite's X or Y coordinate, direction, or custom name, among other choices. This **timer** block holds the timer value. The timer starts running from 0.0 as soon as Scratch is launched and increases by 1 every second; the **reset timer** block sets the timer value back to 0.0. The **username** block holds the username of the user who is logged on to Scratch. Finally, a pair of blocks enable you to ask the user a question, and then store the answer. The **ask What's your name? and wait** block asks the question that you type in its text field, opens an input window on the stage, and waits for the user's input. Scratch then saves the user's input in the **answer** block.

Operators Blocks

The blocks in the **Operators** category (see Figure 7-3) do just what their name implies: Perform operations on the values supplied to them. Sometimes the operations are mathematical, then the block reports the resulting value. Other blocks are Boolean blocks that report whether the indicated operation produced a true or false result. **Operators** blocks all embed into others blocks, which then take action based on the values they report.

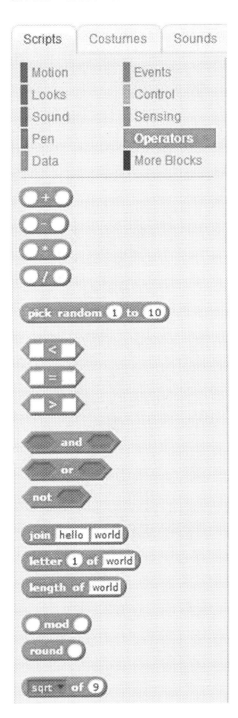

Figure 7-3. Operators blocks

Several blocks in this category perform math then report the result. For instance, the ⬭ block adds the two values that you supply, the ⬭ block subtracts two values, and the ⬭ block divides two values. The ⬭ mod ⬭ block reports the remainder when the first value is divided by the second specified value. For example, when 7 is divided by 3, a remainder of 1 is reported.

The round ⬭ block rounds the specified number to the nearest integer. Decimals that are 0.5 or higher are rounded up. Decimals that 0.5 or less are rounded down, so if you enter 5.3, this block reports 5.

The sqrt ▾ of 9 block reports the result of the selected operation on the specified value. The default is the square root operation, but clicking the pull-down menu displays other mathematical operation choices. In the previous example, the block will report the square root of 9, which is 3. Finally, the

pick random 1 to 10 block picks a random value between the two specified numbers and reports the result.

A second group of blocks in the Operators category perform Boolean comparisons and return a value of true or false. For instance, ⬭ < ⬭ determines whether the first value is smaller than the second value. If it is, the block reports true, otherwise it reports false. The ⬭ > ⬭ block does the opposite, determining whether the first value is larger than the second value. The ⬭ = ⬭ block reports true if the two values are equal. Two blocks, ⬭ and ⬭ and ⬭ or ⬭, enable you to combine and evaluate two Boolean blocks, then return true or false. Both embedded blocks on each side of the ⬭ and ⬭ block need to return true for the condition represented by this block to be true. If one returns false, then this block returns false. For example, on the left side, you use 3 < 4, and on the right side, you use 1 < 3. Both of these Boolean blocks evaluate to true because 3 is less than 4 and 1 is less than 3. Because both sides are true, the ⬭ and ⬭ block evaluates to true. Only one side of the ⬭ or ⬭ block needs to be true, however, for this block to report true. For example, on the left side you use 3 < 4, and on the right side, you use 5 < 3. The left Boolean block evaluates to true because 3 is less than 4, but the right Boolean block evaluates to false, because 5 is less than 3. Because only one side needs to be true, the ⬭ or ⬭ still evaluates to true. The ⬭ not ⬭ block returns the opposite of the result returned by the block embedded within it. If the block embedded within the ⬭ not ⬭ block reports true, therefore, the ⬭ not ⬭ block returns false and vice versa.

The final three blocks in the Operators category work with text. The join hello world block joins the two values that you specify in the block and reports the result. This example returns *hello world*. The letter 1 of world block reports the character in the specified position in the supplied text. The value can consist of text, number, symbol, or even a space. In the previous example, it reports *w*, which is the first letter of the supplied word, *world*. The length of world block reports how many characters the specified value contains.

Examples

Keeping track of three new categories of blocks is a challenge, but trying some examples that put them to use will help. These example scripts are more dynamic than the ones from previous chapters. You'll practice making scripts that interact with the user, check a password, draw with the mouse-pointer, and produce different results depending on the condition that's evaluated.

Example 7-1: What's Your Name?

This example uses Sensing blocks to gather and report on information the user enters. Specifically, the script first asks the user to enter his or her name, then the script displays that name in a speech bubble. When asked for user input (see Figure 7-4), enter a name and press the Enter key on your keyboard.

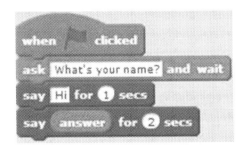

Script 7-1. *What's your name?*

Script 7-1 starts running when the user clicks the green flag. The next block creates a speech bubble that displays *What's your name?*, opens a user input field, and waits for the user's input (see Figure 7-4). The next block creates a speech bubble that displays *Hi* for 1 second. To create the last block, snap the

block onto the script, then drag the answer block over its entry field to embed the Sensing block into the Sound block. Now, the embedded block reports the reader's answer to the

block, which creates a speech bubble for the sprite and displays the user's input for 2 seconds.

Figure 7-4. *User input*

Table 7-1 lists the blocks and describes the actions used in this example.

Table 7-1. *Code Blocks in What's Your Name?*

Blocks	Actions
when ⚑ clicked	Clicking the green flag activates the script. The green flag is the trigger to start the script running.
ask What's your name? and wait	The sprite gets a speech bubble that displays *What's your name?*, opens a user input field, and waits for user input.
say Hi for 1 secs	The sprite gets a speech bubble that displays *Hi* for 1 second.
say ☐ for 2 secs	The sprite gets a speech bubble that displays the specified text for 2 seconds.
answer	Holds the current user input value.

Example 7-2: What's The Correct Answer?

When you combine a C block conditional statement, a sensing block, and an operator, you can produce sophisticated actions with ease. To demonstrate, this script asks the user an easy math question (see Figure 7-5), and then stores and evaluates the answer. If the user answers correctly, then script will display some text in a speech bubble. If the answer is wrong, the script stops running. Although this particular math question is simple, the underlying technique is one that you can use often in your scripts.

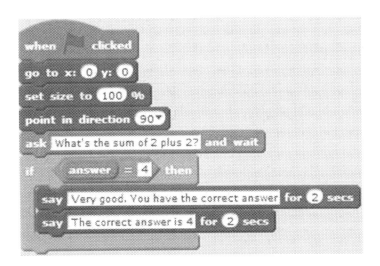

Script 7-2. *Correct answer*

Script 7-2 starts running when the user clicks the green flag. The next three blocks move the sprite to the center of the stage, set the sprite to its default size, and makes the sprite face to the right. The next block creates a speech bubble that displays *What's the sum of 2 plus 2?*, opens a user input field, and waits for the user's input. The C block is a conditional statement that checks if the user's input is equal to 4. If the condition is true, the script will execute the sequence of actions within the C block. If the condition is false, the script stops running. To create this conditional statement, first drag the blocks to the scripts area and embed the user input block ⬤ answer in the left field of the ⬤ = 4 block, and then type **4** in its right field. Next, drag the operator block into ⬤ if then. Block in the scripts area. The first block within the conditional statement creates a speech bubble that displays *Very good. You have the correct answer* for 2 seconds. The last block also creates a speech bubble for the sprite and displays *The correct answer is 4* for 2 seconds.

148

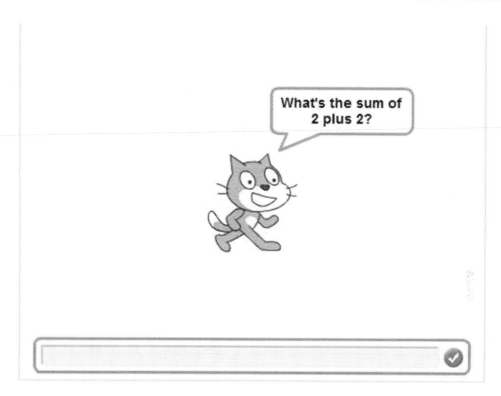

Figure 7-5. *Enter correct answer*

Table 7-2 lists the blocks and describes the actions used in this example.

Table 7-2. *Code Blocks in What's the Correct Answer?*

Blocks	Actions
when ▢ clicked	Clicking the green flag activates the script. The green flag is the trigger to start the script running.
go to x: 0 y: 0	Move the sprite to the position where X = 0 and Y = 0, which is the center of the stage.
set size to 100 %	Set the sprite to its default size.
point in direction 90▾	Make the sprite face to the right.
ask What's the sum of 2 plus 2? and wait	The sprite gets a speech bubble that displays *What's the sum of 2 plus 2?*, opens a user input field, and waits for user input.
if ▢ then	Check if the condition is true. If the condition is true, execute the actions within it. If the condition is false, skip to the next block.
▢ = 4	If the value on the left side is equal to 4, then this condition is true; otherwise, the condition is false.
answer	Hold and report the current user input value.
say Very good. You have the correct answer for 2 secs	The sprite gets a speech bubble that displays *Very good. You have the correct answer* for 2 seconds.
say The correct answer is 4 for 2 secs	The sprite gets a speech bubble that displays *The correct answer is 4* for 2 seconds.

Example 7-3: Please Try Again

In Example 7-2, you created an If/Then conditional statement. This time, try the [if/then/else] block's If/Then/Else conditional statement to control the action in your script based on user input. The script asks the user an easy math question, and then displays a different set of speech bubbles, depending on whether the user answers correctly or incorrectly.

Script 7-3. *Please try again*

Script 7-3 starts running when the user clicks the green flag. The next three blocks move the sprite to the center of the stage, set the sprite to its default size, and makes the sprite face to the right. The next block creates a speech bubble that displays *What's the sum of 2 plus 2?*, opens a user input field, and waits for the user's input. The next block is a conditional statement that checks if the user's input is equal to 4. If the

condition is true, the script will execute the first sequence of actions within the [   ] block (the Then sequence). The first block in the Then sequence creates a speech bubble that displays *Very good. You have the correct answer* for 2 seconds. The second block also creates a speech bubble for the sprite and displays *The correct answer is 4* for 2 seconds. If the condition is false, the script executes the second sequence of blocks contained after the word *else*. The first block in the Else sequence creates a speech bubble that displays *Sorry, wrong answer* for 2 seconds. The second block in the sequence creates a speech bubble that displays *Please try again* for 2 seconds.

Table 7-3 lists the blocks and describes the actions used in this example.

Table 7-3. *Code Blocks in Please Try Again*

Blocks	Actions
when clicked	Clicking the green flag activates the script. The green flag is the trigger to start the script running.
go to x: 0 y: 0	Move the sprite to the position where X = 0 and Y = 0, which is the center of the stage.
set size to 100 %	Set the sprite to its default size.
point in direction 90▾	Make the sprite face to the right.
ask What's the sum of 2 plus 2? and wait	The sprite gets a speech bubble that displays *What's the sum of 2 plus 2?*, opens a user input field and waits for user input.
if then else	Check if the condition is true. If the condition is true, execute the actions within it, before the word *else*. If the condition is false, execute the actions after the word *else* within the block.
☐ = 4	If the value on the left side is equal to 4, then this condition is true; otherwise, the condition is false.
answer	Hold and report the current user input value.
say Very good. You have the correct answer for 2 secs	The sprite gets a speech bubble that displays *Very good. You have the correct answer* for 2 seconds.
say The correct answer is 4 for 2 secs	The sprite gets a speech bubble that displays *The correct answer is 4* for 2 seconds.
say Sorry, wrong answer for 2 secs	The sprite gets a speech bubble that displays *Sorry, wrong answer* for 2 seconds.
say Please try again for 2 secs	The sprite gets a speech bubble that displays *Please try again* for 2 seconds.

Example 7-4: Enter Correct Password

Script 7-4 uses the same technique as you used in the previous example, but this time it evaluates a text answer from the user instead of a number. The script asks the user to enter the correct password. If the user enters *abracadabra*, the script will display some text in a speech bubble, announcing that the answer is right and *You may enter*. If the answers is wrong, the script will also display some text announcing that the answer is wrong and to please try again.

Script 7-4. *Correct Password*

The first four blocks of Script 7-4 are similar to the previous script. The script starts running when the user clicks the green flag. The next three blocks move the sprite to the center of the stage, set the sprite to its default size, and make the sprite face to the right. The next block creates a speech bubble that displays *Please enter the correct password*. It also opens a user input field and waits for the user's input. The next block is an If/Then/Else conditional statement that checks if the user's input is equal to the word *abracadabra*. If the condition is true, the script will execute the Then sequence (the next block within the C block). In this case, it is one block that creates a speech bubble that displays *You may enter* for 2 seconds. If the condition is false, the script executes the two blocks after the word *else*. The first block of the pair creates a speech bubble that displays *Wrong password* for 2 seconds. The second creates a speech bubble that displays *Please try again* for 2 seconds.

Table 7-4 lists the blocks and describes the actions used in this example.

Table 7-4. *Code Blocks in Enter the Correct Password*

Blocks	Actions
when ⚑ clicked	Clicking the green flag activates the script. The green flag is the trigger to start the script running.
go to x: 0 y: 0	Move the sprite to the position where X = 0 and Y = 0, which is the center of the stage.
set size to 100 %	Set the sprite to its default size.
point in direction 90▾	Make the sprite face to the right.
ask Please enter the correct password and wait	The sprite gets a speech bubble that displays *Please enter the correct password*, opens a user input field, and waits for user input.
if ⬡ then else	Check if the condition is true. If the condition is true, execute the actions within it, before the word *else*. If the condition is false, execute the actions after the word *else* within the block.
☐ = abracadabra	If the value on the left side is equal to abracadabra, then this condition is true; otherwise, the condition is false.
answer	Hold and report the current user input value.
say You may enter for 2 secs	The sprite gets a speech bubble that says *You may enter* for 2 seconds.
say Wrong password for 2 secs	The sprite gets a speech bubble that says *Wrong password* for 2 seconds.
say Please try again for 2 secs	The sprite gets a speech bubble that says *Please try again* for 2 seconds.

Example 7-5: Triangle or Square

Remember, trying to figure out what the script does before you create and run it is a good way to learn and understand the blocks and techniques the script uses. Study Script 7-5 for a moment. What do you think it does? Do any of the techniques look familiar from past chapters? They should!

Script 7-5 asks the user whether to draw a triangle or a square. Based on the user's answer, either a triangle or a square is drawn using the repeating C block technique that you learned in Chapter 4.

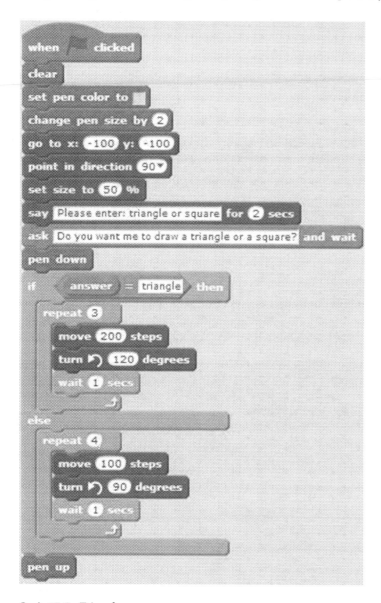

Script 7-5. *Triangle or square*

Script 7-5 starts running when the user clicks the green flag. The second block of code clears the stage of any marks made by the pen or stamp. The third block sets the pen color, and the next block changes the pen size. The next block moves the sprite to the coordinates, (–100, –100). The next block makes the sprite face to the right. The next block sets the sprite to half of its default size, and the block after that creates a speech bubble for the sprite and displays the text *Please enter triangle or square* for 2 seconds. The next block creates a speech bubble with the text *Do you want me to draw a triangle or a square?*, opens a user input field, and waits for the user's input. The **pen down** block means that the pen is on the stage and is ready to draw. The next block is an If/Then/Else conditional statement. If the user input stored in the **answer** block is equal to *triangle*, then the condition is true the script executes the Then sequence of actions (in the top half of the **if then else** block. The sequence draws a triangle using a C block that repeats the sequence of actions within it 3 times: Move the sprite 200 pixels in the direction that it's facing to draw with the pen for 200 pixels, rotates the sprite 120 degrees counterclockwise, and then pauses for 1 second.

If the **answer** block is not equal to triangle, the condition is false and the Else sequence of actions are executed. The first one is a **repeat 4** block that repeats the sequence of actions within it 4 times: Move the sprite 100 pixels in the direction that it's facing, rotate the sprite 90 degrees counterclockwise, and then pause for 1 second.

The last block of this script is **pen up**, which lifts the pen off the stage so if the sprite moves, the pen will not draw.

Table 7-5 lists the blocks and describes the actions used in this example.

Table 7-5. Code Blocks in Triangle or Square

Blocks	Actions
when clicked	Clicking the green flag activates the script. The green flag is the trigger to start the script running.
clear	Remove all marks previously made by the pen or stamp.
set pen color to	Set the pen color to lime color.
change pen size by 2	Change the pen size to 2.
go to x: -100 y: -100	Move the sprite to coordinates (X = -100, Y = -100).
point in direction 90	Make the sprite face to the right.
set size to 50 %	Set the sprite to half its default size.

(continued)

Table 7-5. (*continued*)

Blocks	Actions
say [Please enter: triangle or square] for 2 secs	The sprite gets a speech bubble that displays *Please enter: triangle or square* for 2 seconds.
pen down	The pen is on the stage and is ready to draw.
if [ ] then / else	Check if the condition is true. If the condition is true, execute the actions within it, before the word *else*. If the condition is false, execute the actions after the word *else* within the block.
[ ] = triangle	If the value on the left side is equal to triangle, then this condition is true; otherwise, the condition is false.
answer	Hold and report the current user input value.
repeat 3	Repeat the actions represented by the blocks within this block three times.
move 200 steps	Move the sprite 200 pixels in the direction that it's facing.
turn ↺ 120 degrees	Turn the sprite counterclockwise 120 degrees.
wait 1 secs	The script waits 1 second. No actions are performed for 1 second.
repeat 4	Repeat the actions represented by the blocks within this block four times.
move 100 steps	Move the sprite 100 pixels in the direction that it's facing.
turn ↺ 90 degrees	Turn the sprite counterclockwise 90 degrees.
wait 1 secs	The script waits 1 second. No actions are performed for 1 second.
pen up	The pen is off the stage and cannot draw.

Example 7-6: Secret Mission

This example puts the [repeat until] and [stop all] blocks to work in a script that prompts the user to enter a password, tests it, then gives the user as many tries as needed to enter the correct password.

Script 7-6. *Secret mission*

Script 7-6 also starts running when the user clicks the green flag. The next two blocks both create two-second speech bubbles. First *Please enter the secret code* is displayed and then *to receive the secret mission*. Next, the C block repeats the sequence of actions within it until its condition is true, meaning the user input stored in [answer] is equal to *monkey*. The first block in the sequence creates a speech bubble containing *What's the secret code?*, opens a user input field, and waits for the user's input. The next block is an If/Then conditional statement that also checks whether [answer] is equal to *monkey*. If the condition is true, then the first block within the If/Then conditional statement C block will display a speech bubble with *You entered:* for 1 second. The next block also creates a speech bubble that displays the user input for 2 seconds. The next block creates a third speech bubble with *You're allowed to receive the secret mission now* for 2 seconds. The last block within this sequence stops all scripts in this project from running.

If **answer** is not equal to *monkey*, then the final three blocks in the **repeat until** execute, displaying three consecutive speech bubble that contain *Wrong code, You entered*, the current user input, and *Please try again*, and then the loop repeats. The technique shown in this script can be used any time that you need to test user input for a specific answer.

Table 7-6 lists the blocks and describes the actions used in this example.

Table 7-6. *Code Blocks in Secret Mission*

Blocks	Actions
when ⚑ clicked	Clicking the green flag activates the script. The green flag is the trigger to start the script running.
say Please enter the secret code **for 2 secs**	The sprite gets a speech bubble that displays *Please enter the secret code* for 2 seconds.
say to receive the secret mission **for 2 secs**	The sprite gets a speech bubble that displays *to receive the secret mission* for 2 seconds.
repeat until	Execute the blocks/instructions within this block until the specified condition is true.
▢ = monkey	If the value on the left side is equal to monkey, then this condition is true; otherwise, the condition is false.
answer	Hold and report the current user input value.
ask What's the secret code? **and wait**	The sprite gets a speech bubble that displays *What's the secret code?*, opens a user input field, and waits for user input.
if ▢ **then**	Check if the condition is true. If the condition is true, execute the actions within it. If the condition is false, skip to the next block.
▢ = monkey	If the value on the left side is equal to monkey, then this condition is true; otherwise, the condition is false.

(*continued*)

Table 7-6. (*continued*)

Blocks	Actions
answer	Hold and report the current user input value.
say You entered: for 1 secs	The sprite gets a speech bubble that displays *You entered:* for 1 second.
say ▢ for 2 secs	The sprite gets a speech bubble that displays the specified text for 2 seconds.
answer	Hold and report the current user input value.
say You're allowed to receive the secret mission now for 2 secs	The sprite gets a speech bubble that displays *You're allowed to receive the secret mission now* for 2 seconds.
stop all ▼	Stop all scripts in this project.
say Wrong code. You entered: for 2 secs	The sprite gets a speech bubble that displays *Wrong code. You entered:* for 2 seconds.
say ▢ for 1 secs	The sprite gets a speech bubble that displays the specified text for 1 second.
answer	Hold and report the current user input value.
say Please try again for 1 secs	The sprite gets a speech bubble that displays *Please try again* for 1 second.

Example 7-7: Touching the Edge?

You've used the **if on edge, bounce** block before, but in this example, you're going to script a version of it yourself using your new conditional statement skills.

Script 7-7 starts running when the user clicks the green flag. The next four blocks set the rotation style of the sprite to **left-right**, move the sprite to the center of the stage, make the sprite face to the right, and set the sprite to its default size. Next is a C block that executes the sequence of actions within it forever. The first three blocks in the sequence move the sprite 5 pixels in the direction that it's facing, change the sprite's costume, and pause the script for 0.2 seconds. Next, there is an If/Then conditional statement that evaluates whether the sprite is touching the edge of the stage. If it is (a true result), then the sprite rotates 180 degrees counterclockwise. If the sprite isn't touching an edge (a false result), the action loops back to the **move 5 steps** block and the sequence repeats.

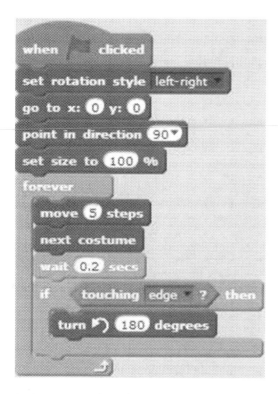

Script 7-7. *Touching the edge*

The movement and costume changes give the illusion as if the sprite is walking. If the sprite hits the edge of the stage, the If/Then conditional statement turns the sprite and moves it in the opposite direction, just like the if on edge, bounce block.

Table 7-7 lists the blocks and describes the actions used in this example.

Table 7-7. *Code Blocks in Touching the Edge?*

Blocks	Actions
when clicked	Clicking the green flag activates the script. The green flag is the trigger to start the script running.
set rotation style left-right	Set the rotation style of the sprite so that it can only face left or right.
go to x: 0 y: 0	Move the sprite to coordinates (X = 0, Y = 0), which is the middle of the stage.
point in direction 90	Make the sprite face to the right.
set size to 100 %	Set the sprite to its default size.
forever	Repeat all the instructions/blocks within this block forever.
move 5 steps	Move the sprite 5 pixels in the direction that it's facing.
next costume	Change the sprite to the next costume in the Costumes tab.
wait 0.2 secs	The script waits 0.2 seconds. No actions are performed for 0.2 seconds.
if then	Check if the condition is true. If the condition is true, execute the actions within it. If the condition is false, skip to the next block.
touching edge ?	Checks if the sprite is touching the edge of the stage. If it is, then this condition is set to true.
turn ↺ 180 degrees	Turn the sprite counterclockwise 180 degrees.

Example 7-8: Key Pressed?

Have you already figured out what Script 7-8 does? This example checks whether the space bar is pressed. Every time the space bar is pressed, the script plays a sound and creates a speech bubble with text. Try it out.

Script 7-8. *Key pressed*

The script starts running when the user clicks the green flag. The next two blocks make the sprite face to the right and move the sprite to the center of the stage. The next block is a C block that loops through the sequence of actions within it forever. That sequence is an If/Then conditional statement that first evaluates whether the space bar is pressed. If it is (a true result), then the **laugh-male1** sound plays and a *Hihihi, again!* speech bubble displays for 2 seconds. If the space bar is not pressed, the action loops back to check for another key press.

Table 7-8 lists the blocks and describes the actions used in this example.

Table 7-8. *Code Blocks in Key Pressed?*

Blocks	Actions
	Clicking the green flag activates the script. The green flag is the trigger to start the script running.
	Make the sprite face to the right.
	Move the sprite to coordinates (X = 0, Y = 0), which is the middle of the stage.
	Repeat all the instructions/blocks within this block forever.
	Check if the condition is true. If the condition is true, execute the actions within it. If the condition is false, skip to the next block.
	Check if the space bar is clicked. If it is, then this condition is set to true.
	Play the sound **laugh-male1**.
	The sprite gets a speech bubble that displays *Hihihi, again!* for 2 seconds.

Example 7-9: Current Time

This example creates some speech bubbles that display the user's name, the current hour, and the current minute, along with other text, to demonstrate two of the reporter blocks in the Sensing category.

Script 7-9. *Current time*

Script 7-9 starts running when the user clicks the green flag. The next block creates a speech bubble that displays *Hello!* for 1 second. The next block creates a speech bubble and displays the username of the user who is logged into Scratch for 2 seconds. The next pair of blocks create a speech bubble that displays *The current time is* followed by a speech bubble that displays the current hour. The next pair of blocks create speech bubbles that display *hours* and then *and*. The last two blocks create speech bubbles that display the current minute and *minutes* for 2 seconds.

Table 7-9 lists the blocks and describes the actions used in this example.

Table 7-9. *Code Blocks in Current Time*

Blocks	Actions
	Clicking the green flag activates the script. The green flag is the trigger to start the script running.
	The sprite gets a speech bubble that displays *Hello!* for 1 seconds.
	The sprite gets a speech bubble that displays the specified text or value for 2 seconds.
	Hold and report the username of the user who has logged in Scratch.

(*continued*)

Table 7-9. (*continued*)

Blocks	Actions
`say The current time is for 2 secs`	The sprite gets a speech bubble that displays *The current time is* for 2 seconds.
`say ⬜ for 1 secs`	The sprite gets a speech bubble that displays the specified text or value for 1 second.
`current hour ▾`	Hold and report the current hour.
`say hours for 2 secs`	The sprite gets a speech bubble that displays *hours* for 2 seconds.
`say and for 1 secs`	The sprite gets a speech bubble that displays *and* for 1 seconds.
`say ⬜ for 1 secs`	The sprite gets a speech bubble that displays the specified text or value for 1 second.
`current minute ▾`	Hold and report the current minute.
`say minutes for 2 secs`	The sprite gets a speech bubble that displays *minutes* for 2 seconds.

Example 7-10: Mouse Coordinates

This example demonstrates how to provide the current X and Y coordinates of the mouse to the code blocks, and then display them on the screen in the stage area.

Script 7-10. *Mouse coordinates*

Script 7-10 also starts running when the user clicks the green flag. The second block creates a speech bubble that displays *The current X-coordinate of the mouse in the stage is* for 2 seconds. The third block also creates a speech bubble and displays the current X coordinate of the mouse on the stage. The last two blocks do the same for the Y coordinate of the mouse on the stage.

You can use this technique whenever you need to report or evaluate the X and Y coordinates. For example, you can use ⬤mouse x⬤, ⬤mouse y⬤, or both blocks in a Boolean block to create a condition and make a decision whether the condition is true or false. For example, if you need to test whether the mouse is in a certain area of the stage, you could evaluate if the X coordinate is greater than 50; for example, by using the ⬤mouse x⬤ block in a Boolean block.

Table 7-10 lists the blocks and describes the actions used in this example.

Table 7-10. *Code Blocks in Mouse Coordinates*

Blocks	Actions
when 🚩 clicked	Clicking the green flag activates the script. The green flag is the trigger to start the script running.
say The current X-coordinate of the mouse in the stage is for 2 secs	The sprite gets a speech bubble that displays *The current X-coordinate of the mouse in the stage is* for 2 seconds.
say ☐ for 2 secs	The sprite gets a speech bubble that displays the specified text or value for 2 seconds.
mouse x	Hold and report the mouse-pointer current X coordinate on the stage.
say The current Y-coordinate of the mouse in stage is for 2 secs	The sprite gets a speech bubble that displays *The current Y-coordinate of the mouse in stage is* for 2 seconds.
say ☐ for 2 secs	The sprite gets a speech bubble that displays the specified text or value for 2 seconds.
mouse y	Hold and report the mouse-pointer current Y coordinate on the stage.

Example 7-11: Let's Do Some Math

This example demonstrates several mathematical blocks from the Operators category, providing the answers to their equations as input for `say ☐ for 2 secs` blocks.

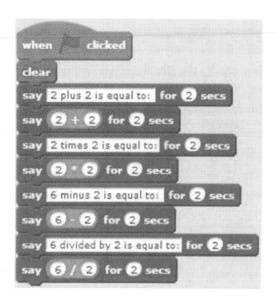

Script 7-11. *Some math*

Script 7-11 starts running when the user clicks the green flag. The second block of code clears the stage, removing any marks made by the pen or stamp. This block is not necessary, but it makes sure you start with a clean stage. The next pair of block create a speech bubble that displays *2 plus 2 is equal to:* for 2 seconds, then create a speech bubble that displays the result of the `2 + 2` operator block. Remember, you need to drag and embed the `2 + 2` into the text field of the `say ☐ for 2 secs` block to provide the result of one as the input to the other. The next three pairs of blocks create a speech bubble that introduce and display the answers for simple multiplication, subtraction, and division questions using the respective operator blocks: `2 * 2`, `6 - 2`, and `6 / 2`.

Table 7-11 lists the blocks and describes the actions used in this example.

Table 7-11. *Code Blocks in Let's Do Some Math*

Blocks	Actions
when clicked	Clicking the green flag activates the script. The green flag is the trigger to start the script running.
clear	Remove all marks previously made by the pen or stamp.
say 2 plus 2 is equal to: for 2 secs	The sprite gets a speech bubble that displays *2 plus 2 is equal to:* for 2 seconds.
say ☐ for 2 secs	The sprite gets a speech bubble that displays the specified text or value for 2 seconds.
(2 + 2)	Add two values (2 + 2) and report the result.
say 2 times 2 is equal to: for 2 secs	The sprite gets a speech bubble that displays *2 times 2 is equal to:* for 2 seconds.
say ☐ for 2 secs	The sprite gets a speech bubble that displays the specified text or value for 2 seconds.
(2 * 2)	Multiply two values (2 * 2) and report the result.
say 6 minus 2 is equal to: for 2 secs	The sprite gets a speech bubble that displays *6 minus 2 is equal to:* for 2 seconds.
say ☐ for 2 secs	The sprite gets a speech bubble that displays the specified text or value for 2 seconds.
(6 - 2)	Subtract one value from another (6 – 2) and report the result.
say 6 divided by 2 is equal to: for 2 secs	The sprite gets a speech bubble that displays *6 divided by 2 is equal to:* for 2 seconds.
say ☐ for 2 secs	The sprite gets a speech bubble that displays the specified text or value for 2 seconds.
(6 / 2)	Divide one value by another (6 / 2) and report the result.

Example 7-12: Math with the Join Block

A more efficient way to produce the same results as Script 7-11 is to use the `join 2 plus 2 is equal to:` block. With this block, you can join two values, and then embed them together into another block. Script 7-12, for example, joins the descriptive text about an equation with its result and embeds both pieces of information into a single `say ☐ for 2 secs` block. The script is now half the size of the previous version!

Script 7-12. *Math with join block*

Script 7-12 starts running when the user clicks the green flag. The second block of code clears the stage area of any marks made by the pen or stamp. Next is the first three-block combination: the 2 + 2 operator block is embedded in the join 2 plus 2 is equal to: block. This newly joined pair is then embedded in the say for 2 secs block in the scripts area. Together they create a speech bubble that displays the text *2 plus 2 is equal to:* and *4* (the sum of 2 + 2) for 2 seconds. The next block is also a three-in-one block that creates a speech bubble that displays the text *2 times 2 is equal to:* and the result of the operator block for 2 seconds. The technique is repeated for the next two blocks, joining the appropriate text with the 6 - 2 and 6 / 2 operators.

Table 7-12 lists the blocks and describes the actions used in this example.

Table 7-12. *Code Blocks in Math with the Join Block*

Blocks	Actions
when clicked	Clicking the green flag activates the script. The green flag is the trigger to start the script running.
clear	Remove all marks previously made by the pen or stamp.
say for 2 secs	The sprite gets a speech bubble that displays the specified text or value for 2 seconds.
join 2 plus 2 is equal to:	Join the two values that have been specified in the block and report the result.
2 + 2	Add two values (2 + 2) and report the result.
say for 2 secs	The sprite gets a speech bubble that displays the specified text or value for 2 seconds.
join 2 times 2 is equal to:	Join the two values that have been specified in the block and report the result.

(*continued*)

Table 7-12. (*continued*)

Blocks	Actions
`2 * 2`	Multiply two values (2 * 2) and report the result.
`say ▢ for 2 secs`	The sprite gets a speech bubble that displays the specified text or value for 2 seconds.
`join 6 minus 2 is equal to: ▢`	Join the two values that have been specified in the block and report the result.
`6 - 2`	Subtract one value from another (6-2) and report the result.
`say ▢ for 2 secs`	The sprite gets a speech bubble that displays the specified text or value for 2 seconds.
`join 6 divided by 2 is equal to: ▢`	Join the two values that have been specified in the block and report the result.
`6 / 2`	Divide one value by another (6 / 2) and report the result.

Example 7-13: Guess the Correct Number

This script demonstrates more ways of joining blocks to produce shorter, more efficient scripts. This example script creates a guessing game. The script asks the user to enter a number between 1 and 10. The correct number to be guessed is 5. The script displays different text, depending on the number that the user guessed—whether it's the correct number, larger than 5, or smaller than 5.

Script 7-13. *Guess the correct number*

Script 7-13 starts running when the user clicks the green flag. The next block creates a speech bubble, displays *Enter a number between 1 and 10*, opens a user input field, and waits for the user's input. The next block pauses the script for 1 second. The [if then] block checks if the user input equals 5. If it does (a true result), the actions within the C block executed: a speech bubble displays the text *The number you have chosen, is* and the user input for 2 seconds, then the [stop all] block stops all scripts in this project from running. If the user input is not equal to 5 (a result of false), the script skips to the If/Then/Else conditional statement block to check if [answer] is greater than 5. If it is, the script executes the actions in the Then portion of the block. Here a four-in-one combination of blocks creates a speech bubble that displays *The number you have chosen,* the user input, and *is larger than 5* for 4 seconds. If [answer] is not greater than 5, the actions in the Else portion of the block are executed instead: A speech bubble displays *The number you have chosen,* the user input, and *is smaller than 5* for 4 seconds.

Table 7-13 lists the blocks and describes the actions used in this example.

Table 7-13. *Code Blocks in Guess the Correct Number*

Blocks	Actions
when [flag] clicked	Clicking the green flag activates the script. The green flag is the trigger to start the script running.
ask Enter a number between 1 and 10 and wait	The sprite gets a speech bubble that displays *Enter a number between 1 and 10*, opens user input field and waits for user input.
wait 1 secs	The script waits 1 second. No actions are performed for 1 second.
if then	Check if the condition is true. If the condition is true, execute the actions within it. If the condition is false, skip to the next block.
☐ = 5	If the value on the left side is equal to 5, then this condition is true; otherwise, the condition is false.
answer	Hold and report the current user input value.
say ☐ for 2 secs	The sprite gets a speech bubble that displays the specified text or value for 2 seconds.
join The number you have chosen, is ☐	Join the two values that have been specified in the block and report the result.
answer	Hold and report the current user input value.
stop all ▾	Stop all scripts in this project.

(*continued*)

Table 7-13. (*continued*)

Blocks	Actions
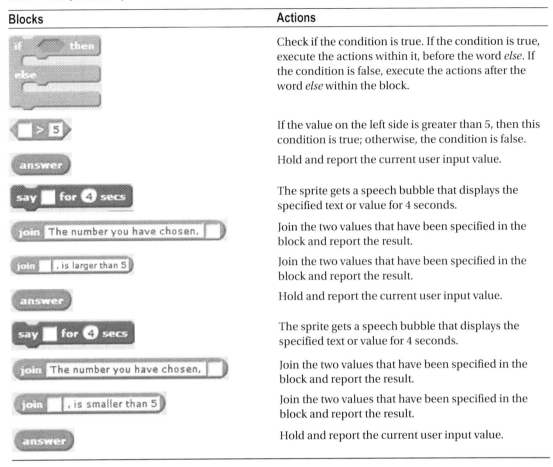	Check if the condition is true. If the condition is true, execute the actions within it, before the word *else*. If the condition is false, execute the actions after the word *else* within the block.
	If the value on the left side is greater than 5, then this condition is true; otherwise, the condition is false.
	Hold and report the current user input value.
	The sprite gets a speech bubble that displays the specified text or value for 4 seconds.
	Join the two values that have been specified in the block and report the result.
	Join the two values that have been specified in the block and report the result.
	Hold and report the current user input value.
	The sprite gets a speech bubble that displays the specified text or value for 4 seconds.
	Join the two values that have been specified in the block and report the result.
	Join the two values that have been specified in the block and report the result.
	Hold and report the current user input value.

Example 7-14: How Many Letters in the Word?

Sometimes you may need to determine the number of characters in a word entered by the user, such as for a password that must be at least a specific length. This example uses the length of ☐ and answer blocks to do just that.

Script 7-14. *How many letters?*

Script 7-14 starts running when the user clicks the green flag. The next block creates a speech bubble, displays the text *Enter a word*, opens a user input field, and waits for the user's input. The next block pauses the script for 1 second. The fourth block embeds several 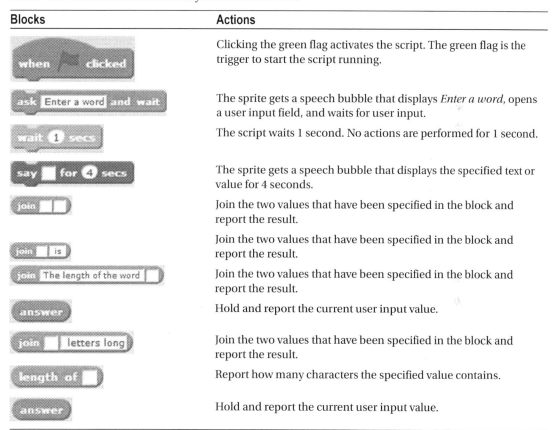blocks within each other to create a speech bubble that displays *The length of the word*, the user input, *is*, the length of the word, and *letters long* for 4 seconds. Embedding the 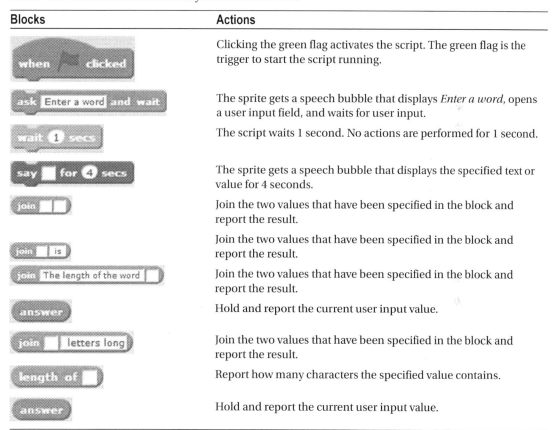 block in the 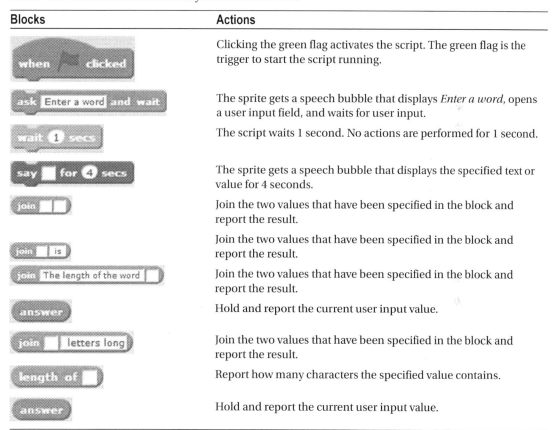 block calculates the length value.

Table 7-14 lists the blocks and describes the actions used in this example.

Table 7-14. *Code Blocks in How Many Letters in the Word?*

Blocks	Actions
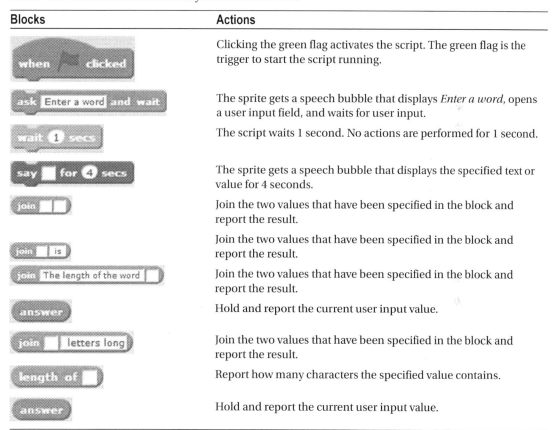	Clicking the green flag activates the script. The green flag is the trigger to start the script running.
	The sprite gets a speech bubble that displays *Enter a word*, opens a user input field, and waits for user input.
	The script waits 1 second. No actions are performed for 1 second.
	The sprite gets a speech bubble that displays the specified text or value for 4 seconds.
	Join the two values that have been specified in the block and report the result.
	Join the two values that have been specified in the block and report the result.
	Join the two values that have been specified in the block and report the result.
	Hold and report the current user input value.
	Join the two values that have been specified in the block and report the result.
	Report how many characters the specified value contains.
	Hold and report the current user input value.

Example 7-15: Pick a Random Number

This example picks a random number between 1 and 100 and displays which number was randomly picked.

Script 7-15. *Pick random number*

Script 7-15 starts running when the user clicks the green flag. The next block does the rest. It creates a speech bubble, picks a random number between 1 and 100 using the **pick random 1 to 100** block, and displays the phrase *My favorite number is*, joined with the number for 2 seconds.

Table 7-15 lists the blocks and describes the actions used in this example.

Table 7-15. *Code Blocks in Pick a Random Number*

Blocks	Actions
when clicked	Clicking the green flag activates the script. The green flag is the trigger to start the script running.
say for 2 secs	The sprite gets a speech bubble that displays the specified text for 2 seconds.
join My favorite number is	Join the two values that have been specified in the block and report the result.
pick random 1 to 100	Pick a random value between the two specified numbers and report the result.

Example 7-16: Timer Trigger

This example starts the timer from 0.0 seconds. When the timer reaches 25 seconds, the script displays a text.

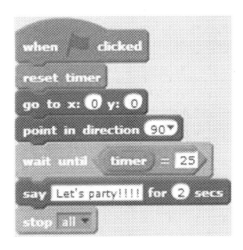

Script 7-16. *Time trigger*

Script 7-16 starts running when the user clicks the green flag. The next block reset the timer to 0.0 seconds. The next block moves the sprite to the center of the stage (0, 0). The next block makes the sprite face to the right. The **wait until** block then evaluates whether **timer** is equal to 25 using embedded blocks. When that condition is true, and the next actions are executed: a speech bubble displays the text *Let's party!!!!* for 2 seconds, then the last block stops all scripts in this project from running.

Table 7-16 lists the blocks and describes the actions used in this example.

Table 7-16. *Code Blocks in Time Trigger*

Blocks	Actions
when clicked	Clicking the green flag activates the script. The green flag is the trigger to start the script running.
reset timer	Reset the timer value back to 0.0.
go to x: ⓪ y: ⓪	Move the sprite to coordinates (X = 0, Y = 0), which is the middle of the stage.
point in direction 90▾	Make the sprite face to the right.
wait until	Pause the script until the specified condition is true.
◼ = 25	If the value on the left side is equal to 25, then this condition is true; otherwise, the condition is false.
timer	Hold and report the timer value.
say Let's party!!!! for ② secs	The sprite gets a speech bubble that displays *Let's party!!!!* for 2 seconds.
stop all ▾	Stop all scripts in this project.

Example 7-17: Move to the Center of the Stage

Being able to check whether your sprite has reached a specific location can be very useful to your scripts, and this script shows you how to do just that. Specifically, Script 7-17 checks whether Sprite1 is at the center of the stage (0, 0), then responds accordingly.

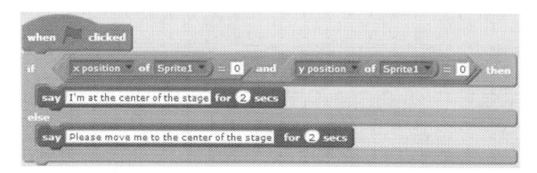

Script 7-17. *Move to center*

Script 7-17 starts running when the user clicks the green flag. The block then checks whether the X and Y coordinates of Sprite1 are both equal to 0. Remember the conditions tested on both sides of the block need to be true for the whole condition to be true. A result of true means the actions in the Then portion activate: the block creates a speech bubble and displays *I'm at the center of the stage* for 2 seconds. If the condition is false, action passes straight to the Else portion and a speech bubble with the text *Please move me to the center of the stage* displays for 2 seconds.

Run the script, and move the sprite along the stage, to see the text change depending on the sprite's position. Remember, you can always see the position of the sprite the top right corner of the scripts area (see Figure 7-6).

Figure 7-6. Sprite's position

Table 7-17 lists the blocks and describes the actions used in this example.

Table 7-17. Code Blocks in Move to the Center of the Stage

Blocks	Actions
when clicked	Clicking the green flag activates the script. The green flag is the trigger to start the script running.
if then else	Check if the condition is true. If the condition is true, execute the actions within it, before the word *else*. If the condition is false, execute the actions after the word *else* within the block.
and	Check both conditions on each side of this block. If both conditions are true, then this condition is true. Any other combination results in this condition being false.

(continued)

Table 7-17. (*continued*)

Blocks	Actions
⟨ □ = 0 ⟩	If the value on the left side is equal to 0, then this condition is true; otherwise, the condition is false.
x position ▾ of Sprite1 ▾	Hold and report the value of the X coordinate of the sprite.
⟨ □ = 0 ⟩	If the value on the left side is equal to 0, then this condition is true; otherwise, the condition is false.
y position ▾ of Sprite1 ▾	Hold and report the value of the Y coordinate of the sprite.
say I'm at the center of the stage for 2 secs	The sprite gets a speech bubble that displays *I'm at the center of the stage* for 2 seconds.
say Please move me to the center of the stage for 2 secs	The sprite gets a speech bubble that displays *Please move me to the center of the stage* for 2 seconds.

Example 7-18: Question

In this example, the script asks the user to answer a question with one of two specific phrases, and then takes different actions depending on the answers. Most of the time, you'll know whether the user of your project is human or alien, but the basic technique is useful for many other types of questions.

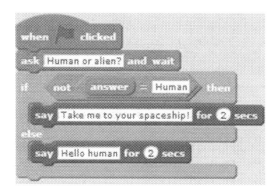

Script 7-18. *Question*

The trigger to start Script 7-18 is the green flag. The next block creates a speech bubble and displays the question *Human or alien?*. This block also opens a user input field and waits for the user's input. Next, an If/Then/Else conditional statement block evaluates whether it is true that the user's answer is **not** Human. The block is snapped in the left field of and the entire assembly is embedded into the block to be evaluated. If the block evaluates as true, then the Then action executes, creating a speech bubble that displays the text *Take me to your spaceship!* for 2 seconds. If the condition is false (meaning the user input does equal human), the Else portion creates a speech bubble that displays the text *Hello human* for 2 seconds.

Table 7-18 lists the blocks and describes the actions used in this example.

Table 7-18. Code Blocks in Question

Blocks	Actions
	Clicking the green flag activates the script. The green flag is the trigger to start the script running.
	The sprite gets a speech bubble that displays *Human or alien?*, opens a user input field, and waits for user input.
	Check if the condition is true. If the condition is true, execute the actions within it, before the word *else*. If the condition is false, execute the actions after the word *else* within the block.
	Check the condition within this block. If the condition within the block is true, return false, otherwise return true.
	If the value on the left side is equal to *Human*, then this condition is true; otherwise, the condition is false.
	Hold and report the current user input value.
	The sprite gets a speech bubble that displays *Take me to your spaceship!* for 2 seconds.
	The sprite gets a speech bubble that displays *Hello human* for 2 seconds.

Example 7-19: Can You Solve It?

This script displays a problem for the user to solve. The user needs to solve for X in the equation X + 4 / 2 = 10. The text response that the script displays depends on if the answer is right or wrong.

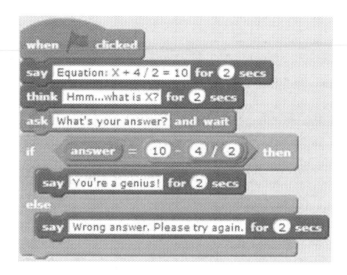

Script 7-19. *Can you solve it?*

Script 7-19 also starts running when the user clicks the green flag. The next block creates a speech bubble and displays the text *Equation: X + 4 / 2 = 10* for 2 seconds. The next block creates a thought bubble and displays the text *Hmm...what is X?* for 2 seconds. The ``ask What's your answer? and wait`` block creates a speech bubble that displays *What's your answer?*, opens a user input field, and waits for the user's input. Next is an If/Then/Else conditional statement that evaluates whether the user input equals the result of 10-4/2. If the condition is true, the block in the Then portion creates a speech bubble and displays the text *You're a genius!* for 2 seconds. If the condition is false, the block in the Else portion block creates a speech bubble that displays the text *Wrong answer. Please try again.* for 2 seconds.

Table 7-19 lists the blocks and describes the actions used in this example.

Table 7-19. *Code Blocks in Can You Solve It?*

Blocks	Actions
when ⚑ clicked	Clicking the green flag activates the script. The green flag is the trigger to start the script running.
say Equation: X + 4 / 2 = 10 for 2 secs	The sprite gets a speech bubble that displays *Equation: X + 4 / 2 = 10* for 2 seconds.
think Hmm...what is X? for 2 secs	The sprite gets a speech bubble that displays *Hmm... what is X?* for 2 seconds.
ask What's your answer? and wait	The sprite gets a speech bubble that displays *What's your answer?*, opens a user input field, and waits for user input.
if then else	Check if the condition is true. If the condition is true, execute the actions within it, before the word *else*. If the condition is false, execute the actions after the word *else* within the block.
☐ = ☐	Check if both sides of the equal sign are equal. If both values are equal, then this condition is true; otherwise, this condition is false.
answer	Hold and report the current user input value.
10 - ☐	Subtract one value from another and report the result.
4 / 2	Divide one value by another (4/2) and report the result.
say You're a genius! for 2 secs	The sprite gets a speech bubble that displays *You're a genius!* for 2 seconds.
say Wrong answer. Please try again. for 2 secs	The sprite gets a speech bubble that displays *Wrong answer. Please try again.* for 2 seconds.

Example 7-20: Drawing with the Mouse-Pointer

This script lets you draw in the stage area. To draw, you need to click the left mouse button, hold it down, and move it around the stage. If the primary mouse button or left mouse button is not pressed then the pen will not draw because the **pen up** block is in effect.

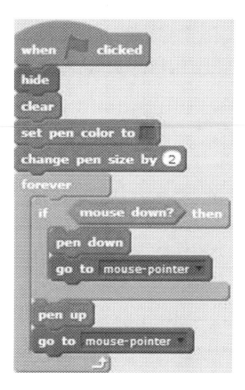

Script 7-20. *Drawing*

Script 7-20 starts running when the user clicks the green flag. The next block makes the sprite disappear from the stage area. The next block clears the stage area of any marks made by the pen or stamp. The next pair of blocks set the pen color and change the pen size. Next is a C block that repeats the sequence of actions within it forever block.

First within this sequence is the block, which checks whether the left mouse button is pressed using the embedded block. If this is true, the sequence within the conditional statement block is executed. The first block places the pen on the stage, ready to draw. The next block moves the pen toward the mouse-pointer. You can use your mouse-pointer to draw in the stage area, because as long as the left mouse button is held down, everywhere the mouse-pointer moves, the pen draws a trail.

When the mouse button is no longer pressed, the script moves out of the [if then] block and the next block lifts the pen from the stage. The last block also moves the pen toward the mouse-pointer, but no drawing is visible because the pen is lifted.

Table 7-20 lists the blocks and describes the actions used in this example.

Table 7-20. *Code Blocks in Drawing with the Mouse-Pointer*

Blocks	Actions
when clicked	Clicking the green flag activates the script. The green flag is the trigger to start the script running.
hide	Make the sprite disappear from the stage.
clear	Remove all marks previously made by the pen or stamp.
set pen color to	Set the pen color to purple color.
change pen size by 2	Change the pen size to 2.
forever	Repeat all the instructions/blocks within this block forever.
if then	Check if the condition is true. If the condition is true, execute the actions within it. If the condition is false, skip to the next block.
mouse down?	Check if the primary mouse button is clicked. If the primary mouse button is clicked, then the condition is true. If not, then the condition is false.
pen down	The pen is on the stage and is ready to draw.
go to mouse-pointer	Move the sprite toward the mouse-pointer.
pen up	The pen is off the stage and cannot draw.
go to mouse-pointer	Move the sprite toward the mouse-pointer.

Summary

In this chapter, you learned about some advanced computer programming concepts, including the following:

- Conditional statements
- Conditions
- Loops
- User input

All programming languages rely on these concepts. The blocks that you need to execute these concepts in Scratch are available in the **Control**, **Operators**, and **Sensing** categories. With them, you can create dynamic scripts that can produce a different result every time they're run, depending on the condition and/or user input.

In the next chapter, you'll investigate another advanced concept: variables, which are items that hold a value that can change. They work similar to the way that the block saves user input.

Exercises

1. Create a script that asks the user for the answer to the equation 10 + 3 – 4 * 2. Use an If/Then/Else conditional statement block to display text depending on if the answer is right or wrong.

2. Create a script that displays the result of each of the following equations:

    2 + 3, 10 – 7, 13 * 4, and 13 / 4. Use join blocks.

■ ■ ■

CHAPTER 8

Variables

To temporarily hold information and pass it to other blocks in your script, you can create variables. Each variable you create in Scratch has a unique name and can hold either a numeric value or a string of characters. A string can be an actual word or any combination of letters, numbers, and symbols, like in a password. For example, you could create a variable called **City** and give it the value *Boston*. Later in your script, you can set **City** to another value, such as *New York*. Variables come in handy whenever you need to use data values that change in a script. For example, suppose that you wanted the cat to count from 1 to 10. You could create a script with a separate `say ▯ for 2 secs` block for each of the 10 values (entering 1, 2, 3, and so on by hand), or you could create one variable that will hold the different values, one at a time, and then use a loop and a single `say ▯ for 2 secs` block with the variable embedded. This is the power of a variable.

Data Blocks and Creating Variables

To create a new variable in Scratch, you need to go to the block palette and select the **Data** blocks category (see Figure 8-1).

Figure 8-1. *Go to the Data category to create a variable*

© Eduardo A. Vlieg 2016
E. A. Vlieg, *Scratch by Example*, DOI 10.1007/978-1-4842-1946-1_8

Once here, you click the **Make a Variable** button (see Figure 8-2) to open the **New Variable** window (see Figure 8-3).

Figure 8-2. *Click Make a Variable*

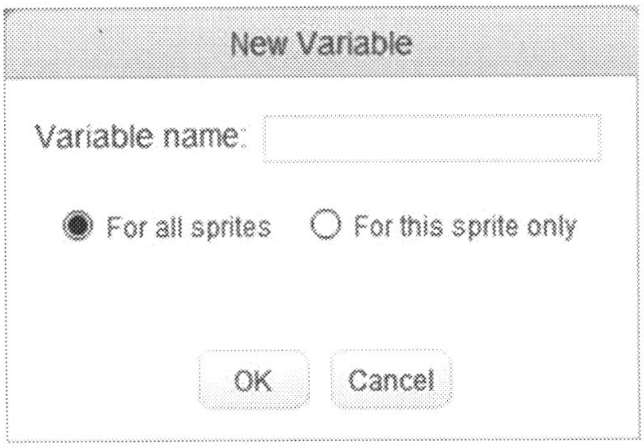

Figure 8-3. *The New Variable dialog*

Here (see Figure 8-3) you enter a name for the variable and select if you want the variable to be available for this sprite only or for all sprites. If you select **For this sprite only**, the variable is considered a *local* variable, meaning that it is only available to the sprite that was selected. If you chose **For all sprites**, the variable is considered a *global* variable. This means that the variable is available to all sprites in the specific project that it was created in. Click the **OK** button when ready. In Figure 8-4, I created a variable named **number**, which we'll use in the examples. A variable, whether local or global, is available per project only. So, you cannot create and use a variable in one project, and then reuse it in another project. You will need to re-create that variable in the second project.

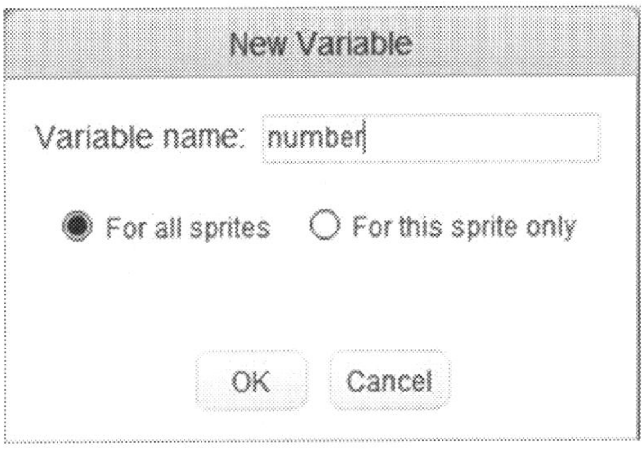

Figure 8-4. *Give the variable a name*

After you create a variable, Scratch adds several other blocks of code to the Data category (see Figure 8-5). These new blocks enable you to work with your variables.

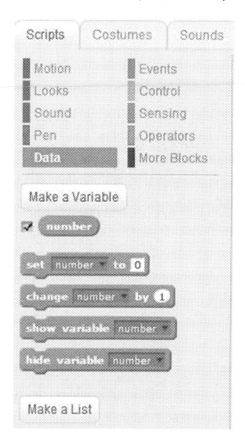

Figure 8-5. *Variable blocks*

The first block you see when you create a variable is a variable reporter block with the same name as your variable, such as **number**. It holds and reports the current value of the variable. To show a reporter window in the stage area that displays the current value of a variable, use the **show variable number** block and choose the desired variable's name from the pull-down menu. Likewise, you can hide the reporter window with the **hide variable number** block. To assign a specific value to your variable, use the **set number to 0** block, choosing the desired variable name from the pull-down menu and enter a value in the field. Here, the variable called **number** is assigned the value 0. You can also embed a reporter block such as **answer** or an operator block such as **pick random 1 to 10** in the block to assign the associated value to the variable. The **change number by 1** block changes the value of the variable by the specified value. This block of code accepts numbers only. It will not work with strings. In this example, the **number** variable is changed by 1, which means that 1 is added to the current value of the variable, and thus the new value for the variable is 2.

Examples

Next, you will create some scripts that show how variables are used. By creating and running these scripts, you will get a better understanding of variables. Remember, after learning how they work, you can always change these scripts to your liking or adapt the techniques for other uses.

Example 8-1: Count to Ten

This script makes the sprite count from 1 to 10. Before you create Script 8-1, be sure to create a new variable in the Data category of the block palette and name it **number**. The script assigns 0 to **number**, and each time through the repeat loop, it adds 1 to the current value of the variable and displays the current value of **number**.

Script 8-1 starts running when the user clicks the green flag. The second block creates a speech bubble for the sprite that displays *I can count to 10* for 2 seconds. The third block assigns the value 0 to the **number** variable. Next is a repeat block that repeats the sequence of actions within it 10 times. The first block in the sequence changes the current value of the **number** variable by 1. The next block creates a speech bubble that displays the current value of the variable for 2 seconds. The last block creates a speech bubble that displays the text *Can you count to 10?* for 2 seconds.

Script 8-1. *Count to ten*

Table 8-1 lists the blocks and describes the actions used in this example.

Table 8-1. *Code Blocks in Count to Ten*

Blocks	Actions
when ⚑ clicked	Clicking the green flag activates the script. The green flag is the trigger to start the script running.
say I can count to 10 for 2 secs	The sprite gets a speech bubble that displays *I can count to 10* for 2 seconds.
set number to 0	Set the current value of the variable called **number** to 0.
repeat 10	Repeat the actions represented by the blocks within this block 10 times.
change number by 1	Add 1 to the current value of the **number** variable.
say ▊ for 2 secs	The sprite gets a speech bubble that displays the specified text or value for 2 seconds.
number	Hold and report the current value of the **number** variable.
say Can you count to 10? for 2 secs	The sprite gets a speech bubble that displays *Can you count to 10?* for 2 seconds.

Example 8-2: Countdown

Remember to try to figure out what the script does before you create and run it. By now you should have enough knowledge to be able to read the script, block by block, and know what it does. (This is the same way that programmers read programs line by line, for example, when troubleshooting a program.) As you probably noticed, you need a **number** variable for this script. If necessary, create one now. Let's walk through the script to see if you figured it out.

Script 8-2 starts running when the user clicks the green flag. The next block creates a speech bubble that displays *The countdown starts now* for 2 seconds. The next block assigns the value 10 to the **number** variable. The fourth block creates a speech bubble that displays the current value of **number** for 1 second. Next, the repeat block repeats the sequence of actions within it 10 times. First, it changes the current value of the **number** variable by –1. Next, it creates a speech bubble that displays the current value of the **number** variable for 1 second. And then the loop repeats. The last block in this script creates a speech bubble that displays *Liftoff. We have liftoff….* for 2 seconds.

Script 8-2. *Countdown*

Did you guess that the script makes the sprite count down from 10? Well done.
Table 8-2 lists the blocks and describes the actions used in this example.

Table 8-2. *Code Blocks in Count Down*

Blocks	Actions
	Clicking the green flag activates the script. The green flag is the trigger to start the script running.
	The sprite gets a speech bubble that displays *The countdown starts now* for 2 seconds.
	Set the current value of the **number** variable to 10.
	The sprite gets a speech bubble that displays the specified text or value for 1 second.
	Hold and report the current value of the **number** variable.
	Repeat the actions represented by the blocks within this block 10 times.
	Subtract 1 from the current value of the **number** variable.
	The sprite gets a speech bubble that displays the specified text or value for 1 second.
	Hold and report the current value of the **number** variable.
	The sprite gets a speech bubble that displays *Liftoff. We have liftoff....* for 2 seconds.

Example 8-3: Odd Numbers

The script assigns the value 1 to the **number** variable and displays this value. Each time through the repeat loop it adds 2 to the current value of the variable and displays the new value. The script displays the values 1, 3, 5, 7, and 9. Again, before you create this script, make sure that the **number** variable is created.

Script 8-3 also starts running when the user clicks the green flag. The next block creates a speech bubble that displays *All the odd numbers from 0 to 10 are?* for 2 seconds. The next block assigns the value 1 to the **number** variable. The next block creates a speech bubble and displays the current value of the **number**

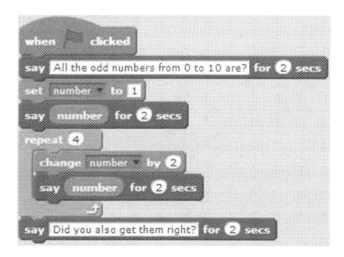

variable for 2 seconds. Next, the ⬚ block that repeats the sequence of actions within it 4 times: change the current value of the variable by 2 and create a speech bubble that displays the current value of the **number** variable for 2 seconds. When the loop is finished, the last block in the script creates a speech bubble that displays *Did you also get them right?* for 2 seconds.

Script 8-3. *Odd numbers*

Table 8-3 lists the blocks and describes the actions used in this example.

Table 8-3. *Code Blocks in Odd Number*

Blocks	Actions
when 🏳 clicked	Clicking the green flag activates the script. The green flag is the trigger to start the script running.
say All the odd numbers from 0 to 10 are? for 2 secs	The sprite gets a speech bubble that displays *All the odd numbers from 0 to 10 are?* for 2 seconds.

(*continued*)

Table 8-3. (*continued*)

Blocks	Actions
set number ▾ to 1	Set the current value of the **number** variable to 1.
say ☐ for 2 secs	The sprite gets a speech bubble that displays the specified text or value for 2 seconds.
number	Hold and report the current value of the **number** variable.
repeat 4	Repeat the actions represented by the blocks within this block four times.
change number ▾ by 2	Add 2 to the current value of the **number** variable.
say ☐ for 2 secs	The sprite gets a speech bubble that displays the specified text or value for 2 seconds.
number	Hold and report the current value of the **number** variable.
say Did you also get them right? for 2 secs	The sprite gets a speech bubble that displays *Did you also get them right?* for 2 seconds.

Example 8-4: String Variable

This simple example demonstrates that variables may contain a string of characters, such as a name. Also, notice how the same variable changes to hold different values as this script progresses.

Before you create this script, you need to create the variable called **name**. Script 8-4 starts running when the user clicks the green flag. The next pair of blocks move the sprite to the center of the stage (0, 0) and make it face to the right. The `set name ▾ to John` block assigns the value *John* to the **name** variable. The next block creates a speech bubble that displays *Hi* for 1 second. The next block creates a speech bubble that displays the current value of **name**, which is *John*, for 2 seconds. The next block assigns the value *Lisa* to the **name** variable. The next block creates a speech bubble that displays the text *Hi there* for 1 second. The next block creates a speech bubble that displays the current value of the **name** variable for 2 seconds; this time the value is *Lisa*. The `set name ▾ to Jim` block then assigns the value *Jim* to the **name** variable. The next block creates a speech bubble that displays *Glad to see you* for 1 second. The final block creates a speech bubble that displays *Jim*, the current value of the **name** variable, for 2 seconds.

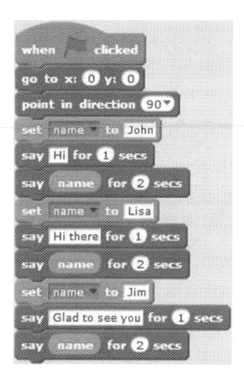

Script 8-4. *String variables*

Table 8-4 lists the blocks and describes the actions used in this example.

Table 8-4. *Code Blocks in String Variable*

Blocks	Actions
when clicked	Clicking the green flag activates the script. The green flag is the trigger to start the script running.
go to x: 0 y: 0	Move the sprite to the position where X = 0 and Y = 0, which is the center of the stage.
point in direction 90▾	Make the sprite face to the right.
set name ▾ to John	Set the current value of the variable called **name** to *John*.
say Hi for 1 secs	The sprite gets a speech bubble that displays *Hi* for 1 second.
say ▢ for 2 secs	The sprite gets a speech bubble that displays the specified text or value for 2 seconds.

(continued)

Table 8-4. (*continued*)

Blocks	Actions
name	Hold and report the current value of the **name** variable.
set name ▾ to Lisa	Set the current value of the **name** variable to *Lisa*.
say Hi there for ① secs	The sprite gets a speech bubble that displays *Hi there* for 1 second.
say ■ for ② secs	The sprite gets a speech bubble that displays the specified text or value for 2 seconds.
name	Hold and report the current value of the **name** variable.
set name ▾ to Jim	Set the current value of the **name** variable to *Jim*.
say Glad to see you for ① secs	The sprite gets a speech bubble that displays *Glad to see you* for 1 second.
say ■ for ② secs	The sprite gets a speech bubble that displays the specified text or value for 2 seconds.
name	Hold and report the current value of the **name** variable.

Example 8-5: Draw an Octagon

Remember Example 4-6 that drew an octagon in Chapter 4? This example does the same thing using a **number** variable to determine the number of sides that the pen should draw and the angles between them. Because Script 8-5 sets the variable to 8, the script draws an octagon, but you could easily draw a square, a pentagon, or a circle with the same script. Just set the variable to 4, 5, or 36 instead. Before you give it a try, make sure that you have the **number** variable created.

Script 8-5. *Draw an octagon*

Script 8-5 script starts when the user clicks the green flag. The second block clears the stage of any marks made by the pen or stamp. The third block sets the pen color, the fourth increase changes the pen size by 2, and the fifth puts the pen on the stage, ready to draw. The next block moves the sprite to the position (0, –100). Because the goal this time is to draw an octagon, which has 8 sides, the next block assigns the value

8 to the **number** variable. The variable block is embedded in the block, meaning the number of times the block repeats the sequenced of actions within it is equal to the value of **number**. In this case that's 8. The first block in the sequence moves the sprite 100 pixels in the direction that it's facing. The next block rotates the sprite a certain amount of degrees counterclockwise. Remember, the angles inside all polygons of four or more sides add up to 360 degrees, so an angle where two sides meet equals 360 divided by the number of sides. To calculate this information and pass it to the block, you need to type **360** in the left field of the operator block, embed in the right field, and then embed this combination in the block. The next block pauses the script for 1 second, and then the action loops back to draw the next side. When the final pass through the loop completes, the script executes the last block, which lifts the pen off the stage so that if the sprite moves, the pen will not draw.

Run the script to draw the octagon, and then try setting the **number** variable to 4 or 5 to draw a square or pentagon. For a real challenge, think about how you might adapt the script to automatically draw several shapes with different numbers of sides or draw a shape with the number of sides specified by user input.

Table 8-5 lists the blocks and describes the actions used in this example.

Table 8-5. *Code Blocks in Draw an Octagon*

Blocks	Actions
when [ ] clicked	Clicking the green flag activates the script. The green flag is the trigger to start the script running.
clear	Remove all marks previously made by the pen or stamp.
set pen color to ▓	Set the pen color to lime color.
change pen size by 2	Change the pen size to 2.
pen down	The pen is on the stage and is ready to draw.
go to x: 0 y: -100	Move the sprite to coordinates (X = 0, Y = –100).
set number ▾ to 8	Set the current value of the **number** variable to 8.
repeat ◯	Repeat the actions represented by the blocks within this block a certain number of times.
number	Hold and report the current value of the **number** variable.
move 100 steps	Move the sprite 100 pixels in the direction that it's facing.
turn ↺ ◯ degrees	Turn the sprite counterclockwise a certain number of degrees.
360 / ◯	Divide one value by another (360 / right field value) and report the result.
number	Hold and report the current value of the **number** variable.
wait 1 secs	The script waits 1 second. No actions are performed for 1 second.
pen up	The pen is off the stage and cannot draw.

Example 8-6: Multiplication

One variable and four 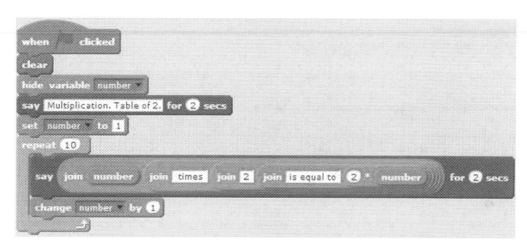 blocks make reciting a multiplication table easy. Before you create Script 8-6, however, make sure that the **number** variable is created.

Script 8-6. *Multiplication*

This script starts running when the user clicks the green flag. The second block clears the stage of any marks made by the pen or stamp. The next block hides the variable reporter window so it will not show up in the stage area. The next block creates a speech bubble that displays *Multiplication. Table of 2* for 2 seconds. The next block assigns the value 1 to the **number** variable. Next there is a repeat block that repeats the sequence of actions within it 10 times. The first block in the sequence creates a speech bubble that for 2 seconds displays the current value of the variable, the text *times 2 is equal to*, and the value of 2 times the current value of the variable. To create this block, start by embedding number into 2 * ⃝, and then embed the combination into join ▢▢, which in turn embeds in another join ▢▢ block with the text *is equal to*. Keep embedding the join ▢▢ blocks and adding text until you have the block shown in Script 8-6. The last block adds 1 to the current value of the **number** variable, and then the sequence loops back to the beginning and repeats. So, the first time through the loop, the script displays *1 times 2 is equal to 2*, and then the value of the variable increases by one and the script displays *2 times 1 is equal to 4*, and so on.

Table 8-6 lists the blocks and describes the actions used in this example.

Table 8-6. *Code Blocks in Multiplication*

Blocks	Actions
when ⚑ clicked	Clicking the green flag activates the script. The green flag is the trigger to start the script running.
clear	Remove all marks previously made by the pen or stamp.
hide variable number ▾	Hide the variable's (**number**) monitor on the stage.
say Multiplication. Table of 2. for 2 secs	The sprite gets a speech bubble that displays *Multiplication. Table of 2.* for 2 seconds.
set number ▾ to 1	Set the current value of the **number** variable to 1.
repeat 10	Repeat the actions represented by the blocks within this block 10 times.
say ▢ for 2 secs	The sprite gets a speech bubble that displays the specified text or value for 2 seconds.
join ▢▢	Join the two values that have been specified in the block and report the result.
number	Hold and report the current value of the **number** variable.
join times ▢	Join the two values that have been specified in the block and report the result.
join 2 ▢	Join the two values that have been specified in the block and report the result.
join is equal to ▢	Join the two values that have been specified in the block and report the result.
2 * ◯	Multiply two values and report the result.
number	Hold and report the current value of the **number** variable.
change number ▾ by 1	Add 1 to the current value of the **number** variable.

Example 8-7: Guess the Correct Number

The script in this example creates a guessing game. The user needs to guess a number between 1 and 10 that is randomly chosen by the script. Depending on the user input (**answer**), a different speech bubble displays. Before you build this script, make sure that a **number** variable is created.

Script 8-7 starts running when the user clicks the green flag. The next block creates a speech bubble and displays the text *Guess the number between 1 and 10*, opens a user input field, and waits for the user's input. The next block assigns a random number between 1 and 10 to the **number** variable. You create this block by embedding **pick random ① to ⑩** in the right field of **set number ▾ to**. Next, there is an If/Then/Else conditional statement block that evaluates whether the user input in **answer** is equal to the current value in **number**. If the condition is true, the block in the Then section creates a speech bubble that displays *Great. You guessed the right number!* for 2 seconds. If the condition is false, the two blocks in the Else section are executed. The first one creates a speech bubble that displays *Please try again.* for 2 seconds. The second block displays *The correct number was* and the current value of the variable for 2 seconds.

Script 8-7. *Guess correct number*

Table 8-7 lists the blocks and describes the actions used in this example.

Table 8-7. *Code Blocks in Guess the Correct Number*

Blocks	Actions
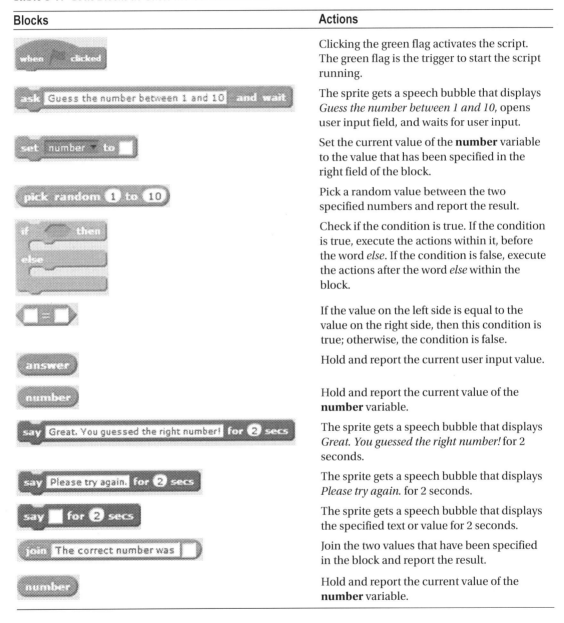	Clicking the green flag activates the script. The green flag is the trigger to start the script running.
	The sprite gets a speech bubble that displays *Guess the number between 1 and 10*, opens user input field, and waits for user input.
	Set the current value of the **number** variable to the value that has been specified in the right field of the block.
	Pick a random value between the two specified numbers and report the result.
	Check if the condition is true. If the condition is true, execute the actions within it, before the word *else*. If the condition is false, execute the actions after the word *else* within the block.
	If the value on the left side is equal to the value on the right side, then this condition is true; otherwise, the condition is false.
	Hold and report the current user input value.
	Hold and report the current value of the **number** variable.
	The sprite gets a speech bubble that displays *Great. You guessed the right number!* for 2 seconds.
	The sprite gets a speech bubble that displays *Please try again.* for 2 seconds.
	The sprite gets a speech bubble that displays the specified text or value for 2 seconds.
	Join the two values that have been specified in the block and report the result.
	Hold and report the current value of the **number** variable.

Example 8-8: Questions and Answers

This script asks the user four questions, assigns the answers to four separate variables, and then combines the variable of the values with text in 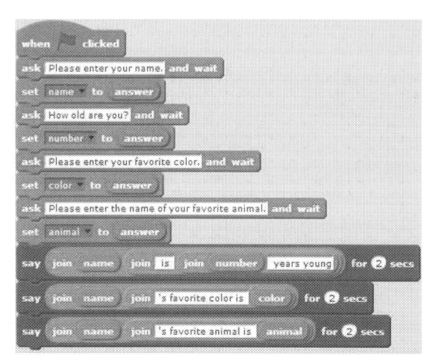 blocks to respond to the user. With this technique you can embed user input into dialog for your sprite. In addition to the **number** and **name** variables that you used in previous examples, create variables named **color** and **animal**.

Script 8-8 starts running when the user clicks the green flag. The next block creates a speech bubble that displays the text *Please enter your name,* opens a user input field, and waits for the user's input. The next block assigns the user input as a value to the **name** variable. The next block creates a speech bubble that displays *How old are you?,* opens a user input field, and waits for the user's answer. The next block assigns the user input as a value to the **number** variable. The next block creates a speech bubble that displays *Please enter your favorite color,* opens a user input field, and waits for the user's input. The next block assigns the user input as a value to the variable called **color**. The next block creates a speech bubble that displays *Please enter the name of your favorite animal*, opens a user input field, and waits for the user's answer. The next block assigns the user input as a value to the variable called **animal**. The next three instructions in the script each use blocks to combine variable values and text into blocks to create 2-second speech bubbles. The first displays the value for the **name** variable, the text *is,* the value of the **number** variable, and the text *years young*. The second displays the value for the **name** variable together with the text *'s favorite color is* and the value of the **color** variable. The third block's speech bubble displays the value for the **name** variable, the text *'s favorite animal is*, and the value of the **animal** variable.

Script 8-8. *Questions and answers*

Table 8-8 lists the blocks and describes the actions used in this example.

Table 8-8. *Code Blocks in Questions and Answers*

Blocks	Actions
when [green flag] clicked	Clicking the green flag activates the script. The green flag is the trigger to start the script running.
ask Please enter your name. and wait	The sprite gets a speech bubble that displays *Please enter your name.*, opens user input field, and waits for user input.
set name to [ ]	Set the current value of the **name** variable to the value that has been specified in the right field of the block.
answer	Hold and report the current user input value.
ask How old are you? and wait	The sprite gets a speech bubble that displays *How old are you?*, opens user input field, and waits for user input.
set number to [ ]	Set the current value of the **number** variable to the value that has been specified in the right field of the block.
answer	Hold and report the current user input value.
ask Please enter your favorite color. and wait	The sprite gets a speech bubble that displays *Please enter your favorite color.*, opens user input field, and waits for user input.
set color to [ ]	Set the current value of the variable called **color** to the value that has been specified in the right field of the block.
answer	Hold and report the current user input value.
ask Please enter the name of your favorite animal. and wait	The sprite gets a speech bubble that displays *Please enter the name of your favorite animal.*, opens user input field, and waits for user input.
set animal to [ ]	Set the current value of the variable called **animal** to the value that has been specified in the right field of the block.
answer	Hold and report the current user input value.
say [ ] for 2 secs	The sprite gets a speech bubble that displays the specified text or value for 2 seconds.

(*continued*)

Table 8-8. (*continued*)

Blocks	Actions
join ▢▢	Join the two values that have been specified in the block and report the result.
name	Hold and report the current value of the **name** variable.
join is ▢	Join the two values that have been specified in the block and report the result.
join ▢ years young	Join the two values that have been specified in the block and report the result.
number	Hold and report the current value of the **number** variable.
say ▢ for ② secs	The sprite gets a speech bubble that displays the specified text or value for 2 seconds.
join ▢▢	Join the two values that have been specified in the block and report the result.
name	Hold and report the current value of the **name** variable.
join 's favorite color is ▢	Join the two values that have been specified in the block and report the result.
color	Hold and report the current value of the **color** variable.
say ▢ for ② secs	The sprite gets a speech bubble that displays the specified text or value for 2 seconds.
join ▢▢	Join the two values that have been specified in the block and report the result.
name	Hold and report the current value of the **name** variable.
join 's favorite animal is ▢	Join the two values that have been specified in the block and report the result.
animal	Hold and report the current value of the **animal** variable.

Example 8-9: How Many Mouse Clicks?

This script keeps track of the number of times that you click the mouse button in 10 seconds. After 10 seconds, the script displays the total number of times that you clicked the mouse button. For Script 8-9, you need the **number** variable.

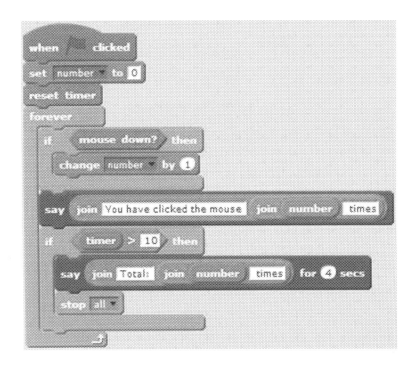

Script 8-9. *How many*

The script starts running when the user clicks the green flag. The next block assigns the value 0 to the **number** variable. The next block resets the timer to 0.0. The next block loops the sequence of actions within it forever, or until the script is manually stopped. The first block within the forever block is an If/Then conditional statement block that checks whether the primary mouse button is clicked. If it is, then the condition is true and the ![change number by 1] block adds 1 to the current value of the **number** variable. Next, the script goes to the ![say] block, which creates a speech bubble that displays *You have clicked the mouse*, the current value of the **number** variable, and *times*. The following block is a second If/Then conditional statement. This one checks whether the *timer* value is greater than 10. If it is, then the condition is true and the sequence of actions within the repeat block executes: the first block displays *Total:*, the value of the **number** variable, and the text *times* for 4 seconds. The second block stops all scripts in this project. If the timer is not greater than 10, the loop repeats again.

204

Table 8-9 lists the blocks and describes the actions used in this example.

Table 8-9. *Code Blocks in How Many Mouse Clicks?*

Blocks	Actions
when clicked	Clicking the green flag activates the script. The green flag is the trigger to start the script running.
set number to 0	Set the current value of the **number** variable to 0.
reset timer	Reset the timer value back to 0.0.
forever	Repeat all the instructions/blocks within this block forever.
if then	Check if the condition is true. If the condition is true, execute the actions within it. If the condition is false, skip to the next block.
mouse down?	Check if the primary mouse button is clicked. If the primary mouse button is clicked, then the condition is true. If not, then the condition is false.
change number by 1	Add 1 to the current value of the **number** variable.
say	The sprite gets a speech bubble that displays the specified text or value.
join You have clicked the mouse	Join the two values that have been specified in the block and report the result.
join times	Join the two values that have been specified in the block and report the result.
number	Hold and report the current value of the **number** variable.
if then	Check if the condition is true. If the condition is true, execute the actions within it. If the condition is false, skip to the next block.
> 10	If the value on the left side is greater than 10, then this condition is true; otherwise, the condition is false.
timer	Hold and report the timer value.
say for 4 secs	The sprite gets a speech bubble that displays the specified text or value for 4 seconds.
join Total:	Join the two values that have been specified in the block and report the result.

(*continued*)

Table 8-9. (*continued*)

Blocks	Actions
join ⬜ times	Join the two values that have been specified in the block and report the result.
number	Hold and report the current value of the **number** variable.
stop all ▼	Stop all scripts in this project.

Example 8-10: Password and Pin Code

Ever wonder what goes on behind the scenes when you log into a website? This example will give you a glimpse! Script 8-10 asks the user to enter a password and pin code, and then assigns the user responses to variables called password and pin. The user is asked to log in with his or her new password and pin, and then the script saves those responses in variables named **pass_login** and **pin_login**. Finally, the script compares the values held in the two pairs of variables to ensure that they match. Before you create the script, be sure to create the variables **password**, **pin**, **passw_login**, and **pin_login**.

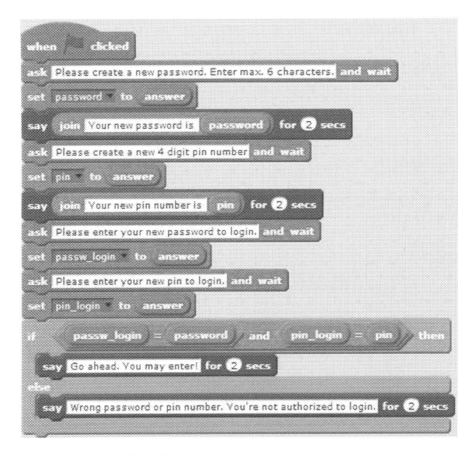

Script 8-10. *Password and pin*

The script starts running when the user clicks the green flag. The next block creates a speech bubble that displays *Please create a new password. Enter max. 6 characters*, opens a user input field, and waits for the user's input. The next block assigns the user input to the **password** variable. The next block creates a speech bubble that displays *Your new password is* and the value of the **password** variable for 2 seconds. The next block creates a speech bubble that displays *Please create a new 4 digit pin number*, opens a user input field, and waits for the user's input. The next block assigns the user input to the **pin** variable. The next block creates a speech bubble that displays *Your new pin number is* and the value of the **pin** variable for 2 seconds. The next block creates a speech bubble that displays *Please enter your new password to log in,* opens a user input field, and waits for the user's input. The next block assigns the user input to the **passw_login** variable. The next block creates a speech bubble that displays *Please enter your new pin to log in,* opens a user input field, and waits for the user's input. The next block assigns the user input to the **pin_login**. The next block is an If/Then/Else conditional statement that evaluates whether the variable **passw_login** variable is equal to the **password** variable and that the **pin_login** variable is equal to the **pin** variable. If both are true, then the Then section is executed: the script creates a speech bubble that displays *Go ahead. You may enter!* for 2 seconds. If the condition is false, meaning one or both pairs of variables don't match, then the Else section is executed: the script creates a speech bubble that displays *Wrong password or pin number. You're not authorized to log in.* for 2 seconds.

Table 8-10 lists the blocks and describes the actions used in this example.

Table 8-10. *Code Blocks in Password and Pin Code*

Blocks	Actions
when clicked	Clicking the green flag activates the script. The green flag is the trigger to start the script running.
ask Please create a new password. Enter max. 6 characters. and wait	The sprite gets a speech bubble that displays *Please create a new password. Enter max. 6 characters.*, opens user input field, and waits for user input.
set password ▾ to	Set the current value of the variable called **password** to the value that has been specified in the right field of the block.
answer	Hold and report the current user input value.
say ▮ for ② secs	The sprite gets a speech bubble that displays the specified text or value for 2 seconds.

(continued)

207

Table 8-10. (*continued*)

Blocks	Actions
join Your new password is ▢	Join the two values that have been specified in the block and report the result.
password	Hold and report the current value of the **password** variable.
ask Please create a new 4 digit pin number and wait	The sprite gets a speech bubble that displays *Please create a new 4 digit pin number*, opens user input field, and waits for user input.
set pin ▾ to ▢	Set the current value of the variable called **pin** to the value that has been specified in the right field of the block.
answer	Hold and report the current user input value.
say ▢ for 2 secs	The sprite gets a speech bubble that displays the specified text or value for 2 seconds.
join Your new pin number is ▢	Join the two values that have been specified in the block and report the result.
pin	Hold and report the current value of the **pin** variable.
ask Please enter your new password to login. and wait	The sprite gets a speech bubble that displays *Please create a new password to log in.*, opens user input field, and waits for user input.
set passw_login ▾ to ▢	Set the current value of the variable called **passw_login** to the value that has been specified in the right field of the block.
answer	Hold and report the current user input value.

(*continued*)

Table 8-10. (*continued*)

Blocks	Actions
ask Please enter your new pin to login. and wait	The sprite gets a speech bubble that displays *Please create a new pin to log in.*, opens user input field, and waits for user input.
set pin_login to	Set the current value of the variable called **pin_login** to the value that has been specified in the right field of the block.
answer	Hold and report the current user input value.
if then else	Check if the condition is true. If the condition is true, execute the actions within it, before the word *else*. If the condition is false, execute the actions after the word *else* within the block.
and	Check both conditions on each side of this block. If both conditions are true, then this condition is true. Any other combination results in this condition being false.
=	If the value on the left side is equal to the value on the right side, then this condition is true; otherwise, the condition is false.
passw_login	Hold and report the current value of the **passw_login** variable.
password	Hold and report the current value of the **password** variable.

Table 8-10. (*continued*)

Blocks	Actions
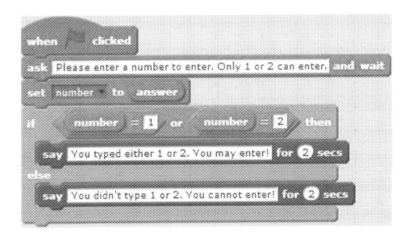	If the value on the left side is equal to the value on the right side, then this condition is true; otherwise, the condition is false.
	Hold and report the current value of the **pin_login** variable.
	Hold and report the current value of the **pin** variable.
	The sprite gets a speech bubble that displays *Go ahead. You may enter!* for 2 seconds.
	The sprite gets a speech bubble that displays *Wrong password or pin number. You're not authorized to log in.* for 2 seconds.

Example 8-11: Only One Correct Answer Required

Script 8-11 follows a pattern that should be familiar by now. Can you figure out what this script does before you create and run it? (Before creating Script 8-11, make sure that the **number** variable is created.)

Script 8-11. *Only one*

The script starts running when the user clicks the green flag. The next block creates a speech bubble that displays *Please enter a number to enter. Only 1 or 2 can enter,* opens a user input field, and waits for the user's input. The next block assigns the user input to the **number** variable. Next, the If/Then/Else conditional statement evaluates whether the **number** variable is equal to 1 or 2. If the variable holds either value, then result is true and the script executes the Then section. It creates a speech bubble that displays *You typed either 1 or 2. You may enter!* for 2 seconds. If the condition is false, the Else section is executed, meaning a speech bubble gets created with the following text for 2 seconds: *You didn't type 1 or 2. You cannot enter!.*

Note that for this condition, just one side of the word *or* needs to be true for the condition to be true. If both sides are false, then the condition is false.

Table 8-11 lists the blocks and describes the actions used in this example.

Table 8-11. *Code Blocks in Only One Correct Answer Required*

Blocks	Actions
when clicked	Clicking the green flag activates the script. The green flag is the trigger to start the script running.
ask Please enter a number to enter. Only 1 or 2 can enter. and wait	The sprite gets a speech bubble that displays *Please enter a number to enter. Only 1 or 2 can enter.*, opens user input field, and waits for user input.
set number ▾ to	Set the current value of the **number** variable to the value that has been specified in the right field of the block.
answer	Hold and report the current user input value.
if then else	Check if the condition is true. If the condition is true, execute the actions within it, before the word *else*. If the condition is false, execute the actions after the word *else* within the block.
or	Check both conditions on each side of the block. If both conditions are true, then this condition is true. Any other combination results in this condition being false.

(*continued*)

Table 8-11. (*continued*)

Blocks	Actions
`◁ ⬜ = 1 ▷`	If the value on the left side is equal to 1, then this condition is true; otherwise, the condition is false.
`number`	Hold and report the current value of the **number** variable.
`◁ ⬜ = 2 ▷`	If the value on the left side is equal to 2, then this condition is true; otherwise, the condition is false.
`number`	Hold and report the current value of the **number** variable.
`say You typed either 1 or 2. You may enter! for 2 secs`	The sprite gets a speech bubble that displays *You typed either 1 or 2. You may enter!*, for 2 seconds.
`say You didn't type 1 or 2. You cannot enter! for 2 secs`	The sprite gets a speech bubble that displays *You didn't type 1 or 2. You cannot enter!*, for 2 seconds.

Example 8-12: Pong Game

In this example, you'll create a version of the Pong game (see Figure 8-6). The game's object is to hit the ball sprite with the paddle sprite (the black bar) as many times as possible during the 20-second time limit and to prevent the ball from hitting the red line at the bottom of the stage area (see Figure 8-7). The user controls the black bar but can move it from left to right only. The ball can bounce against any of the stage area edges. Each time the ball is hit with the black bar you score 1 point. The game stops after the time limit is reached or if the ball hits the red line at the bottom of the stage area. The goal of the game is to score as many points as possible within the time limit of 20 seconds.

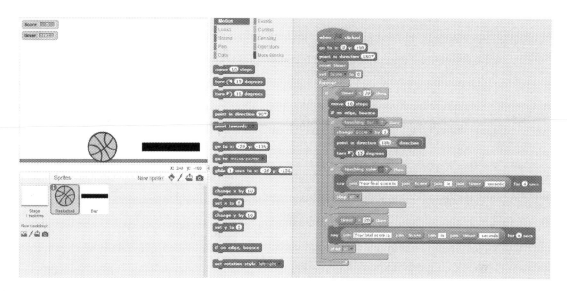

Figure 8-6. *Pong game*

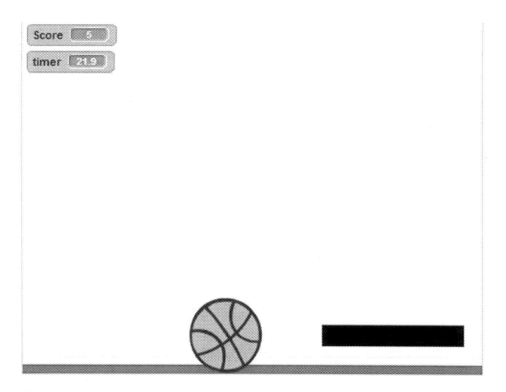

Figure 8-7. *Pong stage*

For this script, you need to select a sprite from the Sprite Library to act as the ball. The sprite called **Basketball** works well (see Figure 8-8).

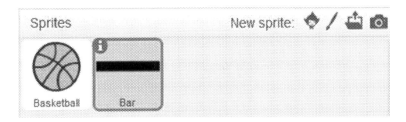

Figure 8-8. Pong sprites

You also need to draw a new sprite to be the paddle that hits the ball. Use Figure 8-9 as an example and call it **Bar**. You also need to create a backdrop with a red rectangle at the bottom of the stage area, as shown in Figure 8-10. (Refer to Chapter 2 if you need a reminder of how to draw a new sprite or backdrop.) Finally, before creating this script, you also need to create a variable called **Score**.

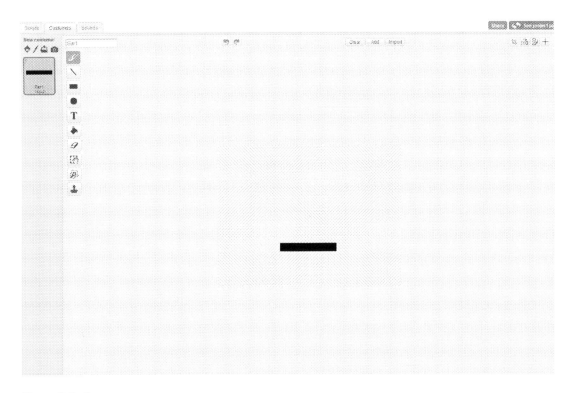

Figure 8-9. Bar

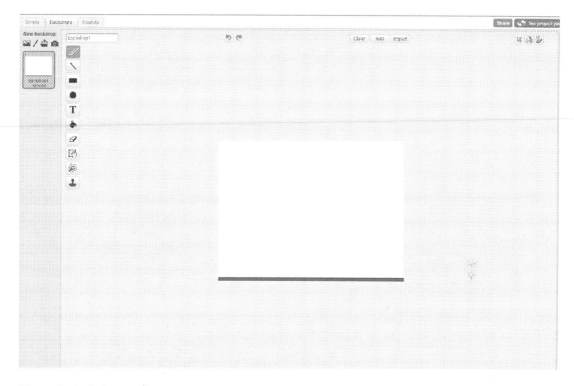

Figure 8-10. *Red rectangle*

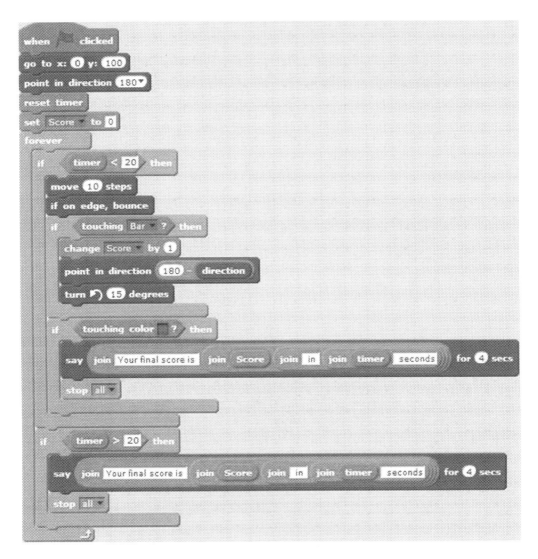

Script 8-12. *Pong game ball script*

Once all your elements are ready, you can start creating the script.

Select the ball in the Sprites pane, because Script 8-11 is assigned to the ball sprite. The script starts running when the user clicks the green flag. The next block moves the sprite to the position (0, 100). The next block makes the sprite face down. The next block resets the timer to 0.0. The next block assigns the value 0 to the **Score** variable. The rest of the script resides in a forever block loop that repeats the sequence of actions within it forever, or until the script is stopped manually. The first block inside is an 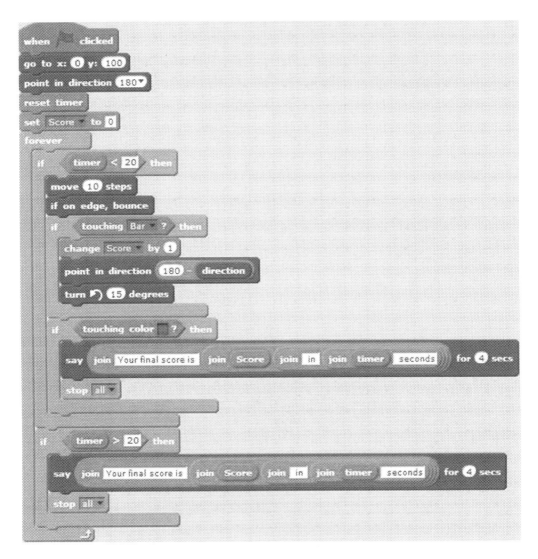 block that checks whether the timer value is less than 20. If this condition is true, then it will execute the sequence of actions within it. The first block within it moves the sprite 10 pixels in the direction that it's facing. The next block bounces the sprite when if it hits any stage edge and makes it travel in the opposite direction. Next

is another [if then] block checks whether the **Basketball** sprite is touching the sprite called **Bar**. If this condition is true, then the value 1 is added to the current value of the **Score** variable. The next block makes the **Basketball** sprite face in a direction that is calculated by subtracting the direction that the sprite is facing from 180. The next block rotates the **Basketball** sprite 15 degrees counterclockwise. Next is a third If/Then C block that checks whether the **Basketball** sprite is touching the color red in the stage area. The only red object in the stage area is the red rectangle at the bottom of the backdrop. If this condition is true, then a speech bubble gets created and displayed for 4 seconds. The text *Your final score is*, the value of the **Score** variable, the text *in*, the value of the timer, and the text *seconds* are displayed in the speech bubble.

The last block in the third [if then] stops all the scripts in this project. The fourth If/Then block checks whether the timer value is greater than 20. If this condition is true then a speech bubble gets created and displayed for 4 seconds. The text *Your final score is*, the value of the **Score** variable, the text *in*, the value of the timer, and the text *seconds* are displayed. The last block stops all the scripts in this project.

Table 8-12 lists the blocks and describes the actions used in this example.

Table 8-12. *Code Blocks in Pong Game Ball*

Blocks	Actions
when clicked	Clicking the green flag activates the script. The green flag is the trigger to start the script running.
go to x: 0 y: 100	Move the sprite to coordinates (X = 0, Y = 100).
point in direction 180	Make the sprite face down.
reset timer	Reset the timer value back to 0.0.
set Score to 0	Set the current value of the variable called **Score** to 0.
forever	Repeat all the instructions/blocks within this block forever.
if then	Check if the condition is true. If the condition is true, execute the actions within it. If the condition is false, skip to the next block.
< 20	If the value on the left side is less than 20, then this condition is true; otherwise, the condition is false.
timer	Hold and report the timer value.

(continued)

217

Table 8-12. (*continued*)

Blocks	Actions
move 10 steps	Move the sprite 10 pixels in the direction that it's facing.
if on edge, bounce	If the sprite reaches the edge of the stage, bounce in the opposite direction.
if ... then	Check if the condition is true. If the condition is true, execute the actions within it. If the condition is false, skip to the next block.
touching Bar ?	Checks if the sprite is touching the sprite called **Bar**. If it is, then this condition is set to true.
change Score by 1	Add 1 to the current value of the **Score** variable.
point in direction	Make the sprite face in the specified direction.
180 - 10	Subtract one value from another (180 – 10) and report the result.
direction	Hold and report the direction value.
turn 15 degrees	Turn the sprite counterclockwise 15 degrees.
if ... then	Check if the condition is true. If the condition is true, execute the actions within it. If the condition is false, skip to the next block.
touching color ?	Checks if the sprite is touching the color red. If it is, then this condition is set to true.
say for 4 secs	The sprite gets a speech bubble that displays the specified text for 4 seconds.
join Your final score is	Join the two values that have been specified in the block and report the result.
join	Join the two values that have been specified in the block and report the result.
Score	Hold and report the current value of the **Score** variable.
join in	Join the two values that have been specified in the block and report the result.
join seconds	Join the two values that have been specified in the block and report the result.
timer	Hold and report the timer value.
stop all	Stop all scripts in this project.

(*continued*)

Table 8-12. (*continued*)

Blocks	Actions
if then	Check if the condition is true. If the condition is true, execute the actions within it. If the condition is false, skip to the next block.
> 20	If the value on the left side is greater than 20, then this condition is true; otherwise, the condition is false.
timer	Hold and report the timer value.
say for 4 secs	The sprite gets a speech bubble that displays the specified text for 4 seconds.
join Your final score is	Join the two values that have been specified in the block and report the result.
join	Join the two values that have been specified in the block and report the result.
Score	Hold and report the current value of the **Score** variable.
join in	Join the two values that have been specified in the block and report the result.
join seconds	Join the two values that have been specified in the block and report the result.
timer	Hold and report the timer value.
stop all	Stop all scripts in this project.

With the ball under control, you're ready to create the three scripts needed to make the **Bar** sprite move (see Figure 8-11). Select the **Bar** sprite to make it the current sprite, and then drag and snap together the following scripts.

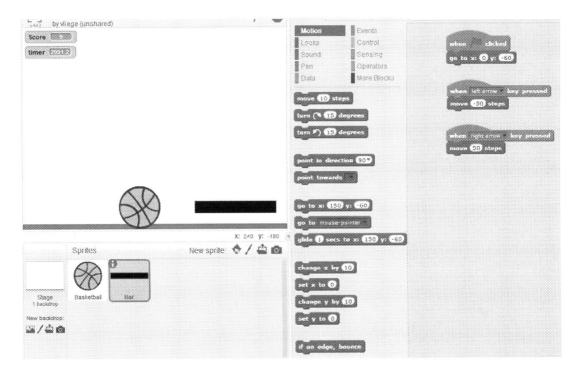

Figure 8-11. *Bar Control*

Script 8-13 moves the bar to a starting position at the beginning of the game. The script starts running when the green flag is clicked. The next block of code moves the **Bar** sprite to the position with coordinates (0, –60).

Script 8-13. *Bar starting position*

220

Table 8-13 lists the blocks and describes the actions used in this example.

Table 8-13. *Code Blocks in Bar Starting Position*

Blocks	Actions
	Clicking the green flag activates the script. The green flag is the trigger to start the script running.
go to x: 0 y: -60	Move the sprite to coordinates (X = 0, Y = –60).

Script 8-14 moves the bar to the left whenever the left arrow key is pressed.

Script 8-14. *Move bar left*

Create Script 8-14 in the same script area as the Script 8-13 but beneath the previous script. This script starts when the left arrow key is pressed. The next block of code moves the **Bar** sprite 50 pixels to the left.

Table 8-14 lists the blocks and describes the actions used in this example.

Table 8-14. *Code Blocks in Move the Bar Sprite Left*

Blocks	Actions
when left arrow key pressed	Pressing the left arrow key activates the script. The left arrow key is the trigger to start the script running.
move -50 steps	Move the sprite 50 pixels in the opposite direction that it's facing.

Script 8-15 moves the bar to the right whenever the right arrow key is pressed.

when right arrow key pressed
move 50 steps

Script 8-15. *Move bar to the right*

Once again, create this script in the same script area but beneath the previous two. Script 8-15 starts when the right arrow key is pressed. The next block of code moves the **Bar** sprite 50 pixels to the right.

Table 8-15 lists the blocks and describes the actions used in this example.

Table 8-15. *Code Blocks in Move the Bar Sprite to the Right*

Blocks	Actions
when right arrow key pressed	Pressing the right arrow key activates the script. The right arrow key is the trigger to start the script running.
move 50 steps	Move the sprite 50 pixels in the direction that it's facing.

Don't be concerned by the multiple scripts in this project. The whole project or game starts running when the green flag is clicked. That is the trigger to start the game. You control the bar with the left and right arrow keys.

Summary

Variables are a very important topic when it comes to computer programming. All computer programming languages use variables, including Scratch. Variables make your programs and Scratch projects more flexible and dynamic. The key to remember is that a variable holds a value, but this value can change while the program runs.

In the next chapter, you'll investigate another important topic called a list. A *list* is similar to a variable. The difference is that a list holds multiple values at one time and a variable holds only one value at a time.

Remember to do the exercises at the end of each chapter. This way you'll put what you learned into practice, and as you probably know, "practice makes perfect."

Exercises

1. Create a script that asks the user to enter a magic word. If the user enters the correct magic word, the script displays a speech bubble with the text *You may enter*. If the user enters the wrong word, the script displays *Please try again.* You need to create a variable for this script.

2. Create a script that makes the sprite count from 1 to 3. At the end the script, create a speech bubble with the text *Ready, steady, go!*.

CHAPTER 9

Lists

Variables give you more flexibility in your scripts, as you learned in Chapter 8, but are limited to storing a single value at any one time. What if you need to store multiple, related values, such as a wish list or a grocery list? You could use several separate variables, but you'd have to create them all ahead of time, which takes time and guess work. Scratch offers another, easier solution: you can create a *list*.

Just like the kind you write on paper, a list in Scratch can store multiple values in one place. Like variables, a list can contain either strings of characters (letters, numbers, or symbols) or numeric values. Each value in a list also has a position, referred to as its *index number*. For example, a list called *grocery* could include the following:

- Bread

- Water

- Peanuts

The *Bread* value is at the first position in the list with index number 1, the *Water* value is at the second position (index number 2), and the *Peanuts* value is at the third and last position (index number 3) in the list. In Scratch, you can modify a list by applying several different actions to it, such as adding, removing, or replacing values. In this chapter, you'll learn all about putting lists to work. I'll start first by showing you how to create lists and discussing the various blocks that control lists. Finally, you can practice with some example scripts where lists are put into action.

Creating and Working with Lists

This section will teach you how to create and control lists. To create a new list in Scratch, the first step is to go to the block palette and select the **Data** category (see Figure 9-1).

© Eduardo A. Vlieg 2016

E. A. Vlieg, *Scratch by Example*, DOI 10.1007/978-1-4842-1946-1_9

Figure 9-1. *Go to the Data category to create a list*

Once there, click the **Make a List** button (see Figure 9-2) to open the **New List** window (see Figure 9-3) .

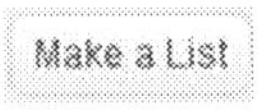

Figure 9-2. *Make list*

Figure 9-3. *The New List window*

In the New List window, you enter a name for the list and choose if you want the list to be available for the currently selected sprite only or for all sprites. Just like for variables, you create a list per project; so if you select **For all sprites**, this means that the list is available for all the sprites in one specific project. If you want to use a list in another project, you'll need to recreate it. Click the **OK** button to create the list. After you do, Scratch automatically creates a number of other blocks of code, which appear in the Data category (see

Figure 9-4), such as the ⬤List⬤ list reporter block that holds and reports the current values of the list. In this example, the name of the list is **List**. There is no limit to the length of an item in a list. There's also no limit to the number of items that a list can hold.

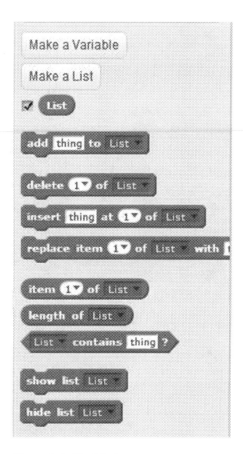

Figure 9-4. *List blocks*

Four blocks in the Data category enable you to control and change the contents of your lists. In each block, you can choose which list to work with using a pull-down menu. The [add thing to List ▼] block adds the value you specific to the end of the list. In this example, the text, *thing*, is added to the end of the list called **List**. The [delete 1▼ of List ▼] block removes the values from specified index numbers in a list. Using the left pull-down menu, you can select the first value in the list, last value in the list, or all the values in the list, or you can type the index number you want to remove. In this example, the value at index number 1 is removed from **List**. Removing items from a list rearranges the list; for example, if a list has four items and you remove the second item, the third item will move up to take the second position (index number 2), and the fourth will move into the third position (index number 3). The [insert thing at 1▼ of List ▼] block inserts a value in a list at the specified position in the list. You can use the left pull-down menu to select the last index number or a random position. You can also type the index number for the position in the list you want to insert the value. In this example, *thing* is inserted at the first position in **List**. If a value was already stored in position 1, it gets moved to position 2, the value originally at position 2 moves to position 3, and so on. The `replace item 1▾ of List▾ with thing` block replaces the value at a specified position in a list with another value you provide. Not only can you use the pull-down menu to select the last or random position, but you can also type the desired position. In this example, the value at position 1 in **List** is replaced by the *thing* value. If position 1 is currently empty, the new value is simply inserted.

The remainder of the **Data** category's blocks provide information about your lists. Again, you can choose which list to monitor using a pull-down menu. The `item 1▾ of List▾` block holds and reports the value at a specified position in a list. In this example, the block reports the value at position 1 in **List**. The `length of List▾` block holds and reports the length of the specified list. The length of a list is the number of values it contains, meaning the length is equal to the highest index number. In this example, the length of the list called **List** is reported. The `List▾ contains thing ?` block searches the specified list for a value you supply. If the value is in the list, the block returns a result of true, otherwise it will return false. In this example, it searches **List** for the *thing* value. Finally, the `show list List▾` and `hide list List▾` blocks show and hide the specified list's monitor in the stage area, respectively. The list's monitor shows all the values in the list, their positions in the list, and the length of the list.

Examples

Now that you know how to create and control lists, you are ready to put what you learned into practice. In this section, you'll be creating and running some scripts that use lists.

Example 9-1: Grocery Shopping List

This script lets the user create a grocery shopping list. The user enters five items, which are added to the list. At the end, the complete list is displayed. Before you create Script 9-1, click the **Make a List** button in the block palette's Data category to create a list called **List**. It doesn't matter if you select **For this sprite only** or **For all sprites**.

Script 9-1. *Grocery shopping list*

Script 9-1 starts running when the user presses the space bar. The second block of code deletes all values in **List**—that is if there were any values in the list. When running a script, if you want to start with an empty list, it's always a good practice to use this block. The next block of code shows the list's monitor in the stage area. The next block of code creates a speech bubble for the sprite that displays the text *I need to create*

a list to go grocery shopping for 2 seconds. Next, a block repeats the sequence actions within it 5 times. The first block within the sequence creates a speech bubble that displays *Please add an item to the grocery list*, opens a user input field, and waits for the user's input (see Figure 9-5). Because the

block is embedded in the block, the script next adds the user input to the end of the list. After five passes through the loop, the script then creates a speech bubble for 2 seconds and

displays *Thank you. The list is ready.* With the help of a block, the last block creates a speech

that displays the text *The list includes the following:* followed by the values held in for 4 seconds.

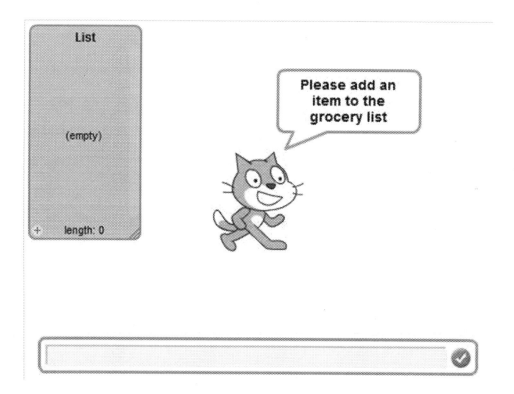

Figure 9-5. *Grocery list creation*

Table 9-1 lists the blocks and describes the actions used in this example.

Table 9-1. *Code Blocks in Grocery Shopping List*

Blocks	Actions
when space ▾ key pressed	Clicking the space bar activates the script. The space bar is the trigger to start the script running.
delete all▾ of List ▾	Delete all values from the list called **List**.
show list List ▾	Show the monitor in the stage area for **List**.
say I need to create a list to go grocery shopping for 2 secs	The sprite gets a speech bubble that displays *I need to create a list to go grocery shopping* for 2 seconds.
repeat 5	Repeat the actions represented by the blocks within this block five times.
ask Please add an item to the grocery list and wait	The sprite gets a speech bubble that displays *Please add an item to the grocery list*, opens a user input field, and waits for user input.
add ▢ to List ▾	Add the specified value to the end of **List**.
answer	Hold and report the current user input value.
say Thank you. The list is ready. for 2 secs	The sprite gets a speech bubble that displays *Thank you. The list is ready.* for 2 seconds.
say ▢ for 4 secs	The sprite gets a speech bubble that displays the specified text or value for 4 seconds.
join The list includes the following: ▢	Join the two values that have been specified in the block and report the result.
List	Hold and report the current values in **List**.

Example 9-2: Add One More Item

This example builds on the last script by first displaying the length of the grocery list called **List**, and then requesting the user to enter another item. The script adds the new item to the end of the list, and then displays the new length of the list. Before creating this script, make sure that **List** is created.

Script 9-2. *Add one more*

Script 9-2 starts running when the user clicks the green flag. The second block is composed of two

blocks and the block embedded within a block.
The result is it creates a speech bubble for the sprite that lasts 2 seconds and displays *The list consists of*, the
length of **List**, and the text *items*. The next block creates a speech bubble that displays the text *Please add one
more item*, opens a user input field, and waits for the user's input. The next block adds the user input to the
end of **List**. The last block creates a speech bubble that lasts 2 seconds and displays *The list consists now of*,
the length of the list, and the text *items*.

Table 9-2 lists the blocks and describes the actions used in this example.

Table 9-2. *Code Blocks in Add One More Item*

Blocks	Actions
	Clicking the green flag activates the script. The green flag is the trigger to start the script running.
	The sprite gets a speech bubble that displays the specified text or value for 2 seconds.
	Join the two values that have been specified in the block and report the result.
	Join the two values that have been specified in the block and report the result.
	Hold and report the length of the specified list.
	The sprite gets a speech bubble that displays *Please add one more item*, opens a user input field, and waits for user input.
	Add the specified value to the end of **List**.
	Hold and report the current user input value.

(continued)

Table 9-2. (*continued*)

Blocks	Actions
say ☐ for ② secs	The sprite gets a speech bubble that displays the specified text or value for 2 seconds.
join The list consists now of ☐	Join the two values that have been specified in the block and report the result.
join ☐ items.	Join the two values that have been specified in the block and report the result.
length of List ▾	Hold and report the length of the specified list.

Example 9-3: Search List

Sometimes you'll need to determine whether your list contains a specific value, and then take different actions depending on the result. This example, for instance, searches the grocery list for the value *ice cream*. If the value is not on the list, it is then added to the list. Before creating Script 9-3, make sure that the list called **List** is created.

Script 9-3. *Search list*

The script starts running when the user clicks the green flag. The second block creates a speech bubble that displays *Please check if ice cream is on the list.* for 2 seconds. The next block also creates a speech bubble that displays *If ice cream is not on the list, please add it to the list.* for 2 seconds. An If/Then conditional statement then checks whether **List** does not contain a value called *ice cream*, as instructed by the embedded and blocks. If the list does not contain a value called *ice cream* then the condition is true, and the script executes the sequence of actions within the C block. The first block in the sequence creates a speech bubble that displays the text *Ice cream is not on the list. Adding ice cream to the list.* for 2 seconds. The next adds the item *ice cream* to the end of the list. The last block creates a speech bubble that displays the text *The list includes the following:* followed by the contents of **List** for 4 seconds.

Table 9-3 lists the blocks and describes the actions used in this example.

Table 9-3. *Code Blocks in Search List*

Blocks	Actions
when clicked	Clicking the green flag activates the script. The green flag is the trigger to start the script running.
say Please check if ice cream is on the list. for 2 secs	The sprite gets a speech bubble that displays *Please check if ice cream is on the list.* for 2 seconds.
say If ice cream is not on the list, please add it to the list. for 2 secs	The sprite gets a speech bubble that displays *If ice cream is not on the list, please add it to the list.* for 2 seconds.
if then	Check if the condition is true. If the condition is true, execute the actions within it. If the condition is false, skip to the next block.
not	Check the condition within this block. If the condition within the block is true, return false; otherwise, return true.
List contains ice cream ?	Search in the specified list, **List**, for the specified value, *ice cream.* If the specified value is in the list, the condition is true; otherwise, it's false.
say Ice cream is not on the list. Adding ice cream to the list. for 2 secs	The sprite gets a speech bubble that displays *Ice cream is not on the list. Adding ice cream to the list.* for 2 seconds.
add ice cream to List	Add the *ice cream* value to the end of **List**.
say for 4 secs	The sprite gets a speech bubble that displays the specified text or value for 4 seconds.
join The list includes the following:	Join the two values that have been specified in the block and report the result.
List	Hold and report the current values in **List**.

Example 9-4: Replace an Item

This example demonstrates replacing the last value of a list. Specifically, Script 9-4 replaces the last item of **List** with the value *Broccoli*. (Make sure that the list is created.)

Script 9-4. *Replace an item*

Script 9-4 starts running when the user presses the A key on the keyboard. The next two blocks create each speech bubbles that display the text for 4 seconds, saying *I don't need ice cream anymore. It's too fattening. I have to stay in shape. I will replace it with broccoli in the list.* The next block replaces the last value in **List** with the *Broccoli* value. Next an If/Then conditional statement block that evaluates whether the list contains the value *Broccoli*. If it does, then the condition is true and the script creates a speech bubble that displays *Broccoli has now been added to the list* for 2 seconds.

Table 9-4 lists the blocks and describes the actions used in this example.

Table 9-4. *Code Blocks in Replace an Item*

Blocks	Actions
	Pressing the A key activates the script. The A key is the trigger to start the script running.
	The sprite gets a speech bubble that displays *I don't need ice cream anymore. It's too fattening.* for 4 seconds.
	The sprite gets a speech bubble that displays *I have to stay in shape. I will replace it with broccoli in the list.* for 4 seconds.

(continued)

Table 9-4. (*continued*)

Blocks	Actions
replace item (last▾) of List ▾ with Broccoli	Replace the last value of **List** with the specified value, *Broccoli*.
if ⬡ then	Check if the condition is true. If the condition is true, execute the actions within it. If the condition is false, skip to the next block.
List ▾ contains Broccoli ?	Search in the specified list, **List**, for the specified value, *Broccoli*. If the specified value is in the list, the condition is true; otherwise, it's false.
say Broccoli has now been added to the list for ② secs	The sprite gets a speech bubble that displays *Broccoli has now been added to the list* for 2 seconds.

Example 9-5: Remove Items

Deleting individual items from a list is simple, as you'll see in Script 9-5. You'll continue to use the grocery list called **List** and remove values at some specific positions in the list.

Script 9-5. *Remove items*

Script 9-5 starts running when the user clicks the green flag. The next block creates a speech bubble that displays *Please remove items 1 and 4 from the list* for 2 seconds. The [delete 1 of List] block removes the value at the first position of **List**, so now the list gets rearranged and all the remaining items get moved one position up the list. The list now consists of 4 items and [delete 4 of List] removes the value at index number 4. The last block creates a speech bubble that displays *The list includes the following:* followed by the contents of **List** for 4 seconds.

Table 9-5 lists the blocks and describes the actions used in this example.

Table 9-5. *Code Blocks in Remove Items*

Blocks	Actions
when [flag] clicked	Clicking the green flag activates the script. The green flag is the trigger to start the script running.
say Please remove items 1 and 4 from the list for 2 secs	The sprite gets a speech bubble that displays *Please remove items 1 and 4 from the list* for 2 seconds.
delete 1 of List	Delete the value at the first position from **List**.
delete 4 of List	Delete the value at the fourth position from **List**.
say [ ] for 4 secs	The sprite gets a speech bubble that displays the specified text or value for 4 seconds.
join The list includes the following: [ ]	Join the two values that have been specified in the block and report the result.
List	Hold and report the current values in **List**.

Example 9-6: Add Items at Specific Positions

Just as you can remove items from specific positions, you can add them too. This script asks for the user's input, and then inserts it at the first and third positions (index numbers 1 and 3) of the list called **List**.

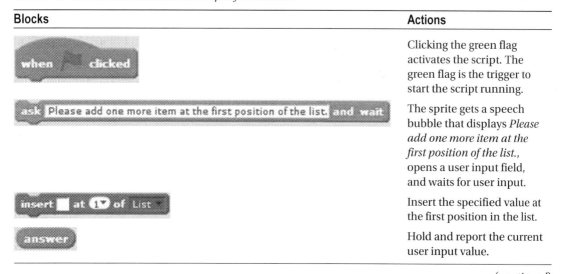

Script 9-6. *Add items*

Script 9-6 starts running when the user clicks the green flag. The next block creates a speech bubble that displays the text *Please add one more item at the first position of the list*, opens a user input field, and waits for the user's input. The next block embeds ⟨answer⟩ in the ⟨insert ⬛ at ① of List⟩ block to insert the user input at the first position of the list. The next block creates a speech bubble that displays the text *Please add one more item at the third position of the list*, opens a user input field, and waits for the user's input. The next block inserts the user input at the third position of the list. The next block creates a speech bubble for the sprite that displays the text *The list consists now of*, the length of the list, and the text *items.* for 4 seconds. The last block creates a speech bubble that displays *The list includes the following:* followed by the contents of the list for 4 seconds.

Table 9-6 lists the blocks and describes the actions used in this example.

Table 9-6. *Code Blocks in Add Items at Specific Positions*

Blocks	Actions
⟨when ▶ clicked⟩	Clicking the green flag activates the script. The green flag is the trigger to start the script running.
⟨ask Please add one more item at the first position of the list. and wait⟩	The sprite gets a speech bubble that displays *Please add one more item at the first position of the list.*, opens a user input field, and waits for user input.
⟨insert ⬛ at ① of List⟩	Insert the specified value at the first position in the list.
⟨answer⟩	Hold and report the current user input value.

(continued)

Table 9-6. (*continued*)

Blocks	Actions
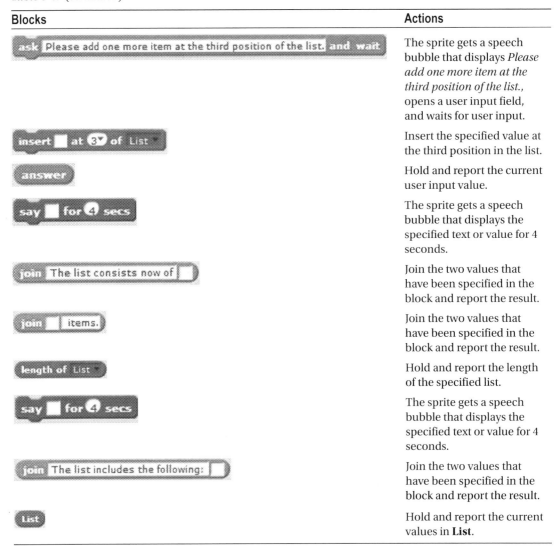	The sprite gets a speech bubble that displays *Please add one more item at the third position of the list.*, opens a user input field, and waits for user input.
	Insert the specified value at the third position in the list.
	Hold and report the current user input value.
	The sprite gets a speech bubble that displays the specified text or value for 4 seconds.
	Join the two values that have been specified in the block and report the result.
	Join the two values that have been specified in the block and report the result.
	Hold and report the length of the specified list.
	The sprite gets a speech bubble that displays the specified text or value for 4 seconds.
	Join the two values that have been specified in the block and report the result.
	Hold and report the current values in **List**.

Example 9-7: Read the List Back to Me

This example shows you how to sequentially display each item in a list along with its index number (position) Once again, it uses the **List** grocery list. In addition, you'll need to create a variable called **number**.

Script 9-7. *Read the list*

Script 9-7 starts running when the user clicks the green flag. The next block hides the list's monitor from the stage area. The next block of code hides the monitor for the **number** variable from the stage area. The next block creates a speech bubble that displays *The list consists now of,* the length of the list, and the text *items.* for 4 seconds. The next block assigns the value 1 to the variable called **number**. Next, by embedding

in a block, you can instruct the C block to repeat the sequence of actions within for all the index numbers in the list. First, it creates a speech bubble that displays the text *Item,* the value of the **number** variable, the text *is,* and the item in the list at the same position as the value of the **number** variable. So, for example, if the current value of the **number** variable is *2,* then the block returns the item in the list at position 2. The next block in the sequence adds 1 to the current value of the **number** variable. After the loop completes all its passes, the next block creates a speech bubble that displays *Ready to go grocery shopping.* for 2 seconds. The last block shows the list's monitor in the stage area.

Table 9-7 lists the blocks and describes the actions used in this example.

Table 9-7. *Code Blocks in Read the List Back to Me*

Blocks	Actions
when clicked	Clicking the green flag activates the script. The green flag is the trigger to start the script running.
hide list List	Hide the specified list's (**List**) monitor from the stage area.
hide variable number	Hide the specified variable's (**number**) monitor from the stage area.
say ☐ for 4 secs	The sprite gets a speech bubble that displays the specified text or value for 4 seconds.
join The list consists now of ☐	Join the two values that have been specified in the block and report the result.
join ☐ items.	Join the two values that have been specified in the block and report the result.
length of List	Hold and report the length of the specified list.
set number to 1	Set the current value of the variable called **number** to 1.
repeat ○	Repeat the actions represented by the blocks within this block a certain number of times.
length of List	Hold and report the length of the specified list.
say ☐ for 2 secs	The sprite gets a speech bubble that displays the specified text or value for 2 seconds.
join Item ☐	Join the two values that have been specified in the block and report the result.
join ☐☐	Join the two values that have been specified in the block and report the result.
number	Hold and report the current value of the **number** variable.
join ☐ is ☐	Join the two values that have been specified in the block and report the result.
item ♥ of List	Hold and report the value at a certain position in **List**.
number	Hold and report the current value of the **number** variable.
change number by 1	Add 1 to the current value of the **number** variable.
say Ready to go grocery shopping. for 2 secs	The sprite gets a speech bubble that displays *Ready to go grocery shopping.* for 2 seconds.
show list List	Show the monitor in the stage area for **List**.

Example 9-8: List of Names

The script asks the user to enter 5 names, which are then added to the list called **Names**. At the end, the contents of the list are displayed. Before creating Script 9-8, make sure that the **Names** list is created.

Script 9-8. *List of names*

The script start running when the user clicks the green flag. The next block deletes all the values in **Names** to ensure that the list is empty. The next block hides the grocery list's monitor (**List**) from the stage

area. The next block shows the monitor for the **Names** list in the stage area. Next, a block repeats the sequence of actions within it 5 times. The first block in the sequence creates a speech bubble that displays the text *Add the names of 5 people*, opens a user input field, and waits for the user's input. The next block adds the user input to the end of the **Names** list. When the loop is finished, action moves to the next block which creates a speech bubble that displays *Thank you. The list is ready.* for 2 seconds. The last block also creates a speech bubble that lasts 4 seconds. The final speech bubble displays the text *The list includes the following:* and the contents of the **Names** list for 4 seconds.

Table 9-8 lists the blocks and describes the actions used in this example.

Table 9-8. *Code Blocks in List of Names*

Blocks	Actions
when clicked	Clicking the green flag activates the script. The green flag is the trigger to start the script running.
delete all of Names	Delete all values from the list called **Names**.
hide list List	Hide the specified list's (**List**) monitor from the stage area.
show list Names	Show the monitor in the stage area for **Names**.
repeat 5	Repeat the actions represented by the blocks within this block five times.
ask Add the names of 5 people and wait	The sprite gets a speech bubble that displays *Add the names of 5 people*, opens a user input field, and waits for user input.
add ▮ to Names	Add the specified value to the end of **Names**.
answer	Hold and report the current user input value.
say Thank you. The list is ready. for 2 secs	The sprite gets a speech bubble that displays *Thank you. The list is ready.* for 2 seconds.
say ▮ for 4 secs	The sprite gets a speech bubble that displays the specified text or value for 4 seconds.
join The list includes the following: ▮	Join the two values that have been specified in the block and report the result.
Names	Hold and report the current values in **Names**.

Example 9-9: Relationship Between Lists

This example demonstrates working with multiple lists. Starting with index number 1, the script sequentially asks the user for the age of each name in the list called **Names** and stores each age at the same index number (position) in a list called **Age**. The script also displays each name from **Names** with its corresponding age from **Age**. Before you begin building Script 9-9, makes sure the lists called **Names** and **Age** are created, as well as the variable called **number**.

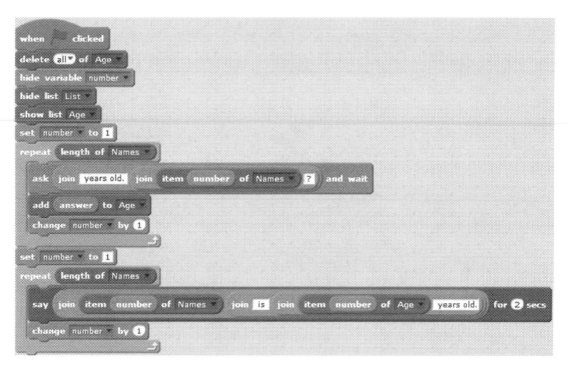

Script 9-9. *Relationship*

Script 9-9 starts running when the user clicks the green flag. The next block deletes all the values in **Age** to ensure that it is empty to start. The next two blocks hide the monitors for the **number** variable and the list called **List** from the stage area. The next block shows the monitor for the **Age** list in the stage area. The next

block assigns the value 1 to the **number** variable. Next, the first ~~repeat~~ block loops through the sequence of actions within it for the length of the **Names list**. The first block in the sequence creates a speech bubble that displays the text *How old is* and the value in the **Names** list at the position equal to the current value of **number** and the *?* symbol (see Figure 9-6). It also opens a user input field and waits for the user's input. The next block adds the user input to end of the **Age list**. The next block adds the value 1 to the

number variable. After the final loop of the sequence completes, the ~~set number to 1~~ block assigns the value 1 to **number** variable. This means that the previous value of the **number** variable is replaced by the value 1. Next, the second repeat block repeats the sequence of actions within it for the length of the **Names** list. The first block in the sequence creates a speech bubble that displays the value in the **Names** list at the position equal to the current value of the **number** variable, the text *is*, the value in the **Age** list at the position equal to the current value of **number**, and the text *years old.* for 2 seconds (see Figure 9-7). The next block adds the value 1 to the **number** variable.

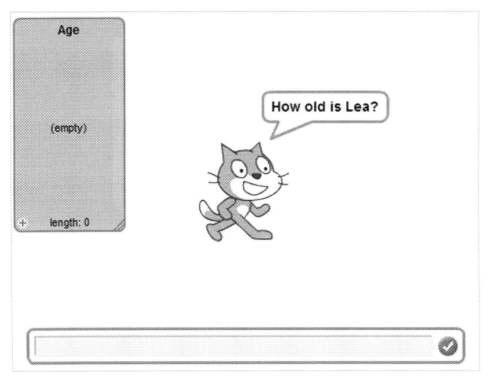

Figure 9-6. *Question*

Figure 9-7. *Display*

Table 9-9 lists the blocks and describes the actions used in this example.

Table 9-9. *Code Blocks in Relationship Between Lists*

Blocks	Actions
when clicked	Clicking the green flag activates the script. The green flag is the trigger to start the script running.
delete all of Age	Delete all values from the list called **Age**.
hide variable number	Hide the specified variable's (**number**) monitor from the stage area.
hide list List	Hide the specified list's (**List**) monitor from the stage area.
show list Age	Show the monitor in the stage area for **Age**.
set number to 1	Set the current value of the variable called **number** to 1.
repeat	Repeat the actions represented by the blocks within this block a certain number of times.
length of Names	Hold and report the length of the specified list.
ask and wait	The sprite gets a speech bubble that displays a certain text, opens a user input field, and waits for user input.
join How old is	Join the two values that have been specified in the block and report the result.
join ?	Join the two values that have been specified in the block and report the result.
item of Names	Hold and report the value at a certain position in **Names**.
number	Hold and report the current value of the **number** variable.
add to Age	Add the specified value to the end of **Age**.
answer	Hold and report the current user input value.
change number by 1	Add 1 to the current value of **number**.
set number to 1	Set the current value of **number** to 1.
repeat	Repeat the actions represented by the blocks within this block a certain number of times.

(*continued*)

Table 9-9. (*continued*)

Blocks	Actions
length of Names ▾	Hold and report the length of the specified list.
say ▢ for ② secs	The sprite gets a speech bubble that displays the specified text or value for 2 seconds.
join ▢▢	Join the two values that have been specified in the block and report the result.
join is ▢	Join the two values that have been specified in the block and report the result.
item ▾ of Names ▾	Hold and report the value at a certain position in **Names**.
number	Hold and report the current value of the **number** variable.
join ▢ old.	Join the two values that have been specified in the block and report the result.
item ▾ of Age ▾	Hold and report the value at a certain position in **Age**.
number	Hold and report the current value of **number**.
change number ▾ by ①	Add 1 to the current value of **number**.

Example 9-10: Replace an Item by User Input

You can also replace specific items in a list with user input. The script asks the user to enter a name and uses this name to replace the value (the previous name) at the first position of the list called **Names**. (Before creating this script, make sure that the **Names** list is created.)

Script 9-10. *Replace an item*

Script 9-10 starts running when the user clicks the green flag. The next block deletes all the values in the **Names** list. The next block hides the monitor for the **Age** list from the stage area. The next block creates a speech bubble that displays the text *Enter one name*, opens a user input field, and waits for the user's input. The next block adds the user input to the end of the **Names** list. The next block creates a speech bubble that displays *Enter another name*, opens a user input field, and waits for the user's input. The next block replaces the value at the first position in the **Names** list with the user input. The next block creates a speech bubble and displays *Enter another name*, opens a user input field, and waits for the user's input. The next block replaces the value at the first position in the **Names** list with the user input.

Table 9-10 lists the blocks and describes the actions used in this example.

Table 9-10. Code Blocks in Replace an Item by User Input

Blocks	Actions
when [🏳] clicked	Clicking the green flag activates the script. The green flag is the trigger to start the script running.
delete (all▾) of Names ▾	Delete all values from the list called **Names**.
hide list Age ▾	Hide the specified list's (**Age**) monitor from the stage area.
ask Enter one name and wait	The sprite gets a speech bubble that displays *Enter one name*, opens a user input field, and waits for user input.
add ☐ to Names ▾	Add the specified value to the end of **Names**.
answer	Hold and report the current user input value.
ask Enter another name and wait	The sprite gets a speech bubble that displays *Enter another name*, opens a user input field, and waits for user input.
replace item (1▾) of Names ▾ with ☐	Replace the value at the first position in **Names** with another value.
answer	Hold and report the current user input value.
ask Enter another name and wait	The sprite gets a speech bubble that displays *Enter another name*, opens a user input field, and waits for user input.
replace item (1▾) of Names ▾ with ☐	Replace the value at the first position in **Names** with another value.
answer	Hold and report the current user input value.

Example 9-11: Replace an Item with a Variable

This example demonstrates that the value in a list can also be the value of a variable. The script replaces the value at the first position in the list called **Names** with the current value of a variable. Before creating Script 9-11, make sure that the list called **Names** and the variable called **name** are created.

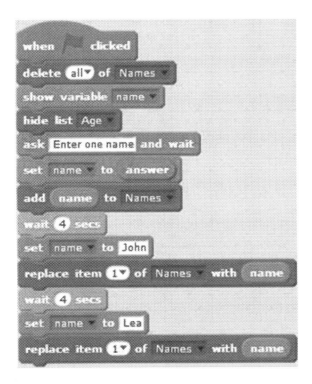

Script 9-11. *Replace with variable*

The script starts running when the user clicks the green flag. The next block deletes all the values in the **Names** list. The next block shows the monitor for the **name** variable on the stage area, and then hides the monitor for the **Age** list from the stage area. The next block creates a speech bubble that displays the text *Enter one name*, opens a user input field, and waits for the user's input. The next block assigns the previous user input to the **name** variable. The next block adds the value of the **name** variable to the end of the list. The next block of code stops the script for 4 seconds. The next block assigns the value *John* to the **name** variable. The next block replaces the value at the first position of the list with the current value (*John*) of the **name** variable. The next block of code stops the script for 4 seconds. The next block of code assigns the value *Lea* to the **name** variable. The next block replaces the value at the first position of the **Names** list with the current value (*Lea*) of the **name** variable.

Table 9-11 lists the blocks and describes the actions used in this example.

Table 9-11. *Code Blocks in Replace an Item with a Variable*

Blocks	Actions
when clicked	Clicking the green flag activates the script. The green flag is the trigger to start the script running.
delete all of Names	Delete all values from the **Names** list.
show variable name	Show the specified variable's (**name**) monitor in the stage area.
hide list Age	Hide the specified list's (**Age**) monitor from the stage area.
ask Enter one name and wait	The sprite gets a speech bubble that displays *Enter one name*, opens a user input field, and waits for user input.
set name to	Set the current value of the variable called **name** to a certain value.
answer	Hold and report the current user input value.
add to Names	Add the specified value to the end of **Names**.
name	Hold and report the current value of the **name** variable.
wait 4 secs	The script waits 4 seconds. No actions are performed for 4 seconds.
set name to John	Set the current value of the **name** variable to the value *John*.
replace item 1 of Names with	Replace the value at the first position in **Names** with another value.
name	Hold and report the current value of the **name** variable.
wait 4 secs	The script waits 4 seconds. No actions are performed for 4 seconds.
set name to Lea	Set the current value of **name** to the value *Lea*.
replace item 1 of Names with	Replace the value at the first position in **Names** with another value.
name	Hold and report the current value of the **name** variable.

Summary

In this chapter, you learned about lists. Most computer programming languages use lists, although they're sometimes called *arrays*. The difference between a list and a variable is that a list can hold multiple values (items) at a time. You learned where to create lists in Scratch. You also learned how to use the blocks of code that control lists.

In the next chapter, you will learn how to use a webcam to interact with Scratch; for example, you'll be using a webcam to control a sprite.

Exercises

1. Create a list of three items. The user is granted three wishes. The user needs to enter his or her three wishes and these wishes will make up the list. Show the list in the stage area.

2. Replace the third wish in the previous list (Exercise 1) with a new user input.

CHAPTER 10

Webcam Interaction

In Scratch, you can control a webcam with a script and make it interact with the objects in a project. Using the blocks of code in the **Sensing** category, for example, you can use a webcam to control a sprite. In this chapter, you will learn how to use these blocks of code. You'll first learn about each block, and then you will apply what you have learned in some examples. To create the examples, you need to have a webcam connected to your computer.

Webcam Blocks

The blocks of code that interact with the webcam are found in the **Sensing** blocks category (see Figure 10-1) in the block palette. One additional block that interacts with the webcam is found in the **Events** block category.

© Eduardo A. Vlieg 2016
E. A. Vlieg, *Scratch by Example*, DOI 10.1007/978-1-4842-1946-1_10

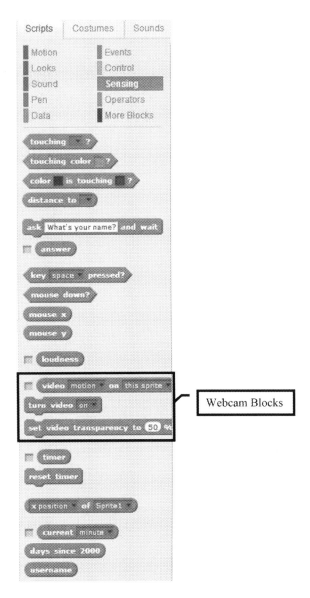

Figure 10-1. *Sensing blocks*

The [turn video on ▼] block activates the webcam. This block instructs Scratch to turn on the webcam. Before the webcam is turned on, the user receives an Adobe Flash Player message (see Figure 10-2) requesting camera and mic access. The user should click **Allow**. When the webcam is turned on, it shows its display on the stage behind the sprite. Clicking the pull-down menu of this block displays two other options: **Off** and **On-flipped**. If **Off** is selected and the block activated, it will turn off the webcam. **On-flipped** turns on the webcam but flips the video to display horizontally. The [set video transparency to ◯ %] block sets the transparency for the video image displayed on the stage, behind the sprite. The higher the value, the

more transparent the video image is. A value of 100% produces a totally white video image. In this
set video transparency to 50 % example, the transparency is set at 50%.

Figure 10-2. *Access request*

The webcam detects video motion and the direction of video motion. The value of video motion ranges from 1 to 100. The faster the video motion, the higher the value. The values are calculated based on a theory called *optical flow*. The **video motion ▾ on this sprite ▾** block detects and reports the value of video motion on the sprite. For example, if you have the webcam pointing at you, the webcam shows this on the stage behind the sprite on the stage behind the sprite. If you move your hand over the sprite, the webcam detects the motion and the block reports its value to the script. Selecting **Stage** from the block's second pull-down menu reports the value of video motion on the stage instead. You can also select **direction** from the block's first pull-down menu. For example, **video direction ▾ on this sprite ▾** detects and reports the direction that the video motion is going when it passes over the sprite.

You can also use a webcam to trigger your script. Found in the **Events** blocks category, the
when video motion ▾ > 50 block is a trigger that activates a script when the webcam detects motion greater than the specified value. In this example, the script starts running if the value of the video motion detected is greater than 50. (The pull-down menu of this block offers other choices like **loudness** and **timer**, as well.) As mentioned, the value of video motion ranges from 1 to 100. This value is the speed of the video motion detected by the webcam, so a slow speed correlates to a lower number and a high speed to a higher number. If you want to see the current value of the video motion, you can always select the box in front of **video motion ▾ on this sprite ▾**. It displays a reporter window on the stage with the current value of video motion.

Examples

The following examples will teach you how to create scripts that interact with the webcam. In order to run these scripts successfully, you need to have a working webcam connected to your computer. Also make sure that the webcam is pointing at you and that you are displayed on the screen.

After practicing the basics, you'll create a game that interacts with your webcam. Remember, that after you have created the following scripts and run them successfully, you can always modify them to your own liking.

Example 10-1: Video Direction

This example teaches you how to use the direction of video motion to control the sprite. The webcam detects which direction the video motion on the sprite is going and points the sprite in that direction.

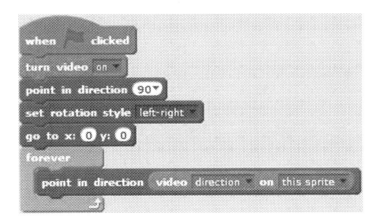

Script 10-1. *Video direction*

Script 10-1 starts running when the user clicks the green flag. The next block of code, turns on the webcam. The webcam display shows up on the stage, behind the sprite. The third block makes the sprite face to the right. The next block sets the rotation style of the sprite to **left-right**. This means that the sprite can only face left or right. The fifth block of code moves the sprite to the middle of the stage. Next, the

block repeats the sequence of actions within it forever, or until the script is manually stopped. You create the action within the forever block by embedding the

block in the point in direction block. This combined block makes the sprite face in the direction that the video motion is going. For example, if you move your hand over the sprite from left to right on the stage, the sprite will face right. If you move your hand over the sprite from right to left on the stage, the sprite will face left.

Table 10-1 lists the blocks and describes the actions used in this example.

Table 10-1. *Code Blocks in Video Direction*

Blocks	Actions
when 🏴 clicked	Clicking the green flag activates the script. The green flag is the trigger to start the script running.
turn video on ▾	Turn the webcam on.
point in direction 90▾	Make the sprite face to the right.
set rotation style left-right ▾	Set the rotation style of the sprite so that it can only face left or right.
go to x: 0 y: 0	Move the sprite to the position where X = 0 and Y = 0.
forever	The actions within the forever block are repeated forever, or until the script is stopped manually.
point in direction ▾	Make the sprite face in the specified direction.
video direction ▾ on this sprite ▾	Hold and report the value of the video motion on the sprite.

Example 10-2: Video Transparency

This example shows you how to control video transparency. Script 10-2 changes the video transparency, first increasing it from 0% (fully opaque) to 100% (fully transparent) and then decreasing it to the setting of 50%. Notice how the webcam display on the stage changes. Before creating the script, make sure that you create a variable called **percentage**. (If you forgot how to create a variable, please consult Chapter 8.)

Script 10-2. *Video transparency*

Script 10-2 starts running when the user clicks the green flag. The next blocks turns on the webcam and shows its display on the stage behind the sprite. The next three blocks make the sprite face to the right, set its rotation style to only face left or right, and move it to the center of the stage. The next block of code assigns

the value 0 to the **percentage** variable. Next, the block repeats the sequence of actions within it 10 times. The block in that sequence adds 10% to the current value of the percentage variable. The next combined block sets the video transparency to the current value of the percentage variable. The last block within the sequence pauses the script for 1 second. After the tenth repeat of the sequence, the value of the percentage variable is 100% and so is the video transparency. Notice how the video display on the stage

is completely blank. The next block repeats the sequence of actions within it 5 times. The first block within the sequence block subtracts 10 from the current value of the percentage variable. The next combined block sets video transparency to the current value of the percentage variable. The last block within the sequence pauses the script for 1 second. At the end of the script, video transparency is at 50%.

Table 10-2 lists the blocks and describes the actions used in this example.

Table 10-2. *Code Blocks in Video Transparency*

Blocks	Actions
when clicked	Clicking the green flag activates the script. The green flag is the trigger to start the script running.
turn video on	Turn the webcam on.
point in direction 90	Make the sprite face to the right.
set rotation style left-right	Set the rotation style of the sprite so that it can only face left or right.
go to x: 0 y: 0	Move the sprite to the position where X = 0 and Y = 0.
set percentage to 0	Set the current value of the **percentage** variable to 0.
repeat 10	Repeat the actions represented by the blocks within this block ten times.
change percentage by 10	Add 10 to the current value of the percentage variable.
set video transparency to ⬤ %	Set video transparency to the specified value.
percentage	Hold and report the current value of the percentage variable.
wait 1 secs	The script waits 1 second. No actions are performed for 1 second.
repeat 5	Repeat the actions represented by the blocks within this block five times.
change percentage by -10	Subtract 10 from the current value of the percentage variable.
set video transparency to ⬤ %	Set video transparency to the specified value.
percentage	Hold and report the current value of the percentage variable.
wait 1 secs	The script waits 1 second. No actions are performed for 1 second.

Example 10-3: Move Sprite

In this example, you'll use the webcam and video motion to move the sprite. For example, if you move your hand over the sprite, the sprite will move in the same direction that your hand moves. The sprite follows your hand.

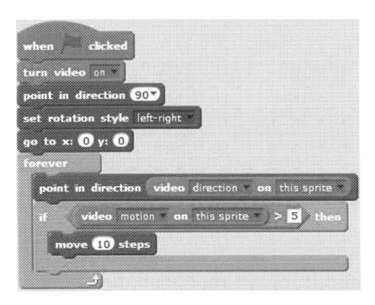

Script 10-3. *Move sprite*

Script 10-3 starts running when the user clicks the green flag. The next block activates the webcam. When the webcam display shows up on the stage, make sure that the webcam is pointing at you. The next three blocks make the sprite face to the right, set its rotation style to **left-right**, and move the sprite to the center of the stage. Next, a [forever] block repeats the sequence of actions within it forever, or until the script is manually stopped. The first block in the loop makes the sprite face in the direction that the video motion is going. Next, there is the [if then] block that evaluates whether the speed of the video motion is greater than 5. If the condition is true (the speed is greater than 5), then the sprite moves 10 pixels in the direction that it's facing. If the condition is false, then the action loops back to the first block in the sequence.

After running the script successfully, modify it to your liking and see how it performs.

Table 10-3 lists the blocks and describes the actions used in this example.

Table 10-3. *Code Blocks in Move Sprite*

Blocks	Actions
when [flag] clicked	Clicking the green flag activates the script. The green flag is the trigger to start the script running.
turn video on	Turn the webcam on.
point in direction 90	Make the sprite face to the right.
set rotation style left-right	Set the rotation style of the sprite so that it can only face left or right.
go to x: 0 y: 0	Move the sprite to the position where X = 0 and Y = 0.
forever	The actions within the forever block are repeated forever, or until the script is stopped manually.
point in direction	Make the sprite face in the specified direction.
video direction on this sprite	Hold and report the direction that the detected motion is going on the sprite.
if then	Check if the condition is true. If the condition is true, execute the actions within it. If the condition is false, skip to the next block.
☐ > 5	If the value on the left side is greater than 5, then this condition is true; otherwise, the condition is false.
video motion on this sprite	Hold and report the value of the video motion on the sprite.
move 10 steps	Move the sprite 10 pixels in the direction that it's facing.

Example 10-4: Motion Detector

Ever wonder how motion detector alarms work? Not only does this example provide the answer, it shows you how to make one. The script plays a sound every time the speed of video motion is detected as being greater than 30. For example, every time that you move your hand over the sprite fast enough that the speed detected is greater than 30, the **meow** sound is played. Go ahead and create Script 10-4 to give it a try.

Script 10-4. *Motion detector*

The script starts running when the user clicks the green flag. The next four blocks are the same as in the previous examples. They activate the webcam, make the sprite face to the right, set the rotation style of the sprite so that it can only face left or right, and move the sprite to the center of the stage. The next block

creates a speech bubble that displays *Hello!*. Next, there is a block with an If/Then conditional statement inside. If the speed of video motion over the sprite is greater than 30, then the condition is true and the **meow** sound is played. If it is false, the loop begins again.

You can create your own motion detector alarm by changing the sound played, and you can even add a

block to create a speech bubble that contains a warning like "Back off" or "You're too close." If someone gets too close to your computer and you have this script running, for example, then motion is detected and a specific action is executed—kind of like a burglar alarm.

Table 10-4 lists the blocks and describes the actions used in this example.

Table 10-4. *Code Blocks in Motion Detector*

Blocks	Actions
when ⚑ clicked	Clicking the green flag activates the script. The green flag is the trigger to start the script running.
turn video on ▾	Turn the webcam on.
point in direction 90▾	Make the sprite face to the right.
set rotation style left-right ▾	Set the rotation style of the sprite so that it can only face left or right.
go to x: 0 y: 0	Move the sprite to the position where X = 0 and Y = 0.
say Hello!	The sprite gets a speech bubble that displays *Hello!*.
forever	The actions within the forever block are repeated forever, or until the script is stopped manually.
if then	Check if the condition is true. If the condition is true, execute the actions within it. If the condition is false, skip to the next block.
[ ] > 30	If the value on the left side is greater than 30, then this condition is true; otherwise, the condition is false.
video motion ▾ on this sprite ▾	Hold and report the value of the video motion on the sprite.
play sound meow ▾	Play the sound **meow**.

Example 10-5: Motion Detector Game

You can also use the motion detecting feature to create a game. Almost the same as Script 10-4, this script moves the sprite around the stage, and then plays the **meow** sound every time that you move your hand; for example, when you move your hand over the sprite at a speed greater than 50.

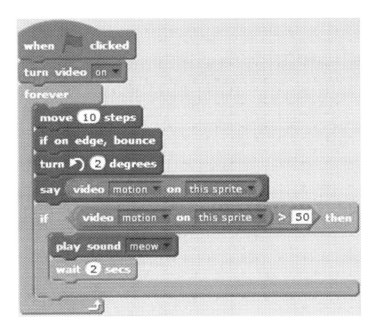

Script 10-5. *Motion detector game*

Script 10-5 activates when the user clicks the green flag. The next block turns on the webcam. Next, a

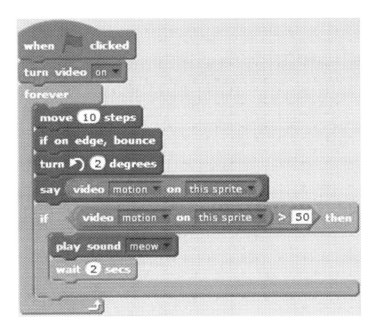 block creates a continuous loop of the sequence of actions within it. The first block within the loop moves the sprite 10 pixels in the direction that it's facing. The next block makes sure that if the sprite hits any of the stage edges, it will bounce and travel in the opposite direction. The next block rotates the sprite 2 degrees counterclockwise. The next compound block creates a speech bubble that displays the current value of the video motion. Next, the If/Then conditional statement evaluates whether the value of the video motion on the sprite is greater than 50. If it is, then the condition is true; the **meow** sound is played and the script pauses for 2 seconds. After the pause, the loop repeats. If the condition is false, the action loops back to the start of the sequence immediately.

Experiment with this script and notice that when you move your hand slowly so that the value of video motion is less than 50, no sound is played and the script is not paused.

Table 10-5 lists the blocks and describes the actions used in this example.

Table 10-5. *Code Blocks in Motion Detector Game*

Blocks	Actions
when clicked	Clicking the green flag activates the script. The green flag is the trigger to start the script running.
turn video on	Turn the webcam on.
forever	The actions within the forever block are repeated forever, or until the script is stopped manually.
move 10 steps	Move the sprite 10 pixels in the direction that it's facing.
if on edge, bounce	If the sprite reaches the edge of the stage, bounce in the opposite direction.
turn ↺ 2 degrees	Turn the sprite counterclockwise 2 degrees.
say	The sprite gets a speech bubble that displays the specified text or value.
video motion on this sprite	Hold and report the value of the video motion on the sprite.
if then	Check if the condition is true. If the condition is true, execute the actions within it. If the condition is false, skip to the next block.
> 50	If the value on the left side is greater than 50, then this condition is true; otherwise, the condition is false.
video motion on this sprite	Hold and report the value of the video motion on the sprite.
play sound meow	Play the sound **meow**.
wait 2 secs	The script waits 2 seconds. No actions are performed for 2 seconds.

Example 10-6: Motion Detector Game 2

In programming, there's always more than one way to produce the same result. This example demonstrates an alternate method to detect video motion in Scratch. It also uses two scripts: the first script handles the sprite's movements and the second script performs the same role as the If/Then conditional statement in Script 10-6, playing a sound when video motion exceeds a specific level. Instead of embedding the

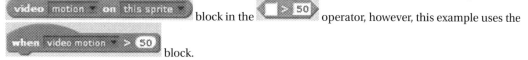 **video motion on this sprite** block in the **> 50** operator, however, this example uses the **when video motion > 50** block.

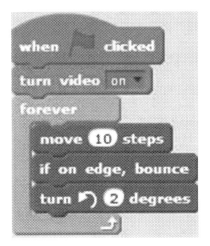

Script 10-6. *Motion Detector Game 2: Sprite Motion*

First, create Script 10-6 to move the sprite around the stage. This script activates when the user clicks the green flag. The next block turns on the webcam. Next, the ![forever block] block loops the sequence of actions inside it indefinitely. The first block in the sequence moves the sprite 10 pixels in the direction that it's moving. The next block makes sure that if the sprite hits any of the stage edges, it will bounce and travel in the opposite direction. The last block in the sequence rotates the sprite 2 degrees counterclockwise.

Table 10-6 lists the blocks and describes the actions used in this example.

Table 10-6. *Code Blocks in Motion Detector Game 2: Sprite Motion*

Blocks	Actions
when clicked	Clicking the green flag activates the script. The green flag is the trigger to start the script running.
turn video on	Turn the webcam on.
forever	The actions within the forever block are repeated forever, or until the script is stopped manually.
move 10 steps	Move the sprite 10 pixels in the direction that it's facing.
if on edge, bounce	If the sprite reaches the edge of the stage, bounce in the opposite direction.
turn 2 degrees	Turn the sprite counterclockwise 2 degrees.

Next, create Script 10-12 beneath Script 10-6 in the scripts area. Script 10-7 is the last script in this project.

Script 10-7. *Motion Detector Game 2: Video motion*

The first block activates the script if the value of the video motion detected is greater than 50. The last block plays the meow sound, only if the script is activated.

Table 10-7 lists the blocks and describes the actions used in this example.

Table 10-7. *Code Blocks in Motion Detector Game 2: Video Motion*

Blocks	Actions
when video motion ▾ > 50	The script gets activated when the webcam detects video motion greater than 50.
play sound meow ▾	Play the sound **meow**.

Example 10-7: Video Game

This last example in this chapter teaches you how to create a game using the webcam (see Figure 10-3). The sprite will move around the stage, and every time that you move your hand over the sprite with a speed greater than 50, you score 1 point and the **meow** sound plays. The goal of the game is to move your hand over the sprite as many times as possible within 10 seconds.

Figure 10-3. *Video game*

You need to create three scripts in the same scripts area (see Figure 10-4). Be sure to select the same sprite when creating all three scripts. The example uses the **Beachball** sprite (see Figure 10-5), but you can select whichever you like. Before you start creating the scripts, you also need to create two variables: **Time** and **Score**. (See Chapter 8 if you need help creating variables.)

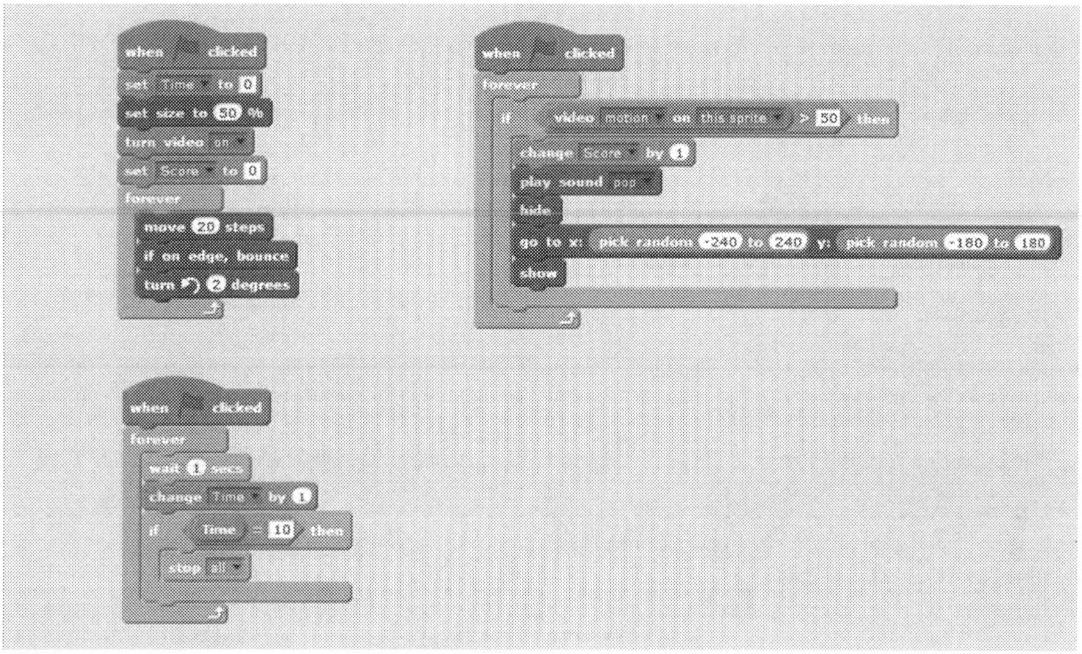
when clicked
set Time to 0
set size to 50 %
turn video on
set Score to 0
forever
move 20 steps
if on edge, bounce
turn 2 degrees
when clicked
forever
if video motion on this sprite > 50 then
change Score by 1
play sound pop
hide
go to x: pick random -240 to 240 y: pick random -180 to 180
show
when clicked
forever
wait 1 secs
change Time by 1
if Time = 10 then
stop all

Figure 10-4. *Video game scripts*

Beachball

Figure 10-5. *Beachball sprite*

The main goal of the first script (Script 10-8) is to control the movement of the sprite.

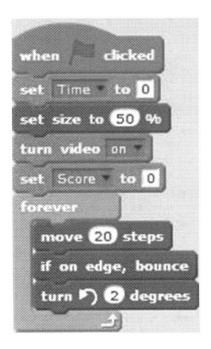

Script 10-8. *Video Game: Motion*

Script 10-8 starts running when the user clicks the green flag. The second block assigns the value 0 to the **Time** variable. The next three blocks shrink the size of the sprite to 50%, turn on the webcam, and assign

the value 0 to the **Score** variable. Then, the sequence of blocks inside the [forever] block controls the sprite's motion. The blocks inside this block move the sprite 20 pixels in the direction that it's facing, make it bounce and travel in the opposite direction if it reaches any of the stage edges, and finally, rotate the sprite 2 degrees counterclockwise. After rotating the sprite, the loop repeats.

Table 10-8 lists the blocks and describes the actions used in this example.

Table 10-8. *Code Blocks in Video Game: Motion*

Blocks	Actions
when clicked	Clicking the green flag activates the script. The green flag is the trigger to start the script running.
set Time ▾ to 0	Set the current value of the variable called **Time** to 0.
set size to 50 %	Shrink the sprite to half its size.
turn video on ▾	Turn the webcam on.
set Score ▾ to 0	Set the current value of the variable called **Score** to 0.
forever	The actions within the forever block are repeated forever, or until the script is stopped manually.
move 20 steps	Move the sprite 20 pixels in the direction that it's facing.
if on edge, bounce	If the sprite reaches the edge of the stage, bounce in the opposite direction.
turn ↺ 2 degrees	Turn the sprite counterclockwise 2 degrees.

Script 10-9 keeps track of the time for the game. When 10 seconds is reached, all the scripts in this project stop.

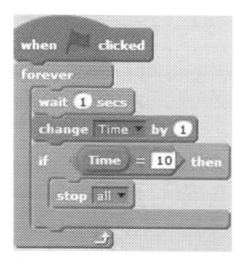

Script 10-9. *Video Game: Time*

Script 10-9 starts running when the user clicks the green flag. The rest of the script's actions loop

inside a block. The first block inside pauses the scripts for 1 second. The next block adds 1 to the current value of **Time**. The next block is an If/Then conditional statement block that evaluates whether the current value of the Time value is equal to 10. If this is true, then all the scripts in this project are stopped. If it is false, the actions repeat.

Table 10-9 lists the blocks and describes the actions used in this example.

Table 10-9. *Code Blocks in Video Game: Time*

Blocks	Actions
	Clicking the green flag activates the script. The green flag is the trigger to start the script running.
	The actions within the forever block are repeated forever, or until the script is stopped manually.
	The script waits 1 second. No actions are performed for 1 second.
	Add 1 to the current value of the **Time** variable.
	Check if the condition is true. If the condition is true, execute the actions within it. If the condition is false, skip to the next block.
	If the value on the left side is equal to 10, then this condition is true; otherwise, the condition is false.
	Hold and report the current value of the Time variable.
	Stop all scripts in this project.

The main goal of the last script for this project (Script 10-10) is to keep track of the score for this game.

Script 10-10. *Video Game: Score*

Script 10-10 activates when the user clicks the green flag. Next, there is a block with an block within it. The condition that it evaluates is whether the value of the video motion is greater than 50. If the condition is true, then the sequence of blocks within the If/Then conditional statement are executed. The first block in the sequence adds 1 to the value of **Score**. The next one plays the **pop** sound. The next block hides the sprite from the stage area and the next block moves the sprite to a position with randomly picked X and Y values. The last block in the sequence displays the sprite in the stage area.

Table 10-10 lists the blocks and describes the actions used in this example.

Table 10-10. *Code Blocks in Video Game: Score*

Blocks	Actions
	Clicking the green flag activates the script. The green flag is the trigger to start the script running.
	The actions within the forever block are repeated forever, or until the script is stopped manually.
	Check if the condition is true. If the condition is true, execute the actions within it. If the condition is false, skip to the next block.
	If the value on the left side is greater than 50, then this condition is true; otherwise, the condition is false.

(*continued*)

Table 10-10. (*continued*)

Blocks	Actions
video motion ▾ on this sprite ▾	Hold and report the value of the video motion on the sprite.
change Score ▾ by 1	Add 1 to the current value of the **Score** variable.
play sound pop ▾	Play the sound **pop**.
hide	Make the sprite disappear from the stage.
go to x: ○ y: ○	Move the sprite to the specified X and Y coordinates.
pick random -240 to 240	Pick a random value between the two specified numbers and report the result.
pick random -180 to 180	Pick a random value between the two specified numbers and report the result.
show	Make the sprite appear on the stage.

Summary

By now, you should realize the power of Scratch. You've progressed from the very simple scripts of Chapter 3 to interacting with the outside world, first through input from the keyboard and now, in this chapter, via a webcam. With Scratch, you can use the webcam as a sensor, or as a motion detector, or to create a game.

Slowly but surely, we are reaching the end of this book. The next chapter teaches you how to make scripts interact with other; for example, one script can trigger another script to start.

Finally, use the knowledge that you gained in this chapter to do these next two exercises.

Exercises

1. Create a script that detects video motion. Each time the video motion on the sprite is greater than 30, make the sprite jump up and down.

2. Create a script that detects video motion. Each time the video motion on the sprite is greater than 30, play a sound.

CHAPTER 11

Broadcast Interaction

By now, you've learned several ways to activate a script besides simply clicking it in the scripts area. For example, you can use hat blocks in the **Events** block category to instruct a script to start when the user clicks the green flag or presses the space bar. But what if you could activate one script automatically from inside another script with no user clicking or key presses required? That's what this chapter teaches you how to do: use a block in one script to broadcast an instruction to another script, telling it to activate.

If you have two sprites in a project, for example, you can create one script for each and make the script you created for one sprite instruct the other sprite's script to start. On the stage, it looks as if the sprites are interacting with each other, which comes in handy when you want to create a project that tells a story. In a game, for example, you could have a sprite's script instruct a backdrop's script to start after the sprite performs a specific action. In this chapter, you will learn about the blocks that allow this interaction by broadcasting instructions between scripts, and then you'll create some scripts that use these blocks.

Broadcast Blocks

The activation of one script by another script consists of two parts: one script broadcasts the start instruction, which Scratch calls a **message**, and the other script receives the message and then activates. Each activation message sent between scripts has a unique name that is specified in both scripts, enabling you to send multiple messages to multiple scripts in a single project, with certainty that the various receiving scripts will start at the appropriate times. The blocks of code you need for both broadcasting and receiving messages are found in the **Events** blocks category (see Figure 11-1).

© Eduardo A. Vlieg 2016
E. A. Vlieg, *Scratch by Example*, DOI 10.1007/978-1-4842-1946-1_11

Figure 11-1. *Events*

To broadcast a message, you have the choice of two blocks. The **broadcast message1** block broadcasts the specified message, and then the action progresses to the next block in the script. As you can see in the block's pull-down menu, the default message name is **message1**. You can create your message name, as well. Simply select **new message...** from the menu (see Figure 11-2), and when the New Message window (see Figure 11-3) opens, give your message a descriptive name and click the **OK** button. Remember, the message you create doesn't contain any value; it's a signal to trigger another script. The name simply helps you differentiate between messages that are being broadcast and received in larger projects. The **broadcast message1 and wait** block also broadcasts the message you specify, but Scratch waits until the receiving script finishes running before performing the action of the next block in the broadcasting script.

Figure 11-2. *Choose to broadcast the default message or to create a new one*

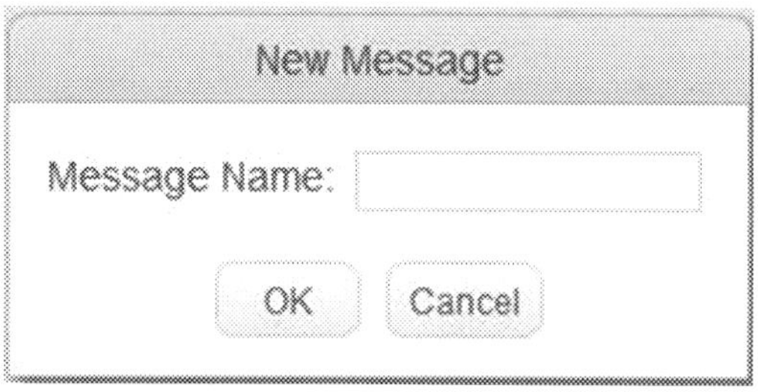

New Message

Message Name: [   ]

OK   Cancel

Figure 11-3. *Name your message in the New Message window*

Remember, for each broadcast block that sends an instruction to activate, you need to add a receiving

block at the top of the script to be activated. The [when I receive message1] block "listens for" the specified message. When it receives that message, the block triggers the script snapped below it and Scratch starts going through the next blocks of code in the script.

Let's go next through a couple of examples showing these blocks in action.

Examples

By creating and running the scripts in the next examples, you will get a better understanding of how broadcasting works and how it can give sprites the illusion of reacting to each other's actions. For instance, you'll set up one sprite's script to broadcast a trigger to another sprite's script to mimic a conversation, as well as create a script for a sprite that sends a message to activate a backdrop-changing script at a key time.

Remember, try to figure out what the script does before you create and run it. This is a good way to learn a programming language.

Example 11-1: Basic Dialog

Without broadcasting messages, setting up interactions between sprites requires building in pauses and guesswork to ensure that the timing of the two sprites' scripts is in sync. To provide a contrast for the broadcast-based examples that follow, this first example sets up a short conversation between two sprites by

adding carefully placed [wait 2 secs] blocks.

Before you create the scripts, add one more sprite to the project. I'll use the Crab sprite, but you can choose whichever one you prefer.

Select the first sprite in the Sprites pane (see Figure 11-4), and snap together Script 11-1 in the scripts area.

Figure 11-4. *Sprites pane*

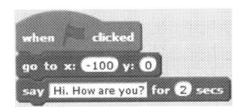

Script 11-1. *Dialog: Sprite 1 speech*

The script activates when the user clicks the green flag. The second block moves the sprite to the position on the stage where the coordinates are (–100, 0). The last block of code creates a speech bubble that displays *Hi. How are you?* for 2 seconds (see Figure 11-5).

Figure 11-5. *The first sprite's line of dialog*

Table 11-1 lists the blocks and describes the actions used in this example.

Table 11-1. *Dialog: Sprite 1 Speech Code Blocks*

Blocks	Actions
when clicked	Clicking the green flag activates the script. The green flag is the trigger to start the script running.
go to x: -100 y: 0	Move the sprite to the position where X = -100 and Y = 0.
say Hi. How are you? for 2 secs	The sprite gets a speech bubble that displays *Hi. How are you?* for 2 seconds.

Now, set up your second sprite's answer. Select the second sprite and create Script 11-2 in the scripts area. The script starts running when the user clicks the green flag. The next block moves the selected sprite to (100, –30). The third block pauses the script for 2 seconds to stay in sync with the first sprite's script, and the last block creates a speech bubble that displays *Fine, thank you!* for 2 seconds.

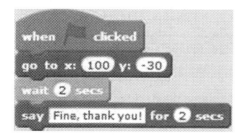

Script 11-2. *Dialog Sprite 2 speech*

Remember, the first sprite's speech bubble displayed for 2 seconds. Because both scripts start at the same time (when the user clicks the green flag), the second sprite's script must pause for 2 seconds before its say Fine, thank you! for 2 secs block so that the second speech bubble displays only after the first one disappears from the stage. Although coordinating speech bubbles and pauses is manageable in this simple example, imagine trying to coordinate the script timing for a longer, more complex conversation—or one among three sprites. Broadcasting messages makes the task much easier, as you'll learn in the next example.

Table 11-2 lists the blocks and describes the actions used in this example.

Table 11-2. *Dialog: Sprite 2 Speech Code Blocks*

Blocks	Actions
when clicked	Clicking the green flag activates the script. The green flag is the trigger to start the script running.
go to x: 100 y: -30	Move the sprite to the position where X = 100 and Y = –30.
wait 2 secs	The script waits 2 seconds. No actions are performed for 2 seconds.
say Fine, thank you! for 2 secs	The sprite gets a speech bubble that displays *Fine, thank you!* for 2 seconds.

Example 11-2: Advanced Conversation

This more efficient example produces the same result as Example 11-1 by using the

broadcast message1 and when I receive message1 blocks. Once again, make sure that you have two sprites added to the project. Select the first sprite in the Sprites pane, and create Script 11-3.

The script starts running when the user clicks the green flag. The next block moves the sprite to the position (100, 0). The third block creates a speech bubble that displays *Hi. How are you?* for 2 seconds. The last block of code broadcasts **message1** to trigger Script 11-5, which controls the second sprite's speech.

Script 11-3. *Conversation: Sprite 1 speech*

Table 11-3 lists the blocks and describes the actions used in this example.

Table 11-3. *Conversation: Sprite 1 Speech Code Blocks*

Blocks	Actions
when ▓ clicked	Clicking the green flag activates the script. The green flag is the trigger to start the script running.
go to x: -100 y: 0	Move the sprite to the position where X = –100 and Y = 0.
say Hi. How are you? for 2 secs	The sprite gets a speech bubble that displays *Hi. How are you?* for 2 seconds.
broadcast message1 ▼	Broadcast **message1**.

Select the second sprite. Create Script 11-4 to control its position and Script 11-5 to control its speech.

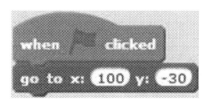

Script 11-4. *Conversation: Sprite 2 position*

Script 11-4 starts running when the user clicks the green flag and moves the sprite to the position (100, –30). Table 11-4 lists the blocks and describes the actions used in this example.

Table 11-4. *Conversation: Sprite 2 Position Code Blocks*

Blocks	Actions
when ▓ clicked	Clicking the green flag activates the script. The green flag is the trigger to start the script running.
go to x: 100 y: -30	Move the sprite to the position where X = 100 and Y = –30.

Script 11-5 activates when it receives the message broadcast by the first sprite.

Script 11-5. *Conversation: Sprite 2 speech*

Specifically, the first block activates the script when it receives **message1**, which Script 11-3 broadcasts after it displays the first sprite's speech bubble. The next block creates a speech bubble for the second sprite that displays *Fine, thank you!* for 2 seconds. The timing of the speech bubbles is coordinated automatically by the scripts—no more figuring out and manually adding pauses. Broadcasting and receiving a message makes coordinating the interaction between scripts easier and more efficient.

Table 11-5 lists the blocks and describes the actions used in this example.

Table 11-5. *Conversation: Sprite 2 Speech Code Blocks*

Blocks	Actions
when I receive message1	Receiving **message1** activates the script.
say Fine, thank you! for 2 secs	The sprite gets a speech bubble that displays *Fine, thank you!* for 2 seconds.

Example 11-3: Dance

This example builds on the concepts in Example 11-2. You will create a conversation between the two sprites in Figure 11-6, and then instruct one of them to dance.

Figure 11-6. *Dance sprites*

Before you create the scripts for this example, make sure that you add the **1080 Hip-Hop** to the Sprites pane (see Figure 11-7). You also need to add the **dance celebrate** sound file from the Sound Library.

Figure 11-7. *The Sprites pane*

To begin, select **Sprite1** and create Script 11-6.

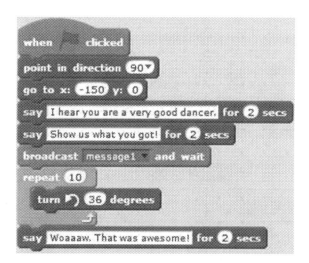

Script 11-6. *Dance: Sprite 1 speech*

Script 11-6 starts running when the user clicks the green flag. The next two blocks make the sprite face to the right and move it to the position (–150, 0). The next two blocks each create a speech bubble that lasts for 2 seconds. The first one displays *I hear you are a very good dancer.*, and then the second one displays *Show us what you got!*. The next block broadcasts **message1** to trigger Script 11-7 (the script that you will create to receive the broadcast) and waits until that script completes. Scratch then executes the next code

block in the broadcasting script, which is a ![repeat 10] block that repeats the single block within it 10 times. That block rotates the sprite 36 degrees counterclockwise. After the loop completes, the last block creates a speech bubble that displays *Woaaaw. That was awesome!* for 2 seconds. Why rotate the sprite by repeating a 36-degree rotation 10 times instead of rotating 360 degrees at once? Because rotating 360 degrees at once wouldn't show the sprite rotating, since the starting and ending position of the sprite would be the same.

Script 11-7. *Dance: Sprite 2 actions*

Table 11-6 lists the blocks and describes the actions used in this example.

Table 11-6. *Dance: Sprite 1 Speech Code Blocks*

Blocks	Actions
when clicked	Clicking the green flag activates the script. The green flag is the trigger to start the script running.
point in direction 90▼	Make the sprite face to the right.
go to x: -150 y: 0	Move the sprite to the position where X = -150 and Y = 0.
say I hear you are a very good dancer. for 2 secs	The sprite gets a speech bubble that displays *I hear you are a very good dancer.* for 2 seconds.
say Show us what you got! for 2 secs	The sprite gets a speech bubble that displays *Show us what you got!* for 2 seconds.
broadcast message1 ▼ and wait	Broadcast **message1** and wait until all the scripts that received the message have finished.
repeat 10	Repeat the actions represented by the blocks within this block ten times.
turn ↺ 36 degrees	Turn the sprite counterclockwise 36 degrees.
say Woaaaw. That was awesome! for 2 secs	The sprite gets a speech bubble that displays *Woaaaw. That was awesome!* for 2 seconds.

The broadcasting script is finished, so now you need to set up the receiving script for the second sprite. Select the **1080 Hip-Hop** sprite and create Script 11-7.

The hat block indicates that Script 11-7 activates when **message1** is received. The next block plays the

dance celebrate sound. The [repeat 35] block repeats the two actions within it 35 times. First, the sprite changes to its next costume, and then the script pauses for 0.2 seconds. The sprite dances while the music plays.

Notice how [broadcast message1 and wait] affects the interaction between the scripts. Because the first sprite's script waits for the second script to complete before it continues, on the stage it appears that the cat prompts and then reacts to the dancer sprite's actions. If you had used

[broadcast message1] instead, the cat would have started spinning and speaking at the same time the dancer began to change costumes.

Table 11-7 lists the blocks and describes the actions used in this example.

Table 11-7. *Dance: Sprite 2 Actions Code Blocks*

Blocks	Actions
when I receive message1	Receiving **message1** activates the script.
play sound dance celebrate	Play the sound **dance celebrate**.
repeat 35	Repeat the actions represented by the blocks within this block 35 times.
next costume	Change the sprite to the next costume in the costumes tab.
wait 0.2 secs	The script waits 0.2 seconds. No actions are performed for 0.2 seconds.

Example 11-4: Math Test

Now that you've mastered broadcasting one message, try broadcasting three. This next example shows interaction amongst five scripts that control a back-and-forth conversation about math between two sprites. One script asks a math question and triggers the script that answers, which in turn triggers a second question that then triggers a second answer. That's a lot of broadcasting and receiving, so you'd better get started.

The first step is to assemble all the elements you need. Make sure that you have two sprites in the Sprites pane. Next, create two additional messages and name them **message2** and **message3**. You can create the new message name, either while the block is still in the block palette or after you have dragged and dropped it in the scripts area. Last but not least, create a variable called **number**.

Next, let's create the scripts that control the sprite that asks the math questions. Select the questioner sprite (I chose the cat), and create Script 11-8, which asks the first math question and broadcasts **message1** to activate the second sprite's first answer script (see Script 11-11).

Script 11-8. *Math Test: Question1*

The script starts running when the user clicks the green flag. The next block moves the sprite to the position (–150, 0). The next block displays the sprite on the stage if it was hidden. If the sprite was not hidden, nothing will happen. The next block creates a speech bubble that displays *Can you count from 1 to 10?* for 2 seconds (see Figure 11-8). The last block of code broadcasts **message1**.

Figure 11-8. *The Math test's first question*

Table 11-8 lists the blocks and describes the actions used in this example.

Table 11-8. *Math Test: Question1 Code Blocks*

Blocks	Actions
when ▢ clicked	Clicking the green flag activates the script. The green flag is the trigger to start the script running.
go to x: -150 y: 0	Move the sprite to the position where X = –150 and Y = 0.
show	Make the sprite appear on the stage.
say Can you count from 1 to 10? for 2 secs	The sprite gets a speech bubble that displays *Can you count from 1 to 10?* for 2 seconds.
broadcast message1	Broadcast **message1**.

With the questioner sprite still selected, create the Script 11-9, which receives **message2** from the second sprite's first answer script (see Script 11-11), asks a second question, and then broadcasts **message3** to the second sprite's second answer script (see Script 11-12).

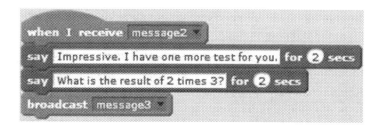

Script 11-9. *Math Test: Question2*

Script 11-9 starts running when it receives **message2**. The next two blocks create speech bubbles. The first bubble displays *Impressive. I have one more test for you.* for 2 seconds, and the second displays *What is the result of 2 times 3?* I for 2 seconds. The last block of code broadcasts **message3** to activate the second sprite's second answer in Script 11-12.

Table 11-9 lists the blocks and describes the actions used in this example.

Table 11-9. *Math Test: Question2 Code Blocks*

Blocks	Actions
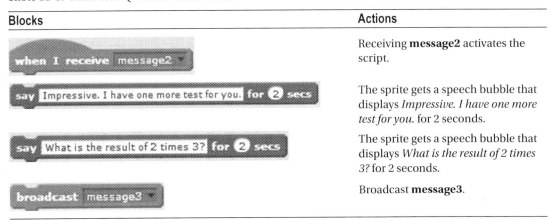	Receiving **message2** activates the script.
	The sprite gets a speech bubble that displays *Impressive. I have one more test for you.* for 2 seconds.
	The sprite gets a speech bubble that displays *What is the result of 2 times 3?* for 2 seconds.
	Broadcast **message3**.

The questioner sprite's scripts are finished, so you're ready to move on to the answering sprite's scripts. Go ahead and select the second sprite. All the scripts you create now in the scripts area will send instructions to this sprite. Start with Script 11-10, which positions the second sprite on the stage.

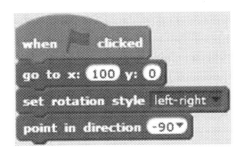

Script 11-10. *Math Test: Position*

Script 11-10 starts running when the user clicks the green flag. The next block moves the sprite to the position (100, 0). The next block sets the rotation style of the sprite to **left-right**. The last block makes the sprite face to the left.

Table 11-10 lists the blocks and describes the actions used in this example.

Table 11-10. *Math Test: Position Code Blocks*

Blocks	Actions
when ⚑ clicked	Clicking the green flag activates the script. The green flag is the trigger to start the script running.
go to x: 100 y: 0	Move the sprite to the position where X = 100 and Y = 0.
set rotation style left-right ▾	Set the rotation style of the sprite, so that it can only turn left or right.
point in direction -90▾	Make the sprite face to the left.

Keeping the second sprite selected, create Script 11-11 with its first math answer, which starts running upon receiving **message1** from Script 11-8 and activates Script 11-9 by broadcasting **message2**.

Script 11-11. *Math Test: Answer1*

Script 11-11 starts running when it receives **message1** broadcast from Script 11-8. The next block creates a speech bubble that displays *Of course!* for 2 seconds. The next block assigns the value 0 to the

number variable. Next, there's a ⟨repeat 10⟩ block that repeats the sequence of actions within it 10 times. The first block in the sequence adds 1 to the current value of **number**, and the second creates a speech bubble that displays the value of **number** for 1 second. After the second sprite counts from 1 to 10 in the loop, the next block creates a speech bubble that displays *There you go. I'm a genius.* for 2 seconds. Finally, the last block of code broadcasts **message2** to trigger Script 11-9.

Table 11-11 lists the blocks and describes the actions used in this example.

Table 11-11. *Math Test: Answer1 Code Blocks*

Blocks	Actions
`when I receive message1`	Receiving **message1** activates the script.
`say Of course! for 2 secs`	The sprite gets a speech bubble that displays *Of course!* for 2 seconds.
`set number to 0`	Set the current value of the variable called **number** to 0.
`repeat 10`	Repeat the actions represented by the blocks within this block ten times.
`change number by 1`	Add 1 to the current value of the **number** variable.
`say ▢ for 1 secs`	The sprite gets a speech bubble that displays the specified text or value.
`number`	Hold and report the current value of the **number** variable.
`say There you go. I'm a genius. for 2 secs`	The sprite gets a speech bubble that displays *There you go. I'm a genius.* for 2 seconds.
`broadcast message2`	Broadcast **message2**.

You're almost done. You just need to create Script 11-12, which receives **message3** from Script 11-9 and gives the second sprite's final math answer. Make sure that the second sprite is still active and snap together the final two blocks in the scripts area.

Script 11-12. *Math Test: Answer2*

The script starts running after it has received **message3**, which is broadcast from Script 11-9. The next block creates a speech bubble that displays the text *2 times 3 is equal to:* and the result of the embedded multiplication operator block for 2 seconds.

Table 11-12 lists the blocks and describes the actions used in this example.

Table 11-12. *Math Test: Answer2 Code Blocks*

Blocks	Actions
when I receive message3 ▼	Receiving **message3** activates the script.
say ▢ for ❷ secs	The sprite gets a speech bubble that displays the specified text or value.
join 2 times 3 is equal to: ▢	Join the two values that have been specified in the block and report the result.
❷ * ❸	Multiply two values (2 * 3) and report the result.

So now that you have learned how to make the scripts and sprites interact with each other automatically, you can create your own stories using the same methods.

Example 11-5: Race

This project illustrates how you can use the broadcasting technique to create a story in which the sprites race each other to a finish line (see Figure 11-9).

Figure 11-9. *Race*

Before creating the scripts, you need to make a few preparations. You'll need three sprites for this project. I added **Sprite1**, **Beetle**, and **Butterfly3** to the Sprites pane from the Scratch library (see Figure 11-10). You will also need to have **message1**, **message2**, and **message3** available for broadcast. Finally, add a vertical red line to the white backdrop (see Figure 11-11) to act as the finish line for the race. (Consult Chapter 2 if you don't remember how to do this.)

Figure 11-10. Race sprites

Figure 11-11. Race backdrop

The cat, **Sprite1**, directs the race between the beetle and the butterfly, so let's begin with the cat's three scripts. First, select **Sprite1** and create Script 11-13, which starts the racers by broadcasting **message1**.

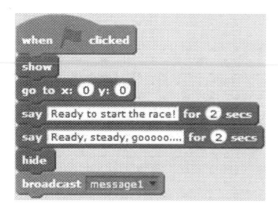

Script 11-13. *Race: Ready*

Script 11-13 starts running when the user clicks the green flag. The next two blocks show the sprite on the stage and move it to the center of the stage. The next pair of blocks create speech bubbles for 2 seconds each, first displaying *Ready to start the race!*, and then *Ready, steady, gooooo.....* The next block hides the sprite from the stage. The last block broadcasts **message1**, which triggers Scripts 11-17 and 11-19.

Table 11-13 lists the blocks and describes the actions used in this example.

Table 11-13. *Race: Ready Code Blocks*

Blocks	Actions
when clicked	Clicking the green flag activates the script. The green flag is the trigger to start the script running.
show	Make the sprite appear on the stage.
go to x: 0 y: 0	Move the sprite to coordinates (X = 0, Y = 0), which is the middle of the stage.
say Ready to start the race! for 2 secs	The sprite gets a speech bubble that displays *Ready to start the race!* for 2 seconds.
say Ready, steady, gooooo.... for 2 secs	The sprite gets a speech bubble that displays *Ready, steady, gooooo....* for 2 seconds.
hide	Make the sprite disappear from the stage.
broadcast message1	Broadcast **message1**.

Beneath the first script and with the cat still selected, create Script 11-14, which announces the beetle as the winner upon receiving **message2**. It then stops all the scripts in the project.

Script 11-14. *Race: Announcement1*

The script starts running after it receives **message2** from Script 11-17. The next block shows the sprite on the stage. The third block creates a speech bubble that displays *The beetle is the winner!!!* for 2 seconds. The last block of code stops all scripts in this project.

Table 11-14 lists the blocks and describes the actions used in this example.

Table 11-14. *Race: Announcement1 Code Blocks*

Blocks	Actions
when I receive message2	Receiving **message2** activates the script.
show	Make the sprite appear on the stage.
say The beetle is the winner!!! for 2 secs	The sprite gets a speech bubble that displays *The beetle is the winner!!!* for 2 seconds.
stop all	Stop all scripts in this project from running.

The last script for Sprite1 announces the butterfly as the winner if it reaches the finish line first.

Script 11-15 starts running if **message3** is received from Script 11-19. The next block shows the sprite on the stage, and the third creates a speech bubble that displays *The butterfly is the winner!!!* for 2 seconds. The last block of code stops all scripts in this project.

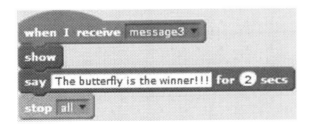

Script 11-15. *Race: Announcement2*

Table 11-15 lists the blocks and describes the actions used in this example.

Table 11-15. *Race: Announcement2 Code Blocks*

Blocks	Actions
when I receive message3	Receiving **message3** activates the script.
show	Make the sprite appear on the stage.
say The butterfly is the winner!!! for 2 secs	The sprite gets a speech bubble that displays *The butterfly is the winner!!!* for 2 seconds.
stop all	Stop all scripts in this project from running.

Next, select the beetle and create Scripts 11-16 and 11-17, one beneath the other. This first script just positions the beetle for the start of the race.

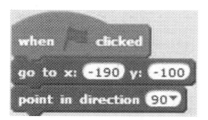

Script 11-16. *Race start Beetle*

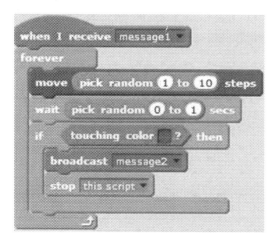

Script 11-17. *Race: Race finish Beetle*

Script 11-16 starts running when the user clicks the green flag. The next two blocks move the beetle to its starting position for the race, which is (–190, –100), and make the beetle face to the right.

Table 11-16 lists the blocks and describes the actions used in this example.

Table 11-16. *Race: Race Start Beetle Code Blocks*

Blocks	Actions
when clicked	Clicking the green flag activates the script. The green flag is the trigger to start the script running.
go to x: -190 y: -100	Move the sprite to coordinates (X = –190, Y = –100).
point in direction 90▾	Point the direction of the sprite to the right.

Upon receipt of **message1**, Script 11-17 starts the Beetle racing toward the finish line and broadcasts **message2** when it reaches the finish line.

Script 11-17 starts running when it receives **message1**, which is broadcast in Script 11-13 as the cat's start sign. The next block is a forever block that repeats the sequence of actions within it forever. The first block in the sequence moves the sprite a random number of pixels (1 to 10) in the direction that it's facing. The next block pauses the script a random number of seconds between 0 and 1. Next there is the If/Then conditional statement checks whether the sprite touches the red color, which is the color of the finish line. If it does, then the condition is true and the sequence of actions within the if then block are executed. The first block within it broadcasts **message2** to Script 11-14, and the last block within it stops this script.

Table 11-17 lists the blocks and describes the actions used in this example.

Table 11-17. *Race: Race Finish Beetle Code Blocks*

Blocks	Actions
when I receive message1 ▾	Receiving **message1** activates the script.
forever	Repeat the actions represented by the blocks within this block forever, until the script is stopped manually.
move ● steps	Move the sprite the amount of specified pixels in the direction that it's facing.

(continued)

292

Table 11-17. (*continued*)

Blocks	Actions
pick random 1 to 10	Pick a random value between the two specified numbers and report the result.
wait ⬤ secs	The script waits a specified number of seconds. No actions are performed in that timespan.
pick random 0 to 1	Pick a random value between the two specified numbers and report the result.
if ⬤ then	Check if the condition is true. If the condition is true, execute the actions within it. If the condition is false, skip to the next block.
touching color ▨ ?	Check if the sprite is touching the red color. If it is, then this condition is true; otherwise, it's false.
broadcast message2	Broadcast **message2**.
stop this script ▾	Stop this script from running.

Next, select the butterfly, and create Scripts 11-18 and 11-19, one beneath the other. As you did for the beetle, you will first create a script that positions the butterfly for the start of the race.

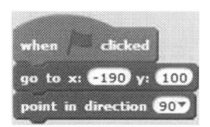

Script 11-18. *Race: Race start Butterfly*

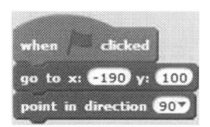

Script 11-19. *Race finish Butterfly*

Script 11-18 starts running when the user clicks the green flag. The next two blocks move the butterfly to its starting position in the race, which is (–190, 100), and make the butterfly face to the right.

Table 11-18 lists the blocks and describes the actions used in this example.

Table 11-18. *Race: Race Start Butterfly Code Blocks*

Blocks	Actions
when ▢ clicked	Clicking the green flag activates the script. The green flag is the trigger to start the script running.
go to x: -190 y: 100	Move the sprite to the position where X = –190 and Y = 100.
point in direction 90▼	Make the sprite face to the right.

The next script starts the Butterfly racing toward the finish line when it receives **message1** and broadcasts **message3** to when it reaches the finish line.

Script 11-19 starts running when it receives **message1**, which is the start sign broadcast from **Sprite1**'s Script 11-13. The next block is a ▢forever block that repeats the sequence of actions within it forever. The first block in the sequence moves the sprite a random number of pixels (1 to 10) in the direction that it's facing. The next block pauses the script a random number of seconds between 0 and 1. The ▢if then block then uses the embedded sensing block to check whether the sprite is touching the red color (the finish line). If it is, then the condition is true and the sequence of actions within the block is executed. The first block in the sequence broadcasts **message3** to trigger Script 11-16. The second block stops the butterfly's script and forever loop.

Table 11-19 lists the blocks and describes the actions used in this example.

Table 11-19. *Race: Race Finish Butterfly Code Blocks*

Blocks	Actions
when I receive message1	Receiving **message1** activates the script.
forever	Repeat the actions represented by the blocks within this block forever, until the script is stopped manually.
move ○ steps	Move the sprite the amount of specified pixels in the direction that it's facing.
pick random ① to ⑩	Pick a random value between the two specified numbers and report the result.
wait ○ secs	The script waits a specified number of seconds. No actions are performed in that timespan.
pick random ⓪ to ①	Pick a random value between the two specified numbers and report the result.
if ○ then	Check if the condition is true. If the condition is true, execute the actions within it. If the condition is false, skip to the next block.
touching color ■ ?	Check if the sprite is touching the red color. If it is, then this condition is true; otherwise, it's false.
broadcast message3	Broadcast **message3**.
stop this script	Stop this script from running.

Notice that multiple messages are used in this example. Each message that is broadcast and received executes different actions and produces different results. This example shows that it would be very difficult to create this project without the broadcasting and receiving blocks. Using the broadcasting block, one script sends a message to activate two scripts; whichever sprite wins the race has a script that broadcasts a message to announce the winner.

Example 11-6: Scenery Change

So far, the example scripts have set up interactions between sprites. This project shows you how you can trigger a backdrop change by broadcasting a message from a sprite's script.

Before creating this project, add two backdrops—**desert** and **slopes**—to the Backdrops pane from the Scratch library (see Figure 11-12). You can keep the default **backdrop1** or you can delete it. You'll also need two messages called **message1** and **message2**.

Figure 11-12. *Backdrops*

Select the sprite, and create Script 11-20. The sprite tells a story, and then the script broadcasts **message1** to Script 11-21, which changes the backdrop.

Script 11-20. *Scenery Change: story*

Script 11-20 starts when the user clicks the green flag. The next block creates a speech bubble that displays *It's very hot here. I better change to a colder climate.* for 2 seconds (see Figure 11-13). The next block broadcasts **message1** to trigger Script 11-22 and the backdrop change. The next block moves the sprite to (0, –180) on the stage. The last block of code creates a speech bubble that displays *Much better. I like this climate much better.* for 2 seconds.

Figure 11-13. *Scenery change*

Table 11-20 lists the blocks and describes the actions used in this example.

Table 11-20. *Scenery Change: Story Code Blocks*

Blocks	Actions
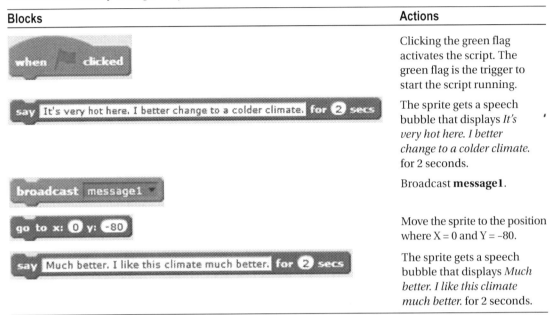	Clicking the green flag activates the script. The green flag is the trigger to start the script running.
	The sprite gets a speech bubble that displays *It's very hot here. I better change to a colder climate.* for 2 seconds.
	Broadcast **message1**.
	Move the sprite to the position where X = 0 and Y = –80.
	The sprite gets a speech bubble that displays *Much better. I like this climate much better.* for 2 seconds.

Now for the backdrops' scripts. Select a backdrop in the Backdrops pane; it doesn't matter which one is showing as a thumbnail, just select one (see Figure 11-14).

Figure 11-14. *Backdrop thumbnail*

Next, create Script 11-21, which sets the starting backdrop for the project.

Script 11-21. *Scenery Change: Desert*

Script 11-21 starts running when the user clicks the green flag. The next block switches the backdrop to **desert**. If the backdrop of the stage is already set to **desert**, then nothing happens.

Table 11-21 lists the blocks and describes the actions used in this example.

Table 11-21. *Scenery Change: Desert Code Blocks*

Blocks	Actions
	Clicking the green flag activates the script. The green flag is the trigger to start the script running.
	Switch the backdrop of the stage area to **desert**.

With the backdrop thumbnail still selected in the Backdrops pane, create Script 11-22 beneath the previous script.

Script 11-22. *Scenery Change: Slopes*

Script 11-22 starts running as soon as it receives **message1** from Script 11-20. The next block switches the backdrop to **slopes**.

Table 11-22 lists the blocks and describes the actions used in this example.

Table 11-22. *Scenery Change: Slopes Code Blocks*

Blocks	Actions
when I receive message1 ▼	Receiving **message1** activates the script.
switch backdrop to slopes ▼	Switch the backdrop of the stage area to **slopes**.

Although this project doesn't illustrate it, a sprite can also receive a message from a backdrop. As an extra challenge, modify this example so that instead of the sprite's script broadcasting a message to the backdrop, the backdrop's script broadcasts a message to the sprite's script to trigger a specific action.

Summary

Now you know how to broadcast messages to trigger scripts. You can make your sprites interact with each other and with backdrops to tell your own stories—with or without user interaction. This is very useful if you want to create a Scratch project that tells a story for a game, movie, or simulation.

You have gathered so much knowledge about Scratch that you can create some great projects. In the next chapter, I will show you how to create your own blocks of code.

Exercises

1. Using the broadcast and receive blocks, create a project that shows two sprites having a conversation with each other.

2. Using the broadcast and receive blocks, create a project that switches backdrops.

CHAPTER 12

Create Your Own Blocks

Congratulations. You have reached the last chapter of this book. You've created a lot of scripts, and we've discussed several ways to make them more efficient. In this chapter, you'll learn another: creating *custom blocks*. The best way to illustrate the power of custom blocks is with an example.

Suppose you want a sprite to jump up and down. That's easy, right? You snap together a sequence of blocks, as shown in Figure 12-1. Now suppose you want several sprites to jump in your project or you frequently write scripts with jumping sprites. Every time, you'd need to go back and forth between categories in the block palette to drag out and snap together these three blocks. Or instead, you could create a custom block called **Jump** (see Figure 12-2) that represents and already includes these three blocks. Save this custom block in the backpack, and then every time you need a sprite to jump, you just snap this one custom block into your script (see Figure 12-3) instead of the three-block sequence.

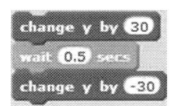

Figure 12-1. Jump script

Figure 12-2. Custom Jump block

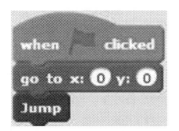

Figure 12-3. Script with custom block

© Eduardo A. Vlieg 2016
E. A. Vlieg, *Scratch by Example*, DOI 10.1007/978-1-4842-1946-1_12

Not only do custom blocks make creating scripts more efficient and faster, but they also make troubleshooting your scripts easier. Because the script is broken down into parts, you can more easily track down and isolate problem areas.

Custom blocks are an example of what high-level languages call *procedures* or *functions*, which are subprograms you can use in other programs. Instead of creating a certain sequence of code every time you need it, you just create it one time by writing a procedure, then call the procedure repeatedly from many other programs. Next, I will show you how to create and use your own custom blocks. After that, you can try out some example scripts that show you different types of custom blocks in action.

Make a Block

To make a custom block, you first create the block itself, and then you define the actions it will perform. To create the block, go to the **More Blocks** category of the block palette (see Figure 12-4) and click the **Make a Block** button (see Figure 12-5).

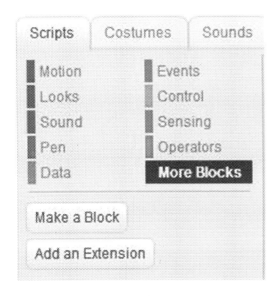

Figure 12-4. *The More Blocks category*

Make a Block

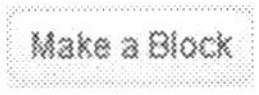

Figure 12-5. *Click Make a Block to begin creating a custom block*

The **New Block** window opens (see Figure 12-6) where you can type a name for the custom block, such as **Jump**, and select any additional options that you require (see Figure 12-7). Click Options to view your choices. The choices are a number input field 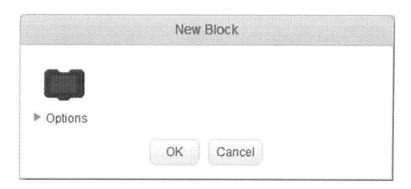, a string input field , or a Boolean input field , as well as a descriptive label, as in .
For example, Figure 12-8 creates a custom block called **Jump** with a number input. The input is given a name, which you can use when instructing other blocks in the custom block's definition script how to use the input. By default, the number input is called **number**. You can always modify the name of the input, whether it is a number, string, or Boolean input. If you change your mind about needing an input option and label, you can delete it by selecting the specified field in the define block and clicking the small **x** in the black circle above the specified field that you want to delete. Once you're done, click the **OK** button to create the custom block.

New Block

▶ Options

OK   Cancel

Figure 12-6. *The New Block window*

New Block

▼ Options

Add number input:

Add string input:

Add boolean input:

Add label text: text

☐ Run without screen refresh

OK   Cancel

Figure 12-7. *Options available for custom blocks*

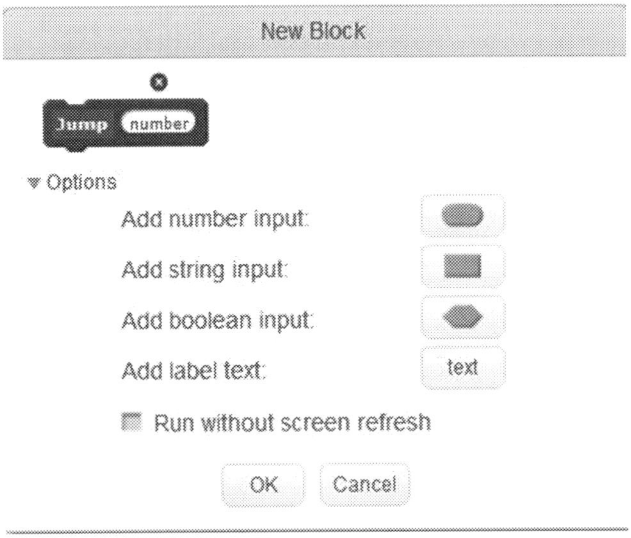

New Block

Jump (number)

▼ Options

Add number input:

Add string input:

Add boolean input:

Add label text: text

☐ Run without screen refresh

OK   Cancel

Figure 12-8. *Creating a block named Jump with a number input*

After you create a custom block, it shows up as a stack type block in the **More Blocks** category below the **Make a Block** button (see Figure 12-9). You use this custom block in your scripts. Because it's a stack type block, you can snap other blocks above and below it. In addition, Scratch creates a new hat block and places it in the scripts area (see Figure 12-10). You'll use this hat block to define the actions the custom block will perform.

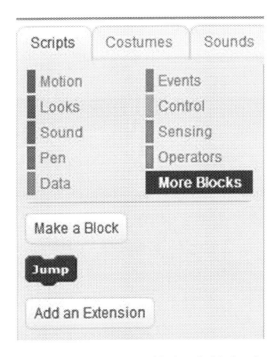

Figure 12-9. *A new custom block in the block palette*

Figure 12-10. *The define block for the new custom block*

Remember, making a custom block consists of two parts. First, you create the block, and then you define it in the scripts area. To define a custom block, snap code blocks to the hat block in the order you want the custom block to execute them when it's activated. For example, drag the three blocks for the jumping script

and snap them below the block, as shown in Figure 12-11. If you want to use this custom block in other projects, be sure to save your definition script in the backpack. To save your custom block in the backpack, just click below the scripts area and open the backpack by clicking the triangle-shaped icon. Drag and drop the definition script into the backpack. If you want to use this custom block in another project, just drag the definition script from the backpack and drop it in the scripts area. If you click the **More Blocks** category, you will see the custom block there.

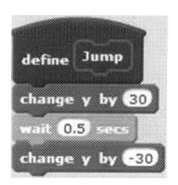

Figure 12-11. *Custom block defined*

Summarizing, you will have two scripts in the scripts area, the definition script (see Figure 12-11) that defines the custom block and the main script that uses the custom block (see Figure 12-3). If the custom block is defined with any input field, then these inputs are passed from the main script in to the definition script.

Let's create some example projects next.

Examples

In the following examples, you will create custom blocks, some with input options and some without, and then put them to work. Remember, you always need have the script that defines the block and the actual script(s) that use the custom block together in the same scripts area.

Example 12-1: Jump

In this example, you'll create a single block of code that makes the sprite jump. First, as discussed in the previous section, go to the **More Blocks** category of the block palette and click **Make a Block** to create a new

block called **Jump**. The block appears in the scripts area.

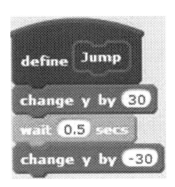

Script 12-1. *Define Jump*

Define the Jump block, by snapping the three blocks shown in Script 12-1 to the [define Jump] block. The first of the three adds 30 to the current Y coordinate of the sprite to raise its position. The next block pauses the script for 0.5 seconds. The last block of code subtracts 30 from the current Y coordinate of the sprite to lower its position.

So, when you use the [Jump] block in a script, it makes the sprite move up and then back down.

Table 12-1 lists the blocks and describes the actions used in this example.

Table 12-1. *Code Blocks in Define Jump*

Blocks	Actions
define Jump	The hat block that defines the block called **Jump**.
change y by 30	Add 30 to the current Y coordinate of the sprite and move it to that new Y coordinate.
wait 0.5 secs	The script waits 0.5 seconds. No actions are performed for 0.5 seconds.
change y by -30	Subtract 30 from the current Y coordinate of the sprite and move it to that new Y coordinate.

Now that the new  block is defined, you are ready to use it in a script.

Script 12-2. *Jump*

Script 12-2 starts running when the user clicks the green flag. The next block of code moves the sprite to the center of the stage. The last block of code makes the sprite move up and back down. Notice that creating your own blocks makes the script shorter. By creating the Jump block, you condensed three blocks of code to just one.

Table 12-2 lists the blocks and describes the actions used in this example.

Table 12-2. *Code Blocks in Jump*

Blocks	Actions
	Clicking the green flag activates the script. The green flag is the trigger to start the script running.
	Move the sprite to coordinates (X = 0, Y = 0), which is the middle of the stage.
	Execute the **Jump** block and make the sprite move up and back down.

Example 12-2: Jump Number Input

This example builds on the previous example by creating a new block and adding a number input field to it. When run, this project asks the user how many times the sprite should jump. The sprite then jumps the requested number of times.

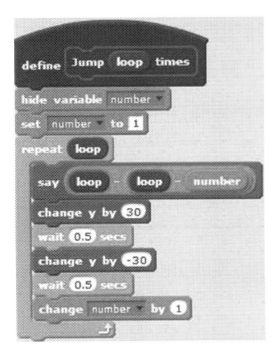

Script 12-3. *Define Jump number input*

Before defining the new block (Script 12-3), you need to create a new block called **Jump** and you need to add a number input (*loop*) and a text label (*times*) to it. You also need to create a variable called **number**. You don't need to create the custom block from scratch. You can modify the previous custom block from Example 12-1. Just right-click the custom block in the **More Blocks** category and select **edit** to open the Edit Block window (see Figure 12-12) Select **Options**, click the number input icon to add the number input field. Click the **OK** button to finish.

```
Edit Block

      ⊗
  Jump (loop) times

▼ Options
        Add number input:      ⬭
        Add string input:       ▭
        Add boolean input:      ⬖
        Add label text:        text
        ☐ Run without screen refresh

              OK    Cancel
```

Figure 12-12. *Jump number input*

After you have created this new block, you'll need to define it. The first block after the **define** block hides the reporter window of the variable called **number** from the stage. The next block assigns the value 1

to the **number** variable. Next, there is a block, which you want to repeat the number of

times specified in the main program and passed to the block via its input. To specify this,

drag the block from into the input field of the

 block. The block then repeats the sequence of actions within it the amount of times that is passed into the block from the script that contains the custom block. The first block in the sequence is a combination block, which is created by embedding a number of blocks within each other. This block creates a speech bubble and displays the result of this

equation . Take note that the inner subtraction operator

block is executed first. Also note that through each repeat of the sequence of

actions, the value of the number input stays the same, but the value of the variable changes. This will make the sprite count up. The next block adds 30 to the current Y coordinate of the sprite and moves the sprite to that new position. The next block pauses the script for 0.5 seconds. The next block subtracts 30 from the current Y coordinate of the sprite and moves the sprite to that new position. The last two blocks pause the script for 0.5 seconds and add 1 to the current value of the **number** variable.

Table 12-3 lists the blocks and describes the actions used in this example.

Table 12-3. Code Blocks in Define Jump Number Input

Blocks	Actions
	The hat block that defines the block called **Jump times**.
	Hide the specified variable's (**number**) monitor from the stage area.
	Set the current value of the **number** variable to 1.
	Repeat the actions represented by the blocks within this block a certain number of times.

(continued)

Table 12-3. (*continued*)

Blocks	Actions
loop	The block that represents the inputted number.
say ▢	The sprite gets a speech bubble and displays the specified text.
◯-◯	Subtract one value from another and report the result.
loop	The block that represents the inputted number.
◯-◯	Subtract one value from another and report the result.
loop	The block that represents the inputted number.
number	Hold and report the current value of the **number** variable.
change y by 30	Add 30 to the current value of the Y coordinate and move the sprite to that new Y coordinate.
wait 0.5 secs	The script waits 0.5 seconds. No actions are performed for 0.5 seconds.
change y by -30	Subtract 30 to the current value of the Y coordinate and move the sprite to that new Y coordinate.
wait 0.5 secs	The script waits 0.5 seconds. No actions are performed for 0.5 seconds.
change number by 1	Add 1 to the current value of the **number** variable.

Now that you have defined the new block, it's time to create a script that uses the new block.

Script 12-4 starts running when the user clicks the green flag. The next block of code moves the sprite to the center of the stage. The next block creates a speech bubble that displays the text *How many times do you want me to jump up and down?*, opens a user input field, and waits for the user's input. The next block creates a speech bubble for 2 seconds and displays *OK, I will jump up and down*, the value of the user input held in ⬤answer , and *times*. The last block calls up the custom block ⬤Jump ◯ times and passes the value in ⬤answer to it. The custom block holds the value from ⬤answer in ⬤loop and uses it to instruct the sprite to jump the number of times that the user requested.

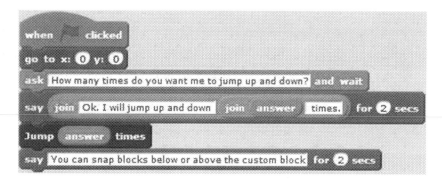

when [flag] clicked
go to x: 0 y: 0
ask How many times do you want me to jump up and down? and wait
say join Ok. I will jump up and down join answer times. for 2 secs
Jump answer times
say You can snap blocks below or above the custom block for 2 secs

Script 12-4. *Jump number input*

You know now how to create a custom block with a number input. Do you remember the backpack? You

define Jump loop times

can drag and drop the   block's definition script into the backpack and use it in other projects.

Table 12-4 lists the blocks and describes the actions used in this example.

Table 12-4. *Code Blocks in Jump Number Input*

Blocks	Actions
when [flag] clicked	Clicking the green flag activates the script. The green flag is the trigger to start the script running.
go to x: 0 y: 0	Move the sprite to coordinates (X = 0, Y = 0), which is the middle of the stage.
ask How many times do you want me to jump up and down? and wait	The sprite gets a speech bubble that displays *How many times do you want me to jump up and down?*, opens a user input field, and waits for user input.
say ▢ for 2 secs	The sprite gets a speech bubble that displays the specified text or value for 2 seconds.
join Ok. I will jump up and down ▢	Join the two values that have been specified in the block and report the result.

(continued)

Table 12-4. (*continued*)

Blocks	Actions
join ▢ times,	Join the two values that have been specified in the block and report the result.
answer	Hold and report the current user input value.
Jump ◯ times	Execute the **Jump times** block and make the sprite jump the specified number of times.
answer	Hold and report the current user input value.
say You can snap blocks below or above the custom block for 2 secs	The sprite gets a speech bubble that displays *You can snap blocks below or above the custom block* for 2 seconds.

Example 12-3: Rotate Number Input

The cat has had enough jumping. Instead, take it for a spin with a custom block that makes the sprite rotate a number of degrees that is specified by the user. This is another example that shows how creating a custom block with a number input can reduce many blocks of code to just one custom block. As before, the first step is to create the new block; this time, call it **Rotate**, name the number input **amount**, and add *degrees back and forth.* as the label.

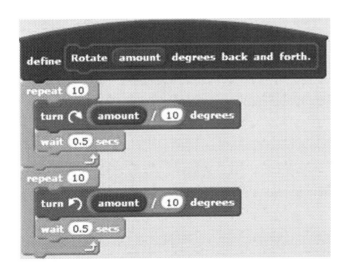

Script 12-5. *Define Rotate number input*

Underneath the 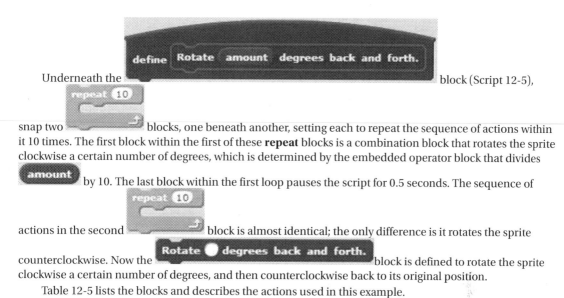 block (Script 12-5),

snap two blocks, one beneath another, setting each to repeat the sequence of actions within it 10 times. The first block within the first of these **repeat** blocks is a combination block that rotates the sprite clockwise a certain number of degrees, which is determined by the embedded operator block that divides

amount by 10. The last block within the first loop pauses the script for 0.5 seconds. The sequence of

actions in the second block is almost identical; the only difference is it rotates the sprite

counterclockwise. Now the **Rotate ◯ degrees back and forth.** block is defined to rotate the sprite clockwise a certain number of degrees, and then counterclockwise back to its original position.

Table 12-5 lists the blocks and describes the actions used in this example.

Table 12-5. *Code Blocks in Define Rotate Number Input*

Blocks	Actions
define Rotate amount degrees back and forth.	The hat block that defines the block called **Rotate degrees back and forth.**
repeat 10	Repeat the actions represented by the blocks within this block ten times.
turn ↻ ◯ degrees	Turn the sprite clockwise a specified number of degrees.
◯ / 10	Divide one value by another and report the result.
amount	The block that represents the inputted amount.
wait 0.5 secs	The script waits 0.5 seconds. No actions are performed for 0.5 seconds.
repeat 10	Repeat the actions represented by the blocks within this block ten times.

(continued)

Table 12-5. (*continued*)

Blocks	Actions
turn ↺ ◯ degrees	Turn the sprite counterclockwise a specified number of degrees.
◯ / 10	Divide one value by another and report the result.
amount	The block that represents the inputted amount.
wait 0.5 secs	The script waits 0.5 seconds. No actions are performed for 0.5 seconds.

Let's create a script that uses this new custom block that makes the sprite rotate back and forth.

Script 12-6 activates when the user clicks the green flag. The next three blocks of code, make the sprite face to the right, move the sprite to the center of the stage, and set its rotation style to **all around**. The next block creates a speech bubble that displays the text *How many degrees do you want me to rotate back and forth?*, opens a user input field, and waits for the user's input. The next block creates a speech bubble for 2 seconds and displays *OK, I will rotate*, the value of the user input, and the text *degrees back and forth..* The last block calls the new custom block and passes it the value in **answer** to instruct the sprite to rotate back and forth the amount of degrees requested by the user.

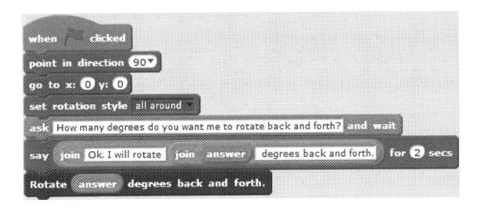

Script 12-6. *Rotate number input*

Table 12-6 lists the blocks and describes the actions used in this example.

Table 12-6. *Code Blocks in Rotate Number Input*

Blocks	Actions
`when clicked`	Clicking the green flag activates the script. The green flag is the trigger to start the script running.
`point in direction 90▼`	Point the direction of the sprite to the right.
`go to x: 0 y: 0`	Move the sprite to coordinates (X = 0, Y = 0), which is the middle of the stage.
`set rotation style all around ▼`	Set the rotation style of the sprite, so it can rotate all around its axis.
`ask How many degrees do you want me to rotate back and forth? and wait`	The sprite gets a speech bubble that displays *How many degrees do you want me to rotate back and forth?*, opens a user input field, and waits for user input.
`say ▯ for 2 secs`	The sprite gets a speech bubble that displays the specified text or value for 2 seconds.
`join Ok. I will rotate ▯`	Join the two values that have been specified in the block and report the result.
`join ▯ degrees back and forth.`	Join the two values that have been specified in the block and report the result.
`answer`	Hold and report the current user input value.
`Rotate ◯ degrees back and forth.`	Execute the **Rotate degrees back and forth** block and make the sprite rotate a specified number of degrees back and forth.
`answer`	Hold and report the current user input value.

Example 12-4: Jump String Input

Creating and using a custom block with a string input is just as easy as adding one with a number input. In this example, the user is asked whether the sprite should jump. Depending whether the user answers, the sprite will jump or not. Start by creating the new custom block called **Jump?**. Add a string input by clicking the appropriate button in the Options area. You can keep the default name of *string1* for the input (see Figure 12-13).

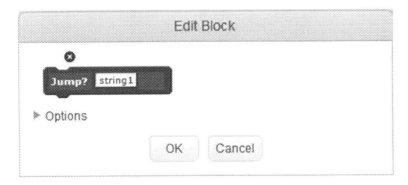

Figure 12-13. *Jump string input*

After you click the **OK** button to create the custom block, the 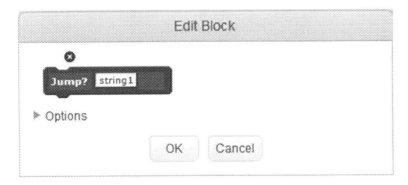 block should appear in the scripts area. Now snap the blocks shown in Script 12-7 to it to define your new block.

Script 12-7. *Define Jump string input*

The first block in the definition is an If/Then/Else conditional statement that first evaluates whether the user input is equal to the string *yes*. To set up this conditional statement, drag the **string1** block, which will hold the user input passed into it. From the **define Jump? string1** block, drop in at the left field of the **= yes** block, and enter **yes** in the right field. Notice that there will still be a copy of **string1** in the **define Jump? string1** block. Finally, embed the whole thing in the **if then else** block. If the condition evaluates true, then Scratch executes the sequence of blocks in the Then section. The first block creates a speech bubble for 2 seconds and displays *OK, I'll jump!*. The next block adds 30 to the current Y coordinate of the sprite and moves the sprite to that position. The third block pauses the script for 0.5 seconds. The last block in the sequence subtracts 30 from the current Y coordinate of the sprite and moves the sprite to that position. If the condition evaluates to false (the user input something other than *yes*), Scratch skips to the block in the Else section and creates a speech bubble for 2 seconds that displays *OK, I won't jump!*.

Table 12-7 lists the blocks and describes the actions used in this example.

Table 12-7. *Code Blocks in Jump Define String Input*

Blocks	Actions
define Jump? string1	The hat block that defines the block called **Jump?**.
if then else	Check if the condition is true. If the condition is true, execute the actions within it, before the word *else*. If the condition is false, execute the actions after the word *else* within the block.
= yes	If the value on the left side is equal to yes, then this condition is true; otherwise, the condition is false.
string1	The block that represents the user input (string).
say Ok, I'll jump! for 2 secs	The sprite gets a speech bubble that displays *OK, I'll jump!* for 2 seconds.
change y by 30	Add 30 to the current value of the Y coordinate and move the sprite to that new Y coordinate.
wait 0.5 secs	The script waits 0.5 seconds. No actions are performed for 0.5 seconds.
change y by -30	Subtract 30 to the current value of the Y coordinate and move the sprite to that new Y coordinate.
say Ok, I won't jump! for 2 secs	The sprite gets a speech bubble that displays *OK, I won't jump!* for 2 seconds.

317

With the custom block defined, you can use it in a script.

Script 12-8 starts running when the user clicks the green flag. The next two blocks move the sprite to the middle of the stage and make it face to the right. The next block creates a speech bubble that displays the text *Do you want me to jump? Enter yes or no*, opens a user input field, and waits for the user's input. The next

block calls the custom block by passing the user input held in 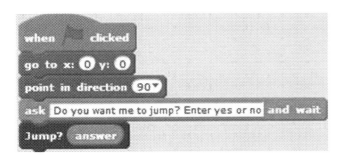 to it.

Script 12-8. *Jump string input*

Table 12-8 lists the blocks and describes the actions used in this example.

Table 12-8. *Code Blocks in Jump String Input*

Blocks	Actions
when ⚑ clicked	Clicking the green flag activates the script. The green flag is the trigger to start the script running.
go to x: 0 y: 0	Move the sprite to coordinates (X = 0, Y = 0), which is the middle of the stage.
point in direction 90▾	Point the direction of the sprite to the right.
ask Do you want me to jump? Enter yes or no and wait	The sprite gets a speech bubble that displays *Do you want me to jump? Enter yes or no*, opens a user input field, and waits for user input.
Jump? ☐	Execute the **Jump?** block and make the sprite jump if the condition is true.
answer	Hold and report the current user input value.

318

Example 12-5: Jump Boolean Input

The last option to try is Boolean input for a custom block. Create a custom block called **test** and add a Boolean input to it. You can use the default name of *boolean1* for the value passed into the block (see Figure 12-14).

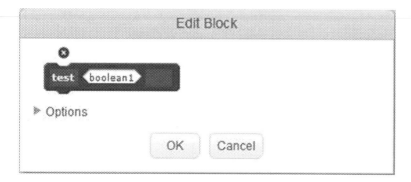

Figure 12-14. *Boolean input test*

Click **OK** to create the custom block and add the hat block ![define test boolean1] to the scripts area.

To define your new custom block, snap together the blocks of code shown in Script 12-9. The first block is an ![if then] block that receives the result of a condition that is passed into it from the main script. Currently, the result of this condition is represented by the ![boolean1] block. The result is a value that is either true or false. Simply drag this block from the ![define test boolean1] block and drop it in the If/Then conditional statement. If ![boolean1] is true, then Scratch performs the sequence of actions within the repeat block. First, it creates a speech bubble that displays *OK, I'll jump.* for 2 seconds. The next blocks add 30 to the current Y coordinate of the sprite to move it to the new position, pause the script for 0.5 seconds, and subtract 30 from the current Y coordinate of the sprite to move it to that new position. If the condition is false, nothing happens.

319

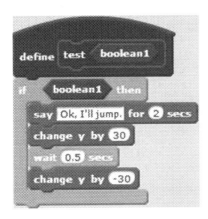

Script 12-9. *Define Jump Boolean input*

Table 12-9 lists the blocks and describes the actions used in this example.

Table 12-9. *Code Blocks in Define Jump Boolean Input*

Blocks	Actions
define test boolean1	The hat block that defines the block called **test**.
if ___ then	Check if the condition is true. If the condition is true, execute the actions within it. If the condition is false, skip to the next block.
boolean1	The block that represents the Boolean condition.
say Ok, I'll jump. for 2 secs	The sprite gets a speech bubble that displays *OK, I'll jump.* for 2 seconds.
change y by 30	Add 30 to the current value of the Y coordinate and move the sprite to that new Y coordinate.
wait 0.5 secs	The script waits 0.5 seconds. No actions are performed for 0.5 seconds.
change y by -30	Subtract 30 to the current value of the Y coordinate and move the sprite to that new Y coordinate.

Let's use the newly define custom block in a script.

Script 12-10 starts running when the user clicks the green flag. The next two blocks move the sprite to the middle of the stage and make the sprite face to the right. The next block creates a speech bubble that displays the text *Do you want me to jump? Enter yes or no*, opens a user input field, and waits for the user's input. The next block passes the result of the condition (true or false) to the custom block. The custom block executes the actions defined for it if the condition is true. If the condition is false, nothing happens and the script ends.

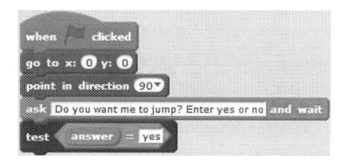

Script 12-10. *Jump Boolean input*

Save this custom block in the backpack if you want to use it later in other future projects.
Table 12-10 lists the blocks and describes the actions used in this example.

Table 12-10. *Code Blocks in Jump Boolean Input*

Blocks	Actions
when clicked	Clicking the green flag activates the script. The green flag is the trigger to start the script running.
go to x: 0 y: 0	Move the sprite to coordinates (X = 0, Y = 0), which is the middle of the stage.
point in direction 90▾	Point the direction of the sprite to the right.
ask Do you want me to jump? Enter yes or no and wait	The sprite gets a speech bubble that displays *Do you want me to jump? Enter yes or no*, opens a user input field, and waits for user input.
test	Execute the **test** block and test if the condition is true. If the condition is true, execute the actions defined in the custom block.
☐ = yes	If the value on the left side is equal to yes, then this condition is true; otherwise, the condition is false.
answer	Hold and report the current user input value.

Summary

Well done. You now know how to create custom blocks in Scratch. Custom blocks are handy, because you can save them in the backpack and reuse them in other projects. Not only do they streamline your scripts by condensing multiple blocks into a single block, they also save you time by enabling you to quickly add frequently used sequences as a single block. After successfully running the scripts in this chapter's examples, and understanding how they work, you can modify the scripts in the examples and create your own project.

This chapter also marks the end of your Scratch lessons, but don't let it stop you from learning. Keep practicing and creating your own projects.

Whether you want to continue with other computer programming languages or your interests lie somewhere else, learning Scratch was worth it. Besides learning about how to program a computer, you learned a new way of thinking when it comes to problem solving. You learned how to break down a larger problem and solve it in small parts. You also learned how to solve problem sequentially.

Congratulations, and have fun creating Scratch projects.

Exercises

1.   Create a new block that makes the sprite face left and right. Create a script and use this new block.

2.   Create a new block that makes the sprite move along the stage and change costumes while moving. Create a script and use this new block.

CHAPTER 13

■ ■ ■

Answers

This chapter has all the answers to the chapter exercises. Remember, usually there's more than one way to produce the same result. So your script doesn't have to look exactly the same as the ones in this chapter. What's important is that it produces the same result. Scripts may be different but produce the same result because there are many ways to produce the same result. For example, there are many ways to make the sprite move. Remember that you can create a very long script, but you can also use repeat blocks to make the script shorter and more efficient. Loops, variables, lists, and custom blocks all help you create a shorter and more efficient script.

Chapter 3: Make the Cat Move

Exercise 1

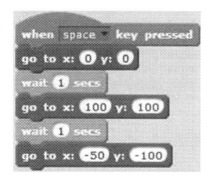

Script 13-1. Move

This script moves the sprite to three different positions, (0, 0), (100, 100), and (-50, -100). It starts running when the user presses the space bar. The next block of code moves the sprite to the position with coordinates (0, 0). The next block pauses the script for 1 second. The  block moves the sprite to the position with coordinates (100, 100). The next block pauses the sprite for 1 second again. The last block moves the sprite to the position with coordinates (-50, -100).

© Eduardo A. Vlieg 2016
E. A. Vlieg, *Scratch by Example*, DOI 10.1007/978-1-4842-1946-1_13

Table 13-1 lists the blocks and describes the actions used in this example.

Table 13-1. *Code Blocks in Move*

Blocks	Actions
when space key pressed	Pressing the space bar activates the script. The space bar is the trigger to start the script running.
go to x: 0 y: 0	Move the sprite to the position where X = 0 and Y = 0.
wait 1 secs	The script waits 1 second. No actions are performed for 1 second.
go to x: 100 y: 100	Move the sprite to the position where X = 100 and Y = 100.
wait 1 secs	The script waits 1 second. No actions are performed for 1 second.
go to x: -50 y: -100	Move the sprite to the position where X = –50 and Y = –100.

Exercise 2

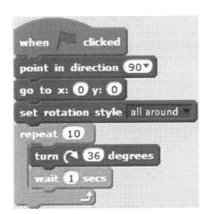

Script 13-2. *Rotate*

This script rotates the sprite 360 degrees on its axis. The script starts running when the user clicks the green flag. The next block makes the sprite face to the right. The block moves the sprite to the center of the stage where the coordinates are (0, 0). The next block sets the rotation style of the sprite to

all around. This means that the sprite will be able to rotate 360 degrees. Next the block repeats the sequence of actions within it, 10 times. The first block in that sequence rotates the sprite 36 degrees clockwise. The next block within it block pauses the script for 1 second.

Table 13-2 lists the blocks and describes the actions used in this example.

Table 13-2. *Code Blocks in Rotate*

Blocks	Actions
	Clicking the green flag activates the script. The green flag is the trigger to start the script running.
	Make the sprite face to the right.
	Move the sprite to the position where X = 0 and Y = 0.
	Set the rotation style of the sprite, so it can rotate all around its axis.
	Repeat the actions represented by the blocks within this block ten times.
	Turn the sprite clockwise 36 degrees.
	The script waits 1 second. No actions are performed for 1 second.

Chapter 4: Make the Cat Draw

Exercise 1

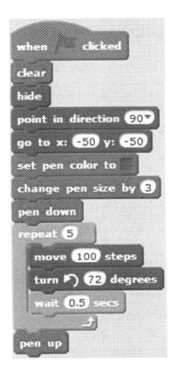

Script 13-3. *Pentagon*

This script draws a pentagon on the stage. It starts running when the user clicks the green flag. The second

block clears the stage by removing all marks made by the pen or stamp. The **hide** block makes the sprite disappear from the stage. The next two blocks make the sprite face to the right, and then move it to position (–50, –50). The next block sets the pen color to blue and the block of code after that changes the pen size to 3, meaning that the width of the line the pen makes is 3 pixels wide. The **pen down** block means that the

pen is on the stage and ready to start drawing. The **repeat 5** block repeats the sequence of actions within it 5 times: move the sprite 100 pixels in the direction that it's facing, turn the sprite 72 degrees

counterclockwise and pause the script for 0.5 seconds. The last block after the loop is **pen up**, which indicates the pen is done drawing. If the sprite moves after this block, the pen will not draw a trail.

Table 13-3 lists the blocks and describes the actions used in this example.

Table 13-3. *Code Blocks in Pentagon*

Blocks	Actions
when ▔ clicked	Clicking the green flag activates the script. The green flag is the trigger to start the script running.
clear	Remove all marks previously made by the pen or stamp.
hide	Make the sprite disappear from the stage.
point in direction 90▾	Make the sprite face to the right.
go to x: -50 y: -50	Move the sprite to the position where X = –50 and Y = –50.
set pen color to ▨	Set the pen color to blue.
change pen size by 3	Change the pen size to 3.
pen down	The pen is on the stage and is ready to draw.
repeat 5	Repeat the actions represented by the blocks within this block five times.
move 100 steps	Move the sprite 100 pixels in the direction that it's facing.
turn ↺ 72 degrees	Turn the sprite counterclockwise 72 degrees.
wait 0.5 secs	The script waits 0.5 seconds. No actions are performed for 0.5 seconds.
pen up	The pen is off the stage and cannot draw.

Exercise 2

Script 13-4. *Three squares*

This script draws three squares of equal size but different colors side by side on the stage. It starts running when the user clicks the green flag. The next block clears the stage by removing all marks made by the pen or stamp. The third block makes the sprite disappear from the stage, and the fourth makes the sprite face to the right. The next block moves the sprite to position (–200, –150). The next two blocks set the pen color to blue,

and then change the pen size to 3. Next is a block that repeats the sequence of actions within

it 3 times. The first block within it is a block, which then repeats the sequence of actions within it 4 times: the sequence of blocks within the inner loop puts the pen on the stage so it's ready to draw, moves the sprite 100 pixels in the direction that it's facing, turns the sprite 90 degrees counterclockwise, and pauses the script for 0.5 seconds. After this loop repeats 4 times, the outer loop continues to the next block in its sequence, which changes the pen color by 30. The subsequent two blocks lift the pen from the stage and move the sprite 150 pixels in the direction that it's facing. Then the entire outer loop repeats twice more.

Table 13-4 lists the blocks and describes the actions used in this example.

Table 13-4. *Code Blocks in Three Squares*

Blocks	Actions
when ▭ clicked	Clicking the green flag activates the script. The green flag is the trigger to start the script running.
clear	Remove all marks previously made by the pen or stamp.
hide	Make the sprite disappear from the stage.
point in direction 90▾	Make the sprite face to the right.
go to x: -200 y: -150	Move the sprite to the position where X = –200 and Y = –150.
set pen color to ▯	Set the pen color to blue.
change pen size by 3	Change the pen size to 3.
repeat 3	Repeat the actions represented by the blocks within this block three times.
repeat 4	Repeat the actions represented by the blocks within this block four times.
pen down	The pen is on the stage and is ready to draw.
move 100 steps	Move the sprite 100 pixels in the direction that it's facing.
turn ↻ 90 degrees	Turn the sprite counterclockwise 90 degrees.
wait 0.5 secs	The script waits 0.5 seconds. No actions are performed for 0.5 seconds.
change pen color by 30	Set the pen color to 30.
pen up	The pen is off the stage and cannot draw.
move 150 steps	Move the sprite 150 pixels in the direction that it's facing.

Chapter 5: The Playful Cat

Exercise 1

Script 13-5. *Change custom*

This script makes the sprite move across the stage back and forth while changing costumes. This gives the illusion as if the sprite is walking. The script starts running when the user presses the space bar. The next block of code moves the sprite to the center of the stage, which is at coordinates (0, 0). The next block of code

makes the sprite face to the right. The next block sets the rotation style to **left-right**. The block repeats the sequence of actions within it forever until the script is manually stopped. The first three blocks in the sequence move the sprite 10 pixels in the direction that it's facing, change the sprite to the next costume, and then pause the script for 0.2 seconds. The last block in the sequence instructs the sprite that if it should reach any edge of the stage, it should bounce and travel in the opposite direction.

Table 13-5 lists the blocks and describes the actions used in this example.

Table 13-5. *Code Blocks in Change Custom*

Blocks	Actions
when space key pressed	Pressing the space bar activates the script. The space bar is the trigger to start the script running.
go to x: 0 y: 0	Move the sprite to the position where X = 0 and Y = 0.
point in direction 90▾	Make the sprite face to the right.
set rotation style left-right ▾	Set the rotation style of the sprite, so it can only turn left or right.
forever	The actions within the forever block is repeated forever, or until the script is stopped manually.
move 10 steps	Move the sprite 10 pixels in the direction that it's facing.
next costume	Change the sprite to the next costume in the costumes tab.
wait 0.2 secs	The script waits 0.2 seconds. No actions are performed for 0.2 seconds.
if on edge, bounce	If the sprite reaches the edge of the stage, bounce in the opposite direction.

Exercise 2

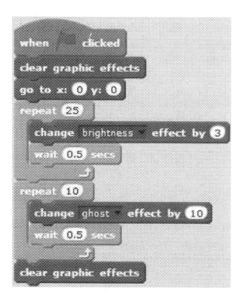

Script 13-6. *Brightness effect*

The script applies the brightness effect to the sprite, causing it to get brighter. Next, the script applies the ghost effect, causing the sprite to disappear completely from the stage. At the end, the sprite reappears on the stage.

The script starts running when the user clicks the green flag. The second block resets all previous graphic effects, so that the sprite will return to its original state. The third moves the sprite to the center of

the stage, which is at (0, 0). The ____ block then repeats the sequence of actions within it 25 times. The first block in the sequence changes the brightness of the sprite by 3, then pauses 0.5 seconds. Each time through the loop, the sprite gets brighter. After 25 repeats, the action moves to the next block in

the script, which is also a ____ block, this time that repeats the sequence of actions within it 10 times. The sequence changes the ghost effect of the sprite by 10, and then pauses the script by 0.5 seconds. Each time through this loop, the sprite disappears more. After the last repeat completes, the final block of this script resets all previous graphic effects and returns the sprite to its original state.

Table 13-6 lists the blocks and describes the actions used in this example.

Table 13-6. Code Blocks in Brightness Effect

Blocks	Actions
when clicked	Clicking the green flag activates the script. The green flag is the trigger to start the script running.
clear graphic effects	Reset all graphic effects on the sprite. It will return the sprite to its original state before any graphic effects were applied to it.
go to x: 0 y: 0	Move the sprite to the position where X = 0 and Y = 0.
repeat 25	Repeat the actions represented by the blocks within this block twenty five times.
change brightness effect by 3	Change the brightness of the sprite by the amount of 3.
wait 0.5 secs	The script waits 0.5 second. No actions are performed for 0.5 second.
repeat 10	Repeat the actions represented by the blocks within this block ten times.
change ghost effect by 10	Change the ghost effect of the sprite by the amount of 10.
wait 0.5 secs	The script waits 0.5 second. No actions are performed for 0.5 second.
clear graphic effects	Reset all graphic effects on the sprite. It will return the sprite to its original state before any graphic effects were applied to it.

Chapter 6: The Noisy Cat

Exercise 1

Script 13-7. *Bird sound*

The script plays the **bird** sound but decreases the volume each time until the volume is all the way down and you can't hear the sound anymore.

Before creating the script, you need to select the bird sound from the Scratch library.

The script starts running when the user clicks the green flag. The next block turns the volume all the

way up. The [repeat 10] block executes the sequence of actions within it 10 times: it plays the **bird** sound, and then decreases the volume by 10%.

Table 13-7 lists the blocks and describes the actions used in this example.

Table 13-7. *Code Blocks in Bird Sound*

Blocks	Actions
when clicked	Clicking the green flag activates the script. The green flag is the trigger to start the script running.
set volume to 100 %	Turn the volume all the way up.
repeat 10	Repeat the actions represented by the blocks within this block ten times.
play sound bird	Play the sound **bird**.
change volume by -10	Decrease the volume by 10%.

Exercise 2

Script 13-8. *Music instruments*

The script selects the piano as the instrument, plays the notes, C, D, and E before pausing, and then plays E, D, and C.

The script starts running when the user clicks the green flag. The next block sets the volume to 100%. The next block selects the piano as the instrument to be played. The next three blocks play the notes, C, D, and E in sequence for 0.5 beats each. The next block pauses the script for 0.2 seconds. The next three blocks play the notes, E, D, and C in sequence, each for 0.5 seconds.

Table 13-8 lists the blocks and describes the actions used in this example.

Table 13-8. *Code Blocks in Music Instruments*

Blocks	Actions
when clicked	Clicking the green flag activates the script. The green flag is the trigger to start the script running.
set volume to 100 %	Turn the volume all the way up.
set instrument to 1	Select piano as instrument.
play note 60 for 0.5 beats	Play note middle C for 0.5 beats.
play note 62 for 0.5 beats	Play note D for 0.5 beats.

(continued)

Table 13-8. (*continued*)

Blocks	Actions
play note 64▾ for 0.5 beats	Play note E for 0.5 beats.
set instrument to 8▾	Select cello as instrument.
wait 0.2 secs	The script waits 0.2 second. No actions are performed for 0.2 second.
play note 64▾ for 0.5 beats	Play note E for 0.5 beats.
play note 62▾ for 0.5 beats	Play note D for 0.5 beats.
play note 60▾ for 0.5 beats	Play note middle C for 0.5 beats.

Chapter 7: Advanced Concepts

Exercise 1

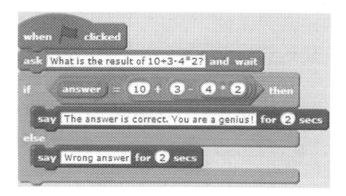

Script 13-9. *Math test*

The script asks the user to solve an equation, and then displays a different speech bubble depending on whether the user's answer is correct or not.

The script starts running when the user clicks the green flag. The second block of code creates a speech bubble that displays *What is the result of 10 + 3 – 4 * 2?*, opens a user input field, and waits for the user's input. The next block is an If/The/Else conditional statement that evaluates an embedded condition. The condition tests whether the user's input, which is held in **answer**, is equal to the result of the equation, 10 + 3 – 4 * 2. If the condition is true, the block in the Then portion is executed, which creates a speech bubble that displays *The answer is correct. You are a genius!* for 2 seconds. If the condition is false, the block in the Else portion is executed, which creates a speech bubble that displays *Wrong answer* for 2 seconds.

Table 13-9 lists the blocks and describes the actions used in this example.

Table 13-9. *Code Blocks in Math Test*

Blocks	Actions
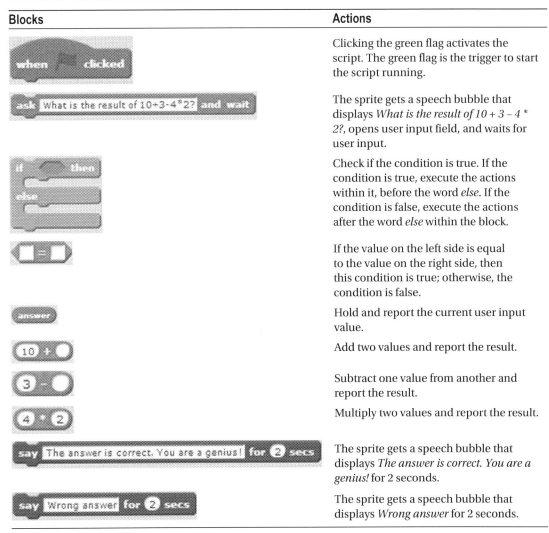	Clicking the green flag activates the script. The green flag is the trigger to start the script running.
	The sprite gets a speech bubble that displays *What is the result of 10 + 3 – 4 * 2?*, opens user input field, and waits for user input.
	Check if the condition is true. If the condition is true, execute the actions within it, before the word *else*. If the condition is false, execute the actions after the word *else* within the block.
	If the value on the left side is equal to the value on the right side, then this condition is true; otherwise, the condition is false.
	Hold and report the current user input value.
	Add two values and report the result.
	Subtract one value from another and report the result.
	Multiply two values and report the result.
	The sprite gets a speech bubble that displays *The answer is correct. You are a genius!* for 2 seconds.
	The sprite gets a speech bubble that displays *Wrong answer* for 2 seconds.

Exercise 2

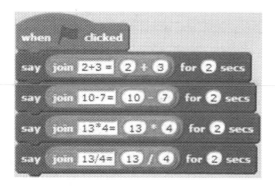

Script 13-10. Math lesson

This script displays four equations paired with their results for 2 seconds each. It script starts running when the user clicks the green flag. The second block of code creates a speech bubble for the sprite that displays 2 + 3 = 5 followed by the result of the equation 2 + 3 for 2 seconds. The third block of code creates a speech bubble that displays the text is 10 – 7 = 3 followed by the result of the equation 10 – 7 for 2 seconds. The third block of code creates a speech bubble that displays 13 * 4 = 52 followed by the result of the equation 13 * 4 for 2 seconds. The last block of code creates a speech bubble that displays 13 / 4 = 3.25 followed by the result of the equation 13 / 4 for 2 seconds.

Table 13-10 lists the blocks and describes the actions used in this example.

Table 13-10. Code Blocks in Math Lesson

Blocks	Actions
when clicked	Clicking the green flag activates the script. The green flag is the trigger to start the script running.
say ☐ for 2 secs	The sprite gets a speech bubble that displays the specified text or value for 2 seconds.
join 2+3 = ☐	Join the two values or that have been specified in the block and report the result.
2 + 3	Add two values (2 + 3) and report the result.
say ☐ for 2 secs	The sprite gets a speech bubble that displays the specified text or value for 2 seconds.
join 10-7= ☐	Join the two values that have been specified in the block and report the result.
10 – 7	Subtract one value from another (10 – 7) and report the result.
say ☐ for 2 secs	The sprite gets a speech bubble that displays the specified text or value for 2 seconds.

(continued)

Table 13-10. (*continued*)

Blocks	Actions
join 13*4=	Join the two values that have been specified in the block and report the result.
13 * 4	Multiply two values (13 * 4) and report the result.
say ▢ for 2 secs	The sprite gets a speech bubble that displays the specified text or value for 2 seconds.
join 13/4=	Join the two values that have been specified in the block and report the result.
13 / 4	Divide one value by another (13 / 4) and report the result.

Chapter 8: Variables

Exercise 1

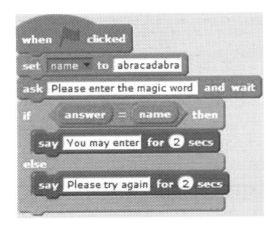

Script 13-11. *Authentication*

The script asks the user for the magic word. If the user answers correctly, the scripts displays *You may enter*; otherwise, the script displays *Please try again*.

The first step is to create a variable called **name** to hold the "magic word." This script starts running when the user clicks the green flag. The next block of code assigns the value *abracadabra* to the **name** variable. The next block creates a speech bubble that displays *Please enter the magic word*, opens a user input field, and waits for the user's input.

Next, there is an [if/then/else] block that evaluates the embedded condition, which tests whether the user input is equal to the current value of the **name** variable. If the condition is true, the Then portion executes and creates a speech bubble for the sprite that displays *You may enter* for 2 seconds. If the condition is false, then the Else portion of the block gets executed, which creates a speech bubble that displays the text *Please try again* for 2 seconds.

Table 13-11 lists the blocks and describes the actions used in this example.

Table 13-11. *Code Blocks in Authentication*

Blocks	Actions
when clicked	Clicking the green flag activates the script. The green flag is the trigger to start the script running.
set name to abracadabra	Set the current value of the **name** variable to *abracadabra*.
ask Please enter the magic word and wait	The sprite gets a speech bubble that displays *Please enter the magic word*, opens user input field, and waits for user input.
if then else	Check if the condition is true. If the condition is true, execute the actions within it, before the word *else*. If the condition is false, execute the actions after the word *else* within the block.
=	If the value on the left side is equal to the value on the right side, then this condition is true; otherwise, the condition is false.
answer	Hold and report the current user input value.
name	Hold and report the current value of the **name** variable.
say You may enter for 2 secs	The sprite gets a speech bubble that displays *You may enter* for 2 seconds.
say Please try again for 2 secs	The sprite gets a speech bubble that displays *Please try again* for 2 seconds.

Exercise 2

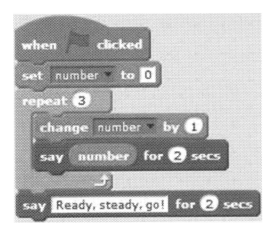

Script 13-12. *Count to 3*

The script makes the sprite count from 1 to 3, and then displays the text *Ready, steady, go!*. It uses a variable named **number**.

This script starts running when the user clicks the green flag. The next block of code assigns the value 0 to the **number** variable. Next, the ![repeat 3] block that repeats the sequence of actions within it 3 times. The first block within the sequence adds the value 1 to the **number** variable. The next block creates a speech bubble that displays the current value of the **number** variable for 2 seconds. The last block creates a speech bubble that displays *Ready, steady, go!* for 2 seconds.

Table 13-12 lists the blocks and describes the actions used in this example.

Table 13-12. *Code Blocks in Count to 3*

Blocks	Actions
when clicked	Clicking the green flag activates the script. The green flag is the trigger to start the script running.
set number to 0	Set the current value of the **number** variable to 0.
repeat 3	Repeat the actions represented by the blocks within this block three times.
change number by 1	Add 1 to the current value of the **number** variable.

(*continued*)

Table 13-12. (*continued*)

Blocks	Actions
say ▢ for ② secs	The sprite gets a speech bubble that displays the specified text or value for 2 seconds.
number	Hold and report the current value of the **number** variable.
say Ready, steady, go! for ② secs	The sprite gets a speech bubble that displays *Ready, steady, go!* for 2 seconds.

Chapter 9: Lists

Exercise 1

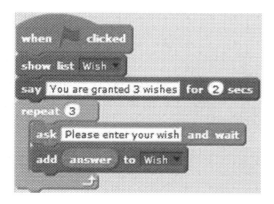

Script 13-13. *Three wishes*

This script creates a list that consists of three user inputs. The first step is to create a list called **Wish**.

This script starts running when the user clicks green flag. The ░show list Wish░ block displays the list's monitor in the stage area. The next block creates a speech bubble that displays *You are granted 3 wishes* for 2 seconds. The next block is a **repeat** ░repeat ③░ block, and then repeats the sequence of actions within it 3 times. The first block in the sequence creates a speech bubble that displays *Please enter your wish*, opens a user input field, and waits for the user's input. The second block in the sequence adds the user input in ░answer░ to the end of the list.

Table 13-13 lists the blocks and describes the actions used in this example.

Table 13-13. *Code Blocks in Three Wishes*

Blocks	Actions
when clicked	Clicking the green flag activates the script. The green flag is the trigger to start the script running.
show list Wish ▾	Show the monitor in the stage area for the list called **Wish**.
say You are granted 3 wishes for 2 secs	The sprite gets a speech bubble that displays *You are granted 3 wishes* for 2 seconds.
repeat 3	Repeat the actions represented by the blocks within this block three times.
ask Please enter your wish and wait	The sprite gets a speech bubble that displays *Please enter your wish*, opens a user input field, and waits for user input.
add ⬜ to Wish ▾	Add the specified value to the end of the list called **Wish**.
answer	Hold and report the current user input value.

Exercise 2

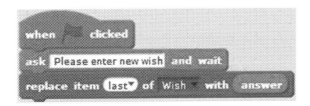

Script 13-14. *Replace wish*

This script replaces an item in the list called **Wish** with user input. It starts running when the user clicks green flag. The next block creates a speech bubble that displays the text *Please enter new wish*, opens a user input field, and waits for the user's input. The `replace item last of Wish with ⬜` block replaces the value at the last position of the list with the user input in `answer`.

Table 13-14 lists the blocks and describes the actions used in this example.

Table 13-14. *Code Blocks in Replace Wish*

Blocks	Actions
when ▢ clicked	Clicking the green flag activates the script. The green flag is the trigger to start the script running.
ask Please enter new wish and wait	The sprite gets a speech bubble that displays *Please enter new wish*, opens a user input field, and waits for user input.
replace item (last▾) of Wish ▾ with ▢	Replace the value at the last position in the list called **Wish** with another value.
answer	Hold and report the current user input value.

Chapter 10: Webcam Interaction

Exercise 1

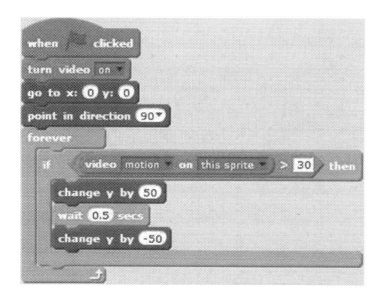

Script 13-15. *Motion detector move*

This script uses receives input from a webcam and checks if the video motion on the sprite is greater than 30. Each time it is, the sprite will jump up and down.

The script starts running when the user clicks the green flag. The **turn video on** block turns on the webcam. The next two blocks move the sprite to the middle of the stage, and then make the sprite face to the

right. The **forever** block repeats the sequence of actions within it forever, or until the script is manually stopped. That sequence begins with an If/Then conditional statement that evaluates whether the video motion on the sprite is greater than 30. If the video motion on the sprite is greater than 30, then the

blocks within the **if then** block are executed: the Y coordinate of the sprite is increased by 50, the script pauses for 0.5 seconds, and the Y coordinate is changed by –50, meaning the sprite jumps up and then goes back to its original position.

Table 13-15 lists the blocks and describes the actions used in this example.

Table 13-15. *Code Blocks in Motion Detector Move*

Blocks	Actions
when clicked	Clicking the green flag activates the script. The green flag is the trigger to start the script running.
turn video on	Turn the webcam on.
go to x: 0 y: 0	Move the sprite to the position where X = 0 and Y = 0.
point in direction 90	Make the sprite face to the right.
forever	The actions within the forever block is repeated forever, or until the script is stopped manually.
if then	Check if the condition is true. If the condition is true, execute the actions within it. If the condition is false, skip to the next block.
> 30	If the value on the left side is greater than 30, then this condition is true; otherwise, the condition is false.
video motion on this sprite	Hold and report the value of the video motion on the sprite.
change y by 50	Add 50 to the current value of the Y coordinate and move the sprite to that new Y coordinate.
wait 0.5 secs	The script waits 0.5 seconds. No actions are performed for 0.5 seconds.
change y by -50	Add –50 to the current value of the Y coordinate and move the sprite to that new Y coordinate.

Exercise 2

Script 13-16. *Motion detector sound*

This script receives input from a webcam and checks if the video motion on the sprite is greater than 30. Each time it is, a sound plays.

    The script starts running when the user clicks the green flag. The next three blocks turn on the webcam, move the sprite to the middle of the stage, and make the sprite face to the right. The [forever] block repeats the sequence of actions within it forever, or until the script is manually stopped. That sequence begins with an If/Then conditional statement that evaluates whether the video motion on the sprite is greater than 30. If the video motion on the sprite is greater than 30, then the block within the [if then] block is executed and the **plunge** sound gets played.

Table 13-16 lists the blocks and describes the actions used in this example.

Table 13-16. *Code Blocks in Motion Detector Sound*

Blocks	Actions
when [flag] clicked	Clicking the green flag activates the script. The green flag is the trigger to start the script running.
turn video on	Turn the webcam on.
go to x: 0 y: 0	Move the sprite to the position where X = 0 and Y = 0.
point in direction 90	Make the sprite face to the right.
forever	The actions within the forever block is repeated forever, or until the script is stopped manually.
if then	Check if the condition is true. If the condition is true, execute the actions within it. If the condition is false, skip to the next block.
[ ] > 30	If the value on the left side is greater than 30, then this condition is true; otherwise, the condition is false.
video motion on this sprite	Hold and report the value of the video motion on the sprite.
play sound plunge	Play the sound file **plunge**.

Chapter 11: Broadcast Interaction

Exercise 1

Composed of five scripts, this exercise uses broadcasting to trigger the scripts of two sprites, enabling the sprites to have a conversation. Two sprites must be in the Sprites pane. The first two scripts apply to the first sprite, so before creating these scripts, select the first sprite.

Script 13-17 starts running when the user presses the space bar. The next block moves the sprite to the position (–150, 0). The next block makes the sprite face to the right. The next block of code creates a speech bubble that displays *Hi, how are you?* for 2 seconds. The last block of code broadcasts **message1** to activate Script 13-20 for the second sprite's answer.

Script 13-17. Question1

Table 13-17 lists the blocks and describes the actions used in this example.

Table 13-17. *Code Blocks in Question1*

Blocks	Actions
when space key pressed	Pressing the space bar activates the script. The space bar is the trigger to start the script running.
go to x: -150 y: 0	Move the sprite to the position where X = –150 and Y = 0.
point in direction 90	Make the sprite face to the right.
say Hi, how are you? for 2 secs	The sprite gets a speech bubble that displays *Hi, how are you?* for 2 seconds.
broadcast message1	Broadcast **message1**.

With the first script still selected, create the following script.

Script 13-18 starts running when it receives **message2** from Script 13-20. The next block of code creates a speech bubble that displays *How old do you think I am?* for 2 seconds. The last block of code broadcasts **message3** to Script 13-21, which contains the second sprite's next answer.

Script 13-18. Question2

Table 13-18 lists the blocks and describes the actions used in this example.

Table 13-18. *Code Blocks in Question2*

Blocks	Actions
when I receive message2	Receiving **message2** activates the script.
say How old do you think I am? for 2 secs	The sprite gets a speech bubble that displays *How old do you think I am?* for 2 seconds.
broadcast message3	Broadcast **message3**.

The next three scripts apply to the second sprite, so you need to select it before creating them.

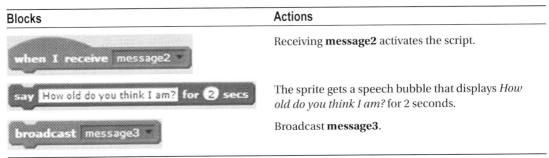

Script 13-19. *Position*

This scripts starts running when the user presses the space bar. The next three blocks of code move the sprite to a position of (150, 0), set the rotation style of the sprite to **left-right**, and make the sprite face to the right.

Table 13-19 lists the blocks and describes the actions used in this example.

Table 13-19. *Code Blocks in Position*

Blocks	Actions
when space key pressed	Pressing the space bar activates the script. The space bar is the trigger to start the script running.
go to x: 150 y: 0	Move the sprite to the position where X = 150 and Y = 0.
set rotation style left-right	Set the rotation style of the sprite so that it can only face left or right.
point in direction -90	Make the sprite face to the left.

With the second sprite still selected, create the script that answers the first sprite's first question and asks one of its own.

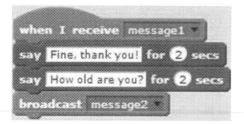

Script 13-20. *Question3*

The script activates when **message1** is received from the first sprite's Script 13-17. The next two blocks each create speech bubbles for 2 seconds. The first one displays *Fine, thank you!* and the second displays *How old are you?*. The last block of code broadcasts **message2** to trigger Script 13-18 for the first sprite's answer.

Table 13-20 lists the blocks and describes the actions used in this example.

Table 13-20. *Code Blocks in Question3*

Blocks	Actions
when I receive message1	Receiving **message1** activates the script.
say Fine, thank you! for 2 secs	The sprite gets a speech bubble that displays *Fine, thank you!* for 2 seconds.
say How old are you? for 2 secs	The sprite gets a speech bubble that displays *How old are you?* for 2 seconds.
broadcast message2	Broadcast **message2**.

The last script for the second sprite answers the first sprite.

Script 13-21. *Answer*

The script starts running when **message3** is received from the first sprite's Script 13-18. The last block creates a speech bubble that displays *Hmmm, I think you are 100 years old. Hahaha, just kidding* for 2 seconds.

Table 13-21 lists the blocks and describes the actions used in this example.

Table 13-21. *Code Blocks in Answer*

Blocks	Actions
when I receive message3	Receiving **message3** activates the script.
say Hmmm, I think you are 100 years old. Hahahaha, just kidding for 5 secs	The sprite gets a speech bubble that displays *Hmmm. I think you are 100 years old. Hahahaha, just kidding* for 2 seconds.

Exercise 2

This exercise broadcasts a message from a sprite's script to a backdrop's script, enabling the sprite to automatically change the backdrop. Two backdrops are used in this exercise: **bedroom1** and **bedroom2**. Make sure that they are in the Backdrops pane, and then start with the sprite's script.

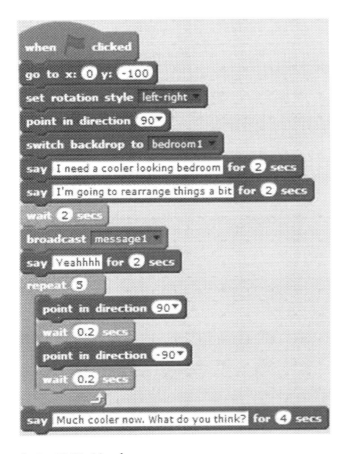

Script 13-22. *Monologue*

Script 13-22 controls the sprite, so make sure that it is selected. The sprite activates when the user clicks the green flag. The next three blocks move the sprite to (0, –1000), set the rotation style of the sprite to **left-right**, and make the sprite face to the right. The next block of code changes the backdrop to **bedroom1**. The next two blocks each create a speech bubble for 2 seconds: first displaying *I need a cooler looking bedroom*, and then *I'm going to rearrange things a bit*. The next block pauses the script for 2 seconds. The next block broadcasts **message1** to trigger Script 13-23, which contains the backdrop change. The next block

creates a speech bubble that displays *Yeahhh* for 2 seconds. The ⟨image⟩ block then executes the sequence of actions within it 5 times: the sprite faces to the right, the script pauses for 0.2 seconds, the sprite faces to the left, and the script pauses for another 0.2 seconds. The last block of the script creates a speech bubble that displays *Much cooler now. What do you think?* for 4 seconds.

Table 13-22 lists the blocks and describes the actions used in this example.

Table 13-22. *Code Blocks in Monologue*

Blocks	Actions
	Clicking the green flag activates the script. The green flag is the trigger to start the script running.
	Move the sprite to the position where X = 0 and Y = –100.
	Set the rotation style of the sprite so that it can only face left or right.
	Make the sprite face to the right.
	Switch the backdrop to **bedroom1**.
	The sprite gets a speech bubble that displays *I need a cooler looking bedroom* for 2 seconds.
	The sprite gets a speech bubble that displays *I'm going to rearrange things a bit* for 2 seconds.
	The script waits 2 second. No actions are performed for 2 second.
	Broadcast **message1**.
	The sprite gets a speech bubble that displays *Yeahhhh* for 2 seconds.

(*continued*)

Table 13-22. (*continued*)

Blocks	Actions
repeat 5	Repeat the actions represented by the blocks within this block five times.
point in direction 90▼	Make the sprite face to the right.
wait 0.2 secs	The script waits 0.2 second. No actions are performed for 0.2 second.
point in direction -90▼	Make the sprite face to the left.
wait 0.2 secs	The script waits 0.2 second. No actions are performed for 0.2 second.
say Much cooler now. What do you think? for 4 secs	The sprite gets a speech bubble that displays *Much cooler now. What do you think?* for 4 seconds.

The following script is for the backdrop, so a backdrop thumbnail needs to be selected in the Backdrops pane. It doesn't matter which backdrop thumbnail.

Script 13-23. *Change backdrop*

Script 13-23 starts running when **message1** is received from the sprite's Script 13-22. The next block of code changes the backdrop to **bedroom2**.

Table 13-23 lists the blocks and describes the actions used in this example.

Table 13-23. *Code Blocks in Change Backdrop*

Blocks	Actions
when I receive message1 ▼	Receiving **message1** activates the script.
switch backdrop to bedroom2 ▼	Switch the backdrop to **bedroom2**.

Chapter 12: Create Own Block

Exercise 1

This exercise creates and uses a custom block called **Look_there** that flips the direction a sprite faces from right to left multiple times. First, create a new custom block called **Look_there** by clicking the **Make a Block** button in the **More Blocks** category of the block palette.

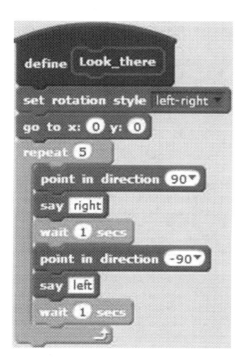

Script 13-24. Define Look_there

Next, define the custom block with Script 13-24. The first two blocks set the rotation style of the sprite to

left-right and move the sprite to the middle of the stage. Next, the block repeats the sequence of actions within it 5 times. The first block in the sequence makes the sprite face to the right. The next block creates a speech bubble that displays *right*. The next block pauses the script for 1 second. The next three blocks make the sprite face to the left, create a speech bubble that displays *left*, and pauses the script for 1 second.

Table 13-24 lists the blocks and describes the actions used in this example.

Table 13-24. *Code Blocks in Define Look_there*

Blocks	Actions
define Look_there	The hat block that defines the block called **Look_there**.
set rotation style left-right ▼	Set the rotation style of the sprite so that it can only face left or right.
go to x: 0 y: 0	Move the sprite to the position where X = 0 and Y = 0.
repeat 5	Repeat the actions represented by the blocks within this block five times.
point in direction 90▼	Make the sprite face to the right.
say right	The sprite gets a speech bubble that displays *right*.
wait 1 secs	The script waits 1 second. No actions are performed for 1 second.
point in direction -90▼	Make the sprite face to the left.
say left	The sprite gets a speech bubble that displays *left*.
wait 1 secs	The script waits 1 second. No actions are performed for 1 second.

Next, create a script to use the custom block.

Script 13-25. *Look_there*

Script 13-25 activates when the user clicks the green flag. The last block activates the 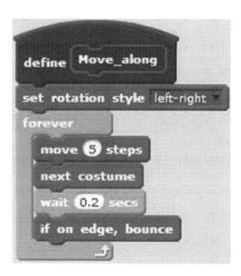**Look_there** custom block.

Table 13-25 lists the blocks and describes the actions used in this example.

Table 13-25. *Code Blocks in Look_there*

Blocks	Actions
when 🏴 clicked	Clicking the green flag activates the script. The green flag is the trigger to start the script running.
Look_there	Execute the **Look_there** block.

Exercise 2

This exercise creates a custom block called **Move_along** that continuously moves the sprite and changes its costume. First, create a new custom block called **Move_along**.

```
define Move_along

set rotation style left-right ▼

forever
    move 5 steps
    next costume
    wait 0.2 secs
    if on edge, bounce
```

Script 13-26. *Define Move_along*

Define the custom block by creating Script 13-26. The first block sets the rotation style of the sprite so that it can only face left or right. Next there is a **forever** block that executes the sequence of actions within it forever. The first block in the sequence moves the sprite 5 pixels in the direction that it's facing. The next block changes the sprite to its next costume. The next block pauses the script for 0.2 seconds, and the last block makes the sprite travel in the opposite direction if it reaches any of the stage edges.

Table 13-26 lists the blocks and describes the actions used in this example.

Table 13-26. *Code Blocks in Define Move_along*

Blocks	Actions
define Move_along	The hat block that defines the block called **Move_along**.
set rotation style left-right	Set the rotation style of the sprite so that it can only face left or right.
forever	The actions within the forever block is repeated forever, or until the script is stopped manually.
move 5 steps	Move the sprite 5 pixels in the direction that it's facing.
next costume	Change the sprite to the next costume in the costumes tab.
wait 0.2 secs	The script waits 0.2 second. No actions are performed for 0.2 second.
if on edge, bounce	If the sprite reaches the edge of the stage, bounce in the opposite direction.

Next, create a script to use the custom block.

Script 13-27 starts running when the user presses the space bar. The next two blocks make the sprite face to the right and move the sprite to the center of the stage. The last block of code activates the

Move_along custom block.

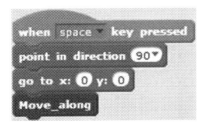

Script 13-27. *Move_along*

Table 13-27 lists the blocks and describes the actions used in this example.

Table 13-27. *Code Blocks in Move_along*

Blocks	Actions
when space key pressed	Pressing the space bar activates the script. The space bar is the trigger to start the script running.
point in direction 90▼	Make the sprite face to the right.
go to x: 0 y: 0	Move the sprite to the position where X = 0 and Y = 0.
Move_along	Execute the **Move_along** block.

CHAPTER 14

▓ ▓ ▓

Conclusion

Congratulations on finishing the book! You have created and run a lot of Scratch scripts and by doing so you have learned how to program using the Scratch programming language. Along the way, you also learned about a lot of advanced programming concepts that Scratch and other languages rely on, such as...

- User input

- Variables

- Conditional statements

- Conditions

- Procedures

- Loops

Scratch is a fun and easy way to start learning about programming. Because all of its commands are represented by blocks of code, Scratch eliminates the possibility of making syntax errors—and the headaches of tracking them down and fixing them. Assuming that you followed all the examples and finished all the chapter exercises, you now have...

- A thorough understanding of the Scratch interface.

- The skills to create different types of Scratch projects by executing a variety of actions, such as movement, adding sound, manipulating user input, drawing, and more.

- A solid foundation upon which you can build to create more advanced Scratch projects.

As you continue experimenting with creating Scratch projects, share them with the Scratch community online. By doing so, you can learn from fellow programmers' feedback; but don't forget to also help fellow programmers by giving them feedback, too. When you're at that point that you feel ready to step up to a more advanced programming language, that transition should be easier. Not only will you know how to program with Scratch, you will be familiar with the common programming concepts that you will encounter in those more advanced languages.

Scratch On!

© Eduardo A. Vlieg 2016
E. A. Vlieg, *Scratch by Example*, DOI 10.1007/978-1-4842-1946-1_14

Index

© Eduardo A. Vlieg 2016
E.A. Vlieg, *Scratch by Example*, DOI 10.1007/978-1-4842-1946-1

▓ T, U

▓ V

Get the eBook for only $5!

Why limit yourself?

Now you can take the weightless companion with you wherever you go and access your content on your PC, phone, tablet, or reader.

Since you've purchased this print book, we're happy to offer you the eBook in all 3 formats for just $5.

Convenient and fully searchable, the PDF version enables you to easily find and copy code—or perform examples by quickly toggling between instructions and applications. The MOBI format is ideal for your Kindle, while the ePUB can be utilized on a variety of mobile devices.

To learn more, go to www.apress.com/companion or contact support@apress.com.